Changing Sports Journalism Practice in the Age of Digital Media

As the funding of journalism moves centre stage as a driver in shaping the new trajectories of journalism in the digital age, this book focuses on how those working in sports journalism have had to adapt and re-invent themselves.

Running through this international collection are key themes related to sports journalism in the digital environment. These include aspects of disruption to established norms of journalistic practice, institutional allegiance, the authority and primary definer role of journalism, and the career structure and development for journalists writing about sport. The book draws on empirically led research that mixes qualitative and quantitative approaches and seeks to better understand and position what is going on across contemporary sports journalism. In so doing, this collection identifies change, but also areas of continuity as well as new opportunities for journalists.

This book was originally published as a special issue of *Digital Journalism*.

Raymond Boyle is a Professor of Communications at the Centre for Cultural Policy Research at the University of Glasgow, UK. He has published widely for many years on sports, media, and journalism. He is a co-Managing Editor of the *Media, Culture and Society* journal, and his most recent book is *The Talent Industry: Television, Cultural Intermediaries and New Digital Pathways* (2018).

Changing Sports Journalism Practice in the Age of Digital Media

Edited by
Raymond Boyle

Routledge
Taylor & Francis Group
LONDON AND NEW YORK

First published 2020
by Routledge
2 Park Square, Milton Park, Abingdon, Oxon, OX14 4RN

and by Routledge
52 Vanderbilt Avenue, New York, NY 10017

Routledge is an imprint of the Taylor & Francis Group, an informa business

British Library Cataloguing-in-Publication Data
A catalogue record for this book is available from the British Library

ISBN13: 978-0-367-36252-2

Typeset in Myriad Pro
by codeMantra

Publisher's Note
The publisher accepts responsibility for any inconsistencies that may have arisen during the conversion of this book from journal articles to book chapters, namely the inclusion of journal terminology.

Disclaimer
Every effort has been made to contact copyright holders for their permission to reprint material in this book. The publishers would be grateful to hear from any copyright holder who is not here acknowledged and will undertake to rectify any errors or omissions in future editions of this book.

Contents

Citation Information

The chapters in this book were originally published in *Digital Journalism*, volume 5, issue 5 (June 2017). When citing this material, please use the original page numbering for each article, as follows:

Introduction

Sports Journalism: Changing journalism practice and digital media
Raymond Boyle
Digital Journalism, volume 5, issue 5 (June 2017) pp. 493–495

Chapter 1

A Community of Practice: Sport journalism, mobile media and institutional change
Brett Hutchins and Raymond Boyle
Digital Journalism, volume 5, issue 5 (June 2017) pp. 496–512

Chapter 2

Controlling the Message and the Medium? The impact of sports organisations' digital and social channels on media access
Merryn Sherwood, Matthew Nicholson and Timothy Marjoribanks
Digital Journalism, volume 5, issue 5 (June 2017) pp. 513–531

Chapter 3

Cheerleaders or Critics? Australian and Indian sports journalists in the contemporary age
Peter English
Digital Journalism, volume 5, issue 5 (June 2017) pp. 532–548

Chapter 4

Playing on the Same Pitch: Attitudes of sports journalists towards fan bloggers
Simon McEnnis
Digital Journalism, volume 5, issue 5 (June 2017) pp. 549–566

Chapter 5

Sports Journalism, Supporters and new Technologies: Challenging the usual complicity between media and football institutions
Ana Carolina Vimieiro
Digital Journalism, volume 5, issue 5 (June 2017) pp. 567–586

Chapter 6

Data Visualisation in Sports Journalism: Opportunities and challenges of data-driven journalism in German football
Thomas Horky and Philipp Pelka
Digital Journalism, volume 5, issue 5 (June 2017) pp. 587–606

Chapter 7

Pressure on Printed Press: How soccer clubs determine journalism in the German Bundesliga
Christoph G. Grimmer
Digital Journalism, volume 5, issue 5 (June 2017) pp. 607–635

Chapter 8

The State of Sport Photojournalism: Concepts, practice and challenges
Richard Haynes, Adrian Hadland and Paul Lambert
Digital Journalism, volume 5, issue 5 (June 2017) pp. 636–651

Chapter 9

Take Five: How Sports Illustrated *and* L'Équipe *redefine the long-form sports journalism genre*
Christopher Tulloch and Xavier Ramon
Digital Journalism, volume 5, issue 5 (June 2017) pp. 652–672

Notes on Contributors

Raymond Boyle is a Professor of Communications at the Centre for Cultural Policy Research at the University of Glasgow, UK. He has published widely for many years on sports, media, and journalism. He is a co-Managing Editor of the *Media, Culture and Society* journal.

Peter English is a Lecturer in Journalism in the Faculty of Arts, Business and Law at the University of the Sunshine Coast, Australia. His chief research area is sports journalism, with an emphasis on its journalists, content, and social media.

Christoph G. Grimmer is a German politician, serving as Mayor of Crailsheim, Germany. He is a Chairman of Stadtwerke Crailsheim and the Franconian Water Service GmbH.

Adrian Hadland is a Professor in the Division of Communications, Media & Culture at the University of Stirling, UK. His research interests include journalism, comparative media systems, digital journalism, democracy, mobile phones and journalism, ethics, photography, biographical writing, and non-fiction.

Richard Haynes is a Professor in the Division of Communications, Media & Culture at the University of Stirling, UK. His principal research interests focus on the inter-relationships between sport, the media, and popular culture.

Thomas Horky is a Professor of Journalism and Sports Communication at the Macromedia University of Applied Sciences, Germany. As a freelance journalist, he has made numerous contributions to newspapers, news and PR agencies, magazines, journals, and TV and radio.

Brett Hutchins is a Professor and the Head of the School of Media, Film & Journalism in the Faculty of Arts at Monash University, Melbourne, Australia. His research investigates who wins, who loses, and how, during processes of technological change.

Paul Lambert is a Professor in the Division of Sociology, Social Policy and Criminology at the University of Stirling, UK. His most common area of applied research is on the theme of 'social stratification', particularly studying occupations and their importance to stratification inequalities.

Timothy Marjoribanks is a Professor in the Department of Management and Marketing in the La Trobe Business School at La Trobe University, Melbourne, Australia. His research focuses on organisational behaviour and transformation, and management practice, both in Australia and internationally, with a particular focus on the media industry, journalism practice, sport, and new technologies.

Simon McEnnis is a Principal Lecturer in the School of Sport and Service Management at the University of Brighton, UK. He is a journalist and academic who has written research articles on sports journalism and professionalism.

Matthew Nicholson is the Director for the Centre for Sport and Social Impact, and a Professor in La Trobe Business School at La Trobe University, Melbourne, Australia. His expertise is in sport policy, the management of community, and state sport organisations, particularly as it relates to the sport-public health nexus; the social impact of sport, recreation and leisure; and the representation of sport through the media.

Philipp Pelka is an Analyst at Spielverlagerung, Germany.

Xavier Ramon is a Lecturer in the Department of Communication at Pompeu Fabra University, Barcelona, Spain. His research and teaching focus on sports media, journalism ethics, media accountability, and Olympic Studies.

Merryn Sherwood is a Senior Lecturer in Journalism in the Department of Communication and Media at La Trobe University, Melbourne, Australia. Her research interests include journalism, newswork, and sports media.

Christopher Tulloch is a Lecturer in the Department of Communication at Pompeu Fabra University, Barcelona, Spain. As a journalist, he is a co-Editor of the Catalan News Agency and has worked for various national and international media.

Ana Carolina Vimieiro is a Postdoctoral Research Fellow in the Department of Communication at the Federal University of Minas Gerais, Belo Horizonte, Brazil. Her research interests include football cultures, digital media, everyday politics, innovative methodologies, and frame analysis.

INTRODUCTION

SPORTS JOURNALISM
Changing journalism practice and digital media

Raymond Boyle

Sports Journalism

A paradox exists at the heart of sports journalism. On one hand, it has over the years often been viewed as the poor relation within journalism, lacking the integrity that journalists often like to associate with their self-image. Sports journalism has been characterised as a form of "soft" journalistic practice, without the rigour and credibility of other forms of "hard" journalism. It was an area of journalism that was viewed as an uncritical booster and promoter of sport and its culture rather than a sector that called the powerful in sport to account. It was a journalism that was more often going to ask the easy and banal question, rather than the penetrating and pertinent one.

At the same time, and here lies the paradox, sports journalism was often one of the most commercially important parts of the newspaper industry. Simply put, while other journalists and academics often decried the lax journalistic standards that they argued could be found in the "back of the book", it was sports journalism's ability to deliver readers, particularly young male readers, that made it such a crucial and integral part of the commercial success of many newspapers.

Of course, this rather stark critique around sports journalism, and the journalists who plied their trade in this sector, often obscured more than it illuminated. As has been argued elsewhere, sports journalists often had more in common with other areas of journalistic practice than many journalists cared to acknowledge (Boyle 2006). As in other areas of journalism, there are huge variations in the range, diversity and quality of the output that gets tagged as sports journalism. The group mentality of the journalistic pack that travels and works closely with its key sources (whose access is crucial) and the conflicts of interest that accompany such relationships are not things specific to the hermetically sealed world of elite sport, but common in political and business journalism. Crucial also in shaping the tenor and tone of the journalism is the institution that you work for and which sets the parameters within which you produce your journalism. The tightly run sports desk of a UK tabloid newspaper offers little latitude for wayward journalistic digressions, while by way of contrast a compact or broadsheet newspaper, often later in coming to valuing its sports coverage, offers more latitude for individual shaping of the tenor of the journalistic output.

National media cultures also shape experience. The sports writer in US journalism occupied a differing, more elevated space than, for example, their UK counterpart did until the last decade or so. Like all journalism, sports has a hierarchy with the Number 1 or sports writer being at the top of the pyramid, while the local sports beat reporter (completely reliant on access to local clubs or associations) traditionally toils at the base of the pyramid.

The last 20 or so years has seen a number of key moments shape sports journalism. The United Kingdom in the 1990s saw a growth in more demand-led journalism driven by pay-TV that was financially underwriting elite sport. As a result, promotion and the expansion of the coverage in sport (football, in particular), saw more journalism (in all its forms) about sport and offered more opportunities for those wishing to develop a career as a sports journalist. An example of the expansion that took place saw the 1986 FIFA World Cup in Mexico, featuring the national teams of England, Scotland and Northern Ireland, covered by the UK *Guardian* newspaper with one page of journalism devoted to events in Mexico, a situation simply unthinkable today.

The digital turn of the 1990s has also dramatically reshaped the journalistic landscape, with sports journalism often being at the leading edge of this transition as journalism moved online and many new (often fan-based) sources of information become available around sports culture. The business crisis in print journalism has arrived at the sports journalists door somewhat later than for other sectors, but arrive it has. As the funding of journalism moves centre stage as a driver in shaping the new trajectories of journalism, those working in sports also have had to adapt and re-invent themselves and it is this process that is the focus of this special issue of *Digital Journalism*.

Mapping the Field

Running through this collection are a number of themes related to sports journalism in the digital environment. These include aspects of disruption to: established norms of journalistic practice, institutional allegiance, the authority and primary definer role of journalism, and the career structure and development for journalists writing about sport. These articles draw on empirically led research that mixes qualitative and quantitative approaches and seek to better understand and position what is going on across contemporary sports journalism. In so doing, this collection identifies change, but also areas of continuity as well as new opportunities for journalists.

Hutchins and Boyle revisit Zelizer's (1993) "community of practice" conceptualisation of journalism practice as their starting point for an examination of shifting practice and culture of sports journalists in the mobile age of content production, distribution and consumption. This contribution, and that of Sherwood et al.'s investigation, highlight the growing complexity that exists between sport and journalism as the media become more embedded in the financial structure of elite sport at a time of technological change. The position of public relations and the importance of sustained institutional support for journalistic output are all highlighted as the front line of sports journalism is examined.

The rise of social media and its impact on culture and practice in differing media markets is the focus of the contributions by English, McEnnis and Vimierio. These identify some of the major themes touched on at the top of this editorial around journalistic rigour, but also the impact that the changing nature of news values and patterns of news consumption are having on journalistic practice and the working environment for the digital sports journalist. Themes of technological disruption as well as new opportunities are examined in research from Germany that tackles debates around the growing impact of data on journalistic practice, while the growth of elite football organisations becoming sports and media businesses are examined in works from Horky and Pelka, and Grimmer. While the neglected area of sport photo-journalism is positioned centre stage by Haynes et al., as they draw from shifting practice in this area from around the globe and highlight the particular challenges that digital practice presents in terms of preserving what has been a key (although undervalued) component of sports journalism over the decades.

Finally, in an edition of *Digital Journalism* that will often focus on the prominence of the short, online, mobile-friendly mode of sports journalism, Tulloch and Ramon, through their study of long-form sports journalism (and its continued commercial and brand value), remind us that the journalistic environment remains diverse and that patterns of continuity can also be found in what is a fast-changing journalistic landscape. This collection then offers a snapshot of a journalistic sector undergoing change, but also one that is adapting to covering one of the most enduring and media-saturated forms of contemporary popular culture, elite sport.

DISCLOSURE STATEMENT

No potential conflict of interest was reported by the author.

REFERENCES

Boyle, Raymond. 2006. *Sports Journalism: Context and Issues*. London: Sage.

Zelizer, Barbie. 1993. "Journalists as Interpretive Communities." *Critical Studies in Mass Communication* 10 (3): 219–237.

A COMMUNITY OF PRACTICE
Sport journalism, mobile media and institutional change

Brett Hutchins and **Raymond Boyle**

Over two decades ago, Barbie Zelizer argued that journalists should be approached as an "interpretive community" in order to understand the processes through which journalists generate shared meanings around major political events. This article refocuses Zelizer's concept in order to analyse the consequences of rapid technological transformation, fraught industry conditions, and disparate audience formations in the context of contemporary news media and journalism. Focusing on the challenges faced by professional sport journalists, we invoke the concept of "community of practice" to make sense of this fluid and commercially volatile context, using it to analyse empirically the experiences of journalists in Australia and Scotland. Informed by the interrelationship that exists between formats of news and the practices that produce it, this paper presents evidence drawn from in-depth semi-structured interviews with journalists, editors, news presenters and commentators who specialise in and/or work across newspapers, radio, television, online and mobile media. Understood as a community of practice, sport journalists are shown to be under pressure because of mutually reinforcing changes in mobile and digital media technologies, journalistic routines and institutional relations.

Introduction

> It's [news] changed in the digital world. Because what is news now? It's anything. If it's on a news website, is that news? I doubt sometimes that it's news. And yet you read stuff and you go, "How is that news?" You read it on social media and ask, "How is this even on here? Why are we writing about this?" … I think for me, if someone's willing to read it, it's news. I know that's a very basic way of looking at it, but if it makes someone learn something or someone read something and they weren't aware of it, that's news. (Sport Editor, interview, 8 October 2015)[1]

This statement by the sport editor of a daily newspaper strikes at the indeterminate status of news under the conditions of informational capitalism. The combined effects of rapidly evolving media and communications technologies, struggling news industry business models and changing audience behaviours are undermining shared understandings of news. As the above quotation indicates, even those charged with producing the news each day lament selected stories circulated by their own publications in the pursuit of reader clicks, social media referrals and advertising revenue. In the eyes of an experienced professional paid to produce it, news has been reduced to "anything" that someone is "willing to read", signalling an erosion of the epistemological status of news and the stories told in its name.

Using sport as a case study, this article aims to make sense of the fluid and volatile conditions that are impacting news and journalism by focusing attention on "media practice" (Couldry 2012)—what news workers do with media and how they articulate their decisions, roles and futures in relation to this practice. Recalling an enduring sociological concern with journalistic practice and the structures in which it takes place (Tumber 2014), the evidence presented in later sections suggests that transformation is a dominant motif of journalism and news at this moment in their history. News is said to be characterised by, all at once, decentralisation, ambience, crisis, chaos, destabilisation and disposability (Crawford 2011; Curran 2011; Hermida 2012; McNair 2006; Meikle and Redden 2011). Yet, the influence of multiple crosscutting forces does not mean that shared practices of news work no longer exist, or that journalists have voluntarily ceded their cultural authority to "the crowd" in determining what counts as news and how it should be produced and delivered.

Borrowing and refocusing Barbie Zelizer's (1993, 219) widely cited formulation of "journalists as interpretive communities", we argue that the work of journalists has moved beyond the "shared discourse and collective interpretations of key public events" in line with a movement away from mass media models of communication. The industrial ructions and audience fragmentation triggered by digital and mobile models of content distribution and consumption are now also forcing journalists to defend their authoritative role as providers of news by reference to practice. This practice is professionally grounded in specialist journalistic training, accumulated experience, technical production skills and quality, cultivation of reliable sources, access to newsroom resources and appeal to sizeable audiences. We invoke the concept of "community of practice"[2] (cf. Cotter 2010; Weiss and Domingo 2010) to describe this shared legitimation process. Based on interview evidence collected from Australian and Scottish sport journalists, editors, presenters and commentators, this term first describes how professional journalists distinguish themselves from so-called semi-professionals, amateurs, enthusiasts and purveyors of sponsored content (e.g. bloggers, citizen journalists, social media commentators, marketers and public relations practitioners), privileging the actions and logics they use to produce knowledge about events in the social world. Second, it captures an important process whereby news workers attempt to make sense of, and locate their role within, the turbulent social, economic and technological conditions that define their workplace experiences. The explanations and justifications of practice offered by journalists are a means of locating what they do and why within publicly articulated traditions of news and journalism, emphasising their longstanding relevance as a domain of specialist skills in the service of informing audiences and wider publics (Curran 2011). For those paid to produce the news, these functions serve to buttress the relevance and effectiveness of their practice, even as they adapt to ongoing changes in the organisation of newsrooms and the skill sets required to work in them (Schlesinger and Doyle 2015).

Methods and Sites of Investigation

The analysis and evidence presented in this article is informed by 10 in-depth semi-structured interviews with journalists, editors, news presenters, commentators and producers who specialise in newspaper, radio, television, online and mobile media reporting. Covering both commercial and public service media, five of these figures work for Australian news outlets and five for Scottish publications and broadcast networks. All specialists in sport reporting, their careers range from 3 to over 30 years in duration. Eight are male and two female, reflecting the historical legacy of male dominance of the sport journalism and news workforce (Boyle 2006). A conspicuous feature of these individuals is that while they often self-identify as a newspaper, radio, television or online reporter, all but two work across multiple platforms and/or formats (e.g. a print journalist who contributes to television and radio programmes, a broadcast journalist who writes a weekly column for an online news site, an online journalist who produces both written reports and video content). These 10 interviews were conducted in Australia and Scotland as part of a larger international research project that investigates mobile media, sport markets and changing communication practices.[3] The focus of this project extends beyond news and journalism. Nonetheless, a broader programme of interviews with sport, media and digital technology industry professionals (N = 65) informs our analysis indirectly and supplies helpful contextual knowledge in the formulation of the arguments presented. This context is particularly relevant in cases where informants such as league and club communications managers (N = 11) interact regularly with journalists, editors and news outlets.

The selection of Australia and Scotland as sites for investigation is indicative of more than where the two co-authors are based, and speaks to analogous sporting cultures and media systems. Often circulated via the news media, popular and populist stories told about sport—of famous victories, brave defeats, heroes, injustices—are key sources of national myth making and the expression of cultural nationalism in both countries. In Australia sport has offered a symbolic means to assert a stunted independence from the greater powers that shadow its history; the United Kingdom in the case of its colonial history and the first half of the twentieth century, and the United States in the post-World War II era where American economic, military and popular culture influences loom large (Mandle 1977). Similarly, for Scotland sport has historically offered a means to express an identity distinct from England, as well as a setting for visible displays of nationalism organised as much around anti-English sentiment as a homogenous sense of nationhood (Whigham 2014). Other commonalities of Australia and Scotland include features of their media systems. Both have limited but highly competitive newspaper, radio and television markets. Commercial media outlets operate alongside a sizeable public service media sector, with the Australian Broadcasting Corporation (ABC) having been modelled on the British Broadcasting Corporation (BBC). From the perspective of globalised media capital, they are geographically located near bigger and more commercially attractive regions (e.g. Southeast Asia, and England and Europe), meaning that the long-term commercial viability of a range of daily newspapers and radio and television networks is a concern for the journalists whose livelihoods depend on them. A related pattern is evident in the digital, online and mobile media industries in terms of where companies and services base their headquarters in the medium-to-long term. By virtue of their small populations compared to the likes of the United States, England, Germany, India or China, both Australia and Scotland struggle to provide the user bases, "scalability", and/or volume of content required to satisfy the demands of venture capital and institutional investors for accelerated market growth and high-yield financial returns (Rushkoff 2016).[4]

Sport News and Journalism: Form, Process and Practice

Despite the credibility and seriousness of sport news coming under constant scrutiny, sport reports and information remain important for media organisations because of their popularity with advertisers and audiences (Boyle, Rowe, and Whannel 2010). Sport is a source of reliable and plentiful content due to the frequent scheduling of events and the regularity of competitions for an array of national and international leagues (including association football, Australian rules, tennis, netball, basketball, cricket, the rugby codes, etc.), high-profile world championship and cup tournaments, and multi-sport global mega-events. Matches and events deliver an exhaustive cycle of reportable results, highlights, press conferences, pre- and post-event interviews, athlete and team profiles, injuries, controversies, analysis and commentary, social media communication, fan actions and reactions, publicity and official statements.

The structures and rhythms of sport have dual consequences for news and journalism. At one level, the appeal and reliability of sport as a source of news means that journalists know their "beat" has a sizeable audience eager to consume content. Their reports and stories are likely to perform well in terms of the online metrics and data analytics that now help to inform editorial decisions and the allocation of space and time for stories (MacGregor 2007) (although it should be noted that data-led logics are also disadvantaging many women's and disability sports that have long struggled for public attention and sponsorship; Hutchins 2015). At another level, sport journalists are struggling with the same pressures that are buffeting journalism in general, including reduced newsroom resources, severe time pressures, the need to produce stories for multiple platforms, the rise of automated content production, and growing competition from content aggregators and "social" news specialists (Allan 2012). Paradoxically, the popularity and volume of sporting fixtures and events that guarantees the employment of sport journalists also presents a burden when they are expected to cover so many of them with limited resources and time across two or more platforms (Hutchins and Rowe 2012).

Recent sport journalism scholarship outlines many of the specific challenges confronted by sport reporters and editors. For example, Peter English presents extensive evidence of falling revenue and staffing levels in newsrooms (English 2014), and anxieties among editorial staff that a focus on speed and "churn" in digital and online publishing is adversely affecting accuracy and fact-checking in reporting (English 2012, 145). These issues make it difficult for many sport reporters to obtain the considerable resources and time needed for in-depth investigations into sly practice and systematic corruption, as the current imbroglio surrounding FIFA and its scandalised former President, Sepp Blatter, demonstrates (Rowe 2016). This situation makes many journalists reliant on a steady stream of "information subsidies" produced by club and league media units to meet their weekly story quotas (Sherwood, Nicholson, and Marjoribanks 2016). Built on public relations strategies and problematic levels of control over access to players and coaches, these information subsidies include polished textual and video content created by in-house league/club media production teams. This content is then recycled in newspaper and television news reports (Sherwood, Nicholson, and Marjoribanks 2016). Journalists and news organisations are also grappling with the vicissitudes of social networking and real-time communication in the delivery of sport news, including via Facebook, Twitter and live blogging (Boyle and Haynes 2013; English 2016; McEnnis 2015; Sherwood and Nicholson 2013). Accelerating the flow of both reliable news and scurrilous rumours, these platforms complicate how journalists present and circulate stories, understand audience expectations, interact with sources and audience members, and present themselves to the public.

Sport news is an underdetermined form given the competing factors detailed in the existing literature. One means of analytically negotiating this problem is to discard the idea of news as a definitive or perhaps even stable cultural form. News is recast as a "processual" outcome of interactions across and between institutional structures, funding models, professional decision making, consumer media technologies and consumption practices (Revers 2014). Judging by the sport journalism literature and the interview data we collected from journalists, it is apparent that an unprecedented diversification at the level of news content and technology links with a countervailing focus on the shared journalism practices used to collect newsworthy information and interpret events. Our deployment of the term community, therefore, encapsulates the self-ascribed specialist character of reporting sport news and the work routines of print, broadcast, online and mobile journalists who produce reports, stories, opinion, commentary and features on controversial issues that occasionally appear in wider news agendas (e.g. drug cheating, match-fixing and financial corruption). This is a community that justifies its contribution and value by seeking to adapt traditional precepts of journalism to a changeable context in which digital and mobile media continue to alter the presentation, economics and parameters of news. This adaptation is evident by reference to perceptive first-hand observation (i.e. "knowing the game and the people who play it"), storytelling and investigative skills, editorial oversight and workplace standards, formal reporting rounds and accreditation, the ability to make and maintain contacts (i.e. find "insider information"), and the telling fact they get paid for their journalism by established news organisations.

The following sections present two key areas that highlight how changing forms of news are assimilated into articulations of journalism practice. The ways in which these professionals describe and explain their activities show that sport journalism practice is: (1) increasingly mobile in format and focus, and (2) impacted by institutional changes that demand adaptability from journalists and influence their workplace conditions and employment.

Mobile Media

Wireless communications networks (e.g. Wi-Fi, 3G, 4G/LTE, WiMAX) and mobile media devices such as smartphones and tablet computers are widely recognised as pivotal but unpredictable factors in determining how news is now produced, presented and consumed. The resulting combination of technological promise and future uncertainty can be partly attributed to the pace of change in consumer technology and telecommunications network innovation. To this can be added fluctuating take-up rates of mobile devices, operating systems and myriad software tools across the news industries and by citizens, with considerable variation evident by region, country and age (Reuters Institute for the Study of Journalism 2015). Another complicating factor is that mobile media is constituted by assemblages of media technologies and practices of direct consequence to the conduct of journalism and the circulation of news (Goggin 2011; Goggin, Martin, and Dwyer 2015; Nel and Westlund 2012; Westlund 2013, 2014). A complex array of mobile software and hardware is penetrating news markets and affecting journalism, including apps, mobile internet, social and locative media, messaging systems, mobile video, live streaming, camera phones and data analytics.

Evidence of the contrasting effects of smartphones and tablets in particular is readily available through high-profile surveys of changing news consumption habits. The Pew Research Center (2015, 4) has found that 39 of the top 50 digital news sites in the United States receive more traffic from mobile devices than desktop computers, although the duration of stay by visitors is often less on mobile sites when compared to desktop. An annual survey of more than 20,000 people across 12 nations, including Australia and the United Kingdom, by the Reuters Institute for the Study of Journalism (2015) offers related results. The latest edition of this report shows that two-thirds of smartphones users surveyed use their devices for news every week (8). This positions the smartphone as "*the* defining device for digital news with a disruptive impact on consumption, formats, and business models" (8, original emphasis).

A related picture of overall yet uneven growth emerges in relation to sport news consumption via smartphones and tablets. A 16-nation survey, *The Global Sports Media Consumption Report* (Perform, Kantar Media, and Sport Business 2014), reveals considerable variation in the use of mobile devices to consume sport news. In China, 55 per cent of surveyed users access news about sport via mobile devices, followed by other countries such as India (46 per cent), Turkey (45 per cent) and South Africa (40 per cent). The United Kingdom and Australia deliver figures of 25 and 22 per cent, respectively (15). Both of these nations also report striking results of over 50 per cent for users who use a tablet or smartphone to access live text commentary during sport events (29; see McEnnis 2015). Sport journalists working in Australia and Scotland confirm these trends. Repeated references were made during our interviews to mobile media as "where the audience is going" (Sportswriter and Broadcaster, interview, 9 November 2015) and the need for news organisations to become "mobile first" in their thinking and output (Head of Digital, interview, 28 March 2014). One of the largest news outlets shared internal figures showing that 50 per cent of their users consume content on a mobile device, with one in four page views and video streams coming through their mobile site. Interestingly, mobile users report slightly higher levels of watching videos until their completion compared to desktop. However, this pattern is offset by average session durations being notably longer on desktop when compared to mobile (12 minutes on desktop versus 3 minutes on the mobile site) (Head of News, email correspondence, 29 October 2014).

The increasing use and "taken-for-grantedness" (Ling 2012) of mobile media and communications represents a critical development in the history of news and journalism. An interrelationship exists between formats of news and the practices that produce it, with each affecting the other to differing degrees depending on available infrastructures, competing commercial interests, intervening government actions and events in the wider world. Communications theorist, James W. Carey (1983), dissected this complex interdependence three decades ago in the course of his seminal examination of the telegraph and its large-scale effects on the circulation of information and ideas in time and space. He argues that the spread of the telegraph across North America in the nineteenth century helped to produce lasting effects on news and journalism. The form of the cable and telegram demanded a "flattened out and standardized" language of journalism, giving rise to a condensed "cablese" noted for its sparse and unadorned written style (310–311). A source of fascination for figures such as Ernest Hemingway, this distinct modification of literary style was imposed on journalists and correspondents as the cost structures and "lingo" of the cable led to an "objective" model of nationalised news denuded of humour, irony and the colloquial. This form of reporting also allowed for a greater volume of news to be communicated quickly across the continent as the telegraph spread word about a "real glut of occurrences", meaning that the frame of news moved outwards from its previously localised and partisan emphasis. The commodifying effects of the telegraph and telegram became obvious over time. In conjunction with the expansion of markets, entrepreneurial endeavours and industrialisation, news became a commodity to be "transported, measured, reduced and timed" (311), recalling an analogue equivalent of online and mobile metrics.

The impact of smartphones and tablets on news arguably follows a parallel logic to the one described by Carey. The format and appearance of news stories are altering in relation to mobile media consumption patterns, the parameters presented by smartphone and tablet functionality and screens, and emergent mobile journalism practices. Interviewees explained that the length of written reports is being reduced to accommodate the tendency of users to "skim" the news on mobile devices for short periods of time. For instance, editors acknowledge that their audiences and readers use mobile devices in escalating numbers, even if they also consume print and/or broadcast stories from the same news outlet. According to a Head of Content for an online news organisation charged with managing the presentation of stories across different media (desktop, social, mobile, video and audio/podcast), this means adapting written stories for smartphone screens and the shorter session times associated with mobile device use:

> We've got to accept that eventually our audience will be in the majority on these devices. So we've got to write a little bit shorter because our news stories might go to 18 pars [paragraphs], but 10 to 12 pars is probably the "sweet spot" for someone standing at the train station. (Interview, 11 April 2014)

The popularity of mobile devices is leading other editors and journalists to claim that longer sport stories written for desktop consumption "will not matter in a couple of years" (Head of Digital, interview, 28 March 2014). While this claim is disputable, it signals that mobile media and communications are central to how news producers think about the presentation of stories and content into the future.

The triumvirate of shorter usage sessions, concise stories and compact mobile screens is changing the practice of journalists and, in the process, their expectations. An experienced Sportswriter and Broadcaster made reference to a belief that most people "will not read more than 900 words on their mobile [phone] or their tablet" (interview, 9 November 2015). This length entails a pragmatic acceptance on his behalf, as he had spent much of his career writing features of anywhere between 1000 and 3000 words:

> I go back to the point about splitting the text up and making it digestible and readable for that [mobile] device because people are not going to go through lots and lots [of words] ... it does have that practical impact. There's no point writing a piece of 2000 words. It's just wasting everybody's time really. (Sportswriter and Broadcaster, interview, 9 November 2015)

Other sportswriters have a less accepting attitude towards the effects of mobile media on their journalism. A Senior Online Sportswriter and Broadcaster outlined how the presentation constraints presented by the mobile phone and tablet have, at the behest of his news directors, changed how he writes match reports in a way that is "depressing" (interview, 9 November 2015). In the movement from print to mobile reporting, the first four paragraphs of match reports have been reduced "to more or less one sentence paragraphs with all the key details" (e.g. teams, score, star player, the decisive moment in the game). He explained that the rest of the report can resume a more traditional style, but "a child of 10" could do the opening because "they [his outlet] just want the details so they can sit on the screen of a mobile phone".

Similar to correspondents needing to learn "cablese" and report via telegraph during the nineteenth century, a challenge faced by sport journalists in the new millennium is learning how to report for and via mobile media. For most journalists, this involves internalising the requirements of story formats on mobile devices and incorporating mobile social media into their research and reporting practices. However, we also found an example of an early "adapter"—the Sportswriter and Broadcaster (radio and television) discussed above—who has become adept at using a tablet computer and smartphone to file stories with both written and audio components. His level of proficiency appears unusual, but is nonetheless worth detailing as an indicator of the technical skills that sport journalists may need to develop in the coming years. His embrace of mobile reporting practices is motivated by his continual movement around a football stadium on match day to attend press conferences, interview players and coaches, and relay scores and updates for both television and radio. He describes a shrinking in the size of his computing devices that is assisted by the shorter reports now preferred by his news outlet:

> If I'm at a press conference on my own I'll record it on my phone. I'll ping it back [to the office], so there's just a technical app that we use. So they'll get audio quality back here over a Wi-Fi signal in 10 minutes if it's a 5-minute press conference. I'll then quickly write up a news line, a top line for the press conference, three or four pars and send that over. They will put that up very quickly on to the Web and on to Twitter. While still sitting in my car or wherever, I'll then transcribe the full thing and write up the full news story ... I just got fed up lugging my laptop about, which was heavy. And then my laptop died on me and I got an iPad so I was using my iPad quite a lot. And I flipped between having a keyboard for that and just writing on the screen. I can write a match report on my phone. The match reports here are all under 500 words, but I have written 900 word pieces on my phone. I don't mind it. (Sportswriter and Broadcaster, interview, 9 November 2015)

This description speaks to an adaptability that has become a requirement of sport news and journalism. In contemplating her career trajectory and that of her peers, another television, radio and online Sport Journalist observed that a willingness to adapt is essential in an industry where "journalism is a performance in some ways and you're commissioned to be a certain type of journalist", with the commissioning process entailing intermittent shifts in focus depending on the job and outlet (interview, 21 April 2016).

Changes in journalism practice are easier to identify and describe than comparatively opaque transformations in news as a textual system that exercises social and cultural authority in the construction of reality (Meikle and Redden 2011). However, the spread of mobile media is altering this textual system, triggering questions about how an event is awarded the status of reportable news. The Online Sport Editor for a newspaper revealed that mobile device use is, in some cases, refashioning which stories are selected for publication. The question of what people want from a story presented on a smartphone compared to a newspaper is a factor in editorial decision making:

> You need to be a bit snappier because people aren't looking for long reads on a mobile phone. It's maybe not so much the way sports journalism is done in terms of writing that has been affected. It's probably more in the selecting of stories. If people are out on a weekend, you're trying to envisage what sort of information they are using their mobile phone for. And they're probably trying to find out scores and what's going on, and they want that in a fairly easily digestible manner. (Interview, 31 August 2015)

Other informants confirm this impressionistic account of how stories are chosen. The stunning popularity of mobile video (Goggin 2014) means that, for those outlets with ready access to content, stories accompanied by short-form video featuring pre-roll advertisements are prioritised (Head of Digital, interview, 28 March 2014). This focus on mobile video produces a bias towards footage that is most likely to be watched until the end and shared on social media. A dispiriting result of this preference is that, for a major national news organisation, the most popular videos often involve sporting violence: "That's what people want. Going back to that notion of 'if it bleeds it leads', people want to see violence" (Head of News, interview, 29 October 2014).

The following section widens the scope of the analysis presented so far by examining how this community of practice is responding to changes in the organisation of newsrooms, and the challenges faced by news organisations and journalists when confronted by an expanding range of competitors.

Institutional Change

Variance in the practices and norms of contemporary sport journalism are related to widespread transformations across the news industries as organisations scramble to find sustainable structures and business models. Under the conditions fostered by industrial capitalism and mass communications for much of the twentieth century, news media came to exercise institutionalised power by the accretion of a putatively objective authority built from the systematic administration of news production and the applied expertise of journalists, thereby ensuring the reliability and timeliness of reports (cf. Weber 1991 [1948]). The new millennium has seen the health of this industrial model deteriorate following a splintering of the companies, groups and individuals that supply, circulate, recycle and remediate news, confusing the once comparatively stable organisational logics of print and broadcast news media (Singer et al. 2011). Sport news both leads and is subject to a tide change in personalised news presentation and multi-platform consumption. It is, for example, available from a growing range of digital, mobile media and telecommunications companies and intermediaries such as Copa90, Perform, SendtoNews, The Players' Tribune, BT Sport, Telstra Media, Apple News, YouTube, Snapchat, Twitter and Facebook. As already mentioned, to these can be added the multiplication of quasi-news services operated in-house by leagues and clubs, including the likes of MLB Advanced Media, AFL Media and Celtic TV. The institutional power and authority to produce news is atomised in this environment, affecting how newsrooms are organised and the ways in which journalists exercise their craft.

The practice of professional journalists is challenged significantly by the proliferation of news provision and a concomitant dispersal of authority in determining what news is (and is not). The impact of these processes is most obvious in the expansion of information supplied by public relations practices throughout professional sport. A Senior Sports Writer for a national newspaper is critical of promotional strategies and policies designed to protect the brands of associations, leagues and clubs by limiting journalist access to athletes, which also serves to advantage their own branded "news" and online information services. Sardonically referring to communications and public relations figures as "media prevention officers", he believes that their actions devalue the potential benefits of journalism and are deleterious to the public image of sportsmen and women:

> They're a disaster for sportspeople as much as they are for sportswriters because what they're doing is preventing personalities from being conveyed. It makes for duller copy and it's much harder for sportspeople to actually portray themselves as individuals—as people with proper personalities—because they never develop any relationships with journalists or anyone else for that matter it seems. They're constantly protected. They live in little bubbles and increasingly think that's who they should be as well. (Senior Sports Writer, interview, 9 November 2015)

This opinion is indicative of the fact that it is much harder for journalists to find good leads and reliable sources in the midst of a structural shift in the employment market towards public relations and corporate communications. For example, in the same week that the UK national newspaper, *The Independent*, closed its print edition after 30 years, with the loss of 100 journalism jobs, *PRWeek* magazine noted the defection of senior journalists and editors to the corporate communications sector (Rogers 2016). Career opportunities in communications and public relations are "booming" compared to journalism (Lloyd and Toogood 2015), as the spread of league and club communications units and media operations attest.

The rise of public relations strategies creates a double bind for sport journalists in the area of source relations. Journalists find it harder to access major sporting figures reliably, forcing them to seek alternative sources for stories and reports. When combined with considerable workloads, this lack of access generates a pull towards more easily accessed source material on social media and, in the process, weakens the experience and skills needed to cultivate and maintain dependable "insider" sources. This dynamic almost inevitably edges sport reporting ever closer to "churnalism" and an emphasis on "nowness" that hollows out the value of journalism performed in the service of an informed and engaged public (Davies 2011; Lewis 2013). In this regard, it is worth quoting the observations of distinguished newspaper journalist, Hugh McIlvanney, at length, as he draws on his nearly six decades of experience:

> No doubt the Scottish connection helped to secure educational sessions with Sir Matt Busby, Bill Shankly, Jock Stein and Sir Alex Ferguson ... But that privileged access is firmly associated in my mind with the atmosphere and ethos of those days, a time when the links between journalists writing about sport and the subjects of their pieces were more relaxed and more real. It was all a far cry from having to create a story from some player's brief babblings on Twitter. Technology has delivered many a boon to the working reporter but in sport, especially, there are penalties. The demand for instant information and comment for the internet in addition to the copy transmitted to the newspaper must eat into the opportunities for the ferreting around that I always found productive in the immediate aftermath of an event. (McIlvanney 2016)

The nostalgia of McIlvanney's account is underpinned by the centrality of extensive source relations to effective journalism practice, and the difficulties that arise when there is limited time to "ferret around".

However, as with the case of mobile media, there is evidence of adaptation to combat impediments to the cultivation of sources. This involves the use of the (admittedly contested) cultural status of professional journalism in social media environments, displacing the relatively flat user hierarchies engineered by the operators of these connective platforms. By virtue of their public visibility, journalists often stand out on the likes of Facebook and Twitter because of their follower numbers, possession of "verified" accounts, and widespread awareness of the news organisations and brands attached to their profiles (Hanusch and Bruns 2016). These features assist when journalists contact sporting figures via social media, allowing them to develop relationships at a distance and receive responses to at least some of their inquiries. The Senior Online Sportswriter and Broadcaster discussed earlier administers a Twitter profile with over 30,000 followers, and uses this service to make direct contact with athletes and famous figures. Employing Twitter as an introduction tool, he describes how his persistence led to a "phenomenal interview" and three-page newspaper feature on the boxer Buster Douglas, the fighter who once defeated the then heavyweight world champion, Mike Tyson. Success in the case of Douglas prompted similar approaches:

> Margaret Court was another one, the great Australian tennis player. That happened in a similar way [contact made via Twitter]. Again [it led to] a two-page interview and there's a few others similar to that. So you can use it [Twitter]. I know my main producer has generated a lot of radio interviews on the back of contacting people on Twitter, and he has maintained those contacts over the years. He's prolific at it. (Interview, 9 November 2015)

Other forms of adaptation to reduced source access are evident. Twitter has, for instance, been used to stimulate the development of source networks. The Sport Editor quoted at the outset of this article initiated a weekly column that curated messages published on this service as a way of summarising events in a local football competition. Initially aimed at generating content for the Friday edition of his newspaper, the column was an unanticipated success:

> The column got a cult following … I was producing this compilation of the best tweets of the week. It was 300 words. You'd probably get 10 to 12 tweets in there. I just watched this world expand … this column just became insane … There was this expectation that people on a Friday would flick to it. It was one of the popular things in the paper each week. It was fascinating because it was something readers had access to online, but it was almost linking the online and print worlds. (Sport Editor, interview, 8 October 2015)

The benefit that flowed from this weekly column was significant. It positioned the Editor as a "gatekeeper" in terms of judging the most important tweets of the week and, by extension, interpretation of events across the league. Different members of the football league who read the column initiated contact with him via Twitter and entered into discussions with him when he was completing his reporting rounds and covering games: "By doing that I got to meet people that I'd never met before in the sporting industry."

The combined effects of public relations on the news industries and the adaptability required to practise journalism produces uncertainty in two ways. First, it makes it difficult for some journalists to envision a long-term career. As mentioned earlier, the process of being "commissioned to be a certain type of journalist" can entail precarious employment conditions forced by regular changes of focus in terms of routine, platform and/or outlet (even within the same news organisation). This situation is manifest in the case of a Freelance Sportswriter who has been writing for newspapers and online news sites for a few years. Stating that she has "doesn't really have a long-term [career] plan because I don't really know what is going to happen" (interview, 10 November 2015), she goes on to explain that the variable income produced by her freelance status spurs a tension between needing to pursue work to earn money, but not so much work that it dilutes the quality of her journalism:

> I kind of like things like that [work from a particular news outlet] and that's a bit of extra money. But I would never count on it because one month I could get 600 quid easily from them and then the next month I get nothing. So you can never bank on the fact that's going to be coming in. But I'm also quite conscious that I don't want to start trying to do lots of stuff and do none of it properly because … someone like [names journalist] can sit down and [quickly] bash out a 900-word article and it's really good. But I can't do that. (Freelance Sportswriter, interview, 10 November 2015)

Second, this type of insecure work produces flow-on effects in terms of journalism training. Beyond adaptability, the question of the skills that novice journalists need when they enter the field presents hurdles for those seeking to train graduate journalists for the realities of workplace conditions and expectations in newsrooms, but also in league and club media units and corporate communications departments. It is a question confronted by a Sport Journalist who worked for many years in a major news organisation and now divides her time between teaching journalism at a university and producing content for a football club media unit. She is keenly aware of the complexities and contradictions that exist across all these roles:

> [When you're] running a club channel, you're very aware that you're not critical of the club in any way, and it's quite hard because I'm training journalists to be critical … And then you're saying [to the trainees], "Okay, so this weekend you're working for [a club] and it's a different kind of journalism where you're not critical, where your job is

> to promote your employers" … It's an uncomfortable mix of PR and journalism and traditionally within the club it has been PR departments who have performed that function. But now, because they're also content creators, journalists are the ones with the skills to edit football packages together. They're the storytellers, so people are training as journalists and then going in-house somewhere and basically being asked, "Could you leave those bits of journalism at the door? Because that's not what you're being paid to do." (Sport Journalist, interview, 21 April 2016)

This quotation highlights the intersecting institutional pressures impacting sport journalism, including multiplying news and content providers, the strength of public relations strategies and promotional cultures in sport, and the tangled expectations confronted by journalists who produce news and attempt to make a living from it. The notion of practice—of acting, doing and making news via variegated technologies and outlets—has then become a key means of making sense of professional experience in unwieldy news and media ecosystems.

Conclusion

We have employed the concept of "community of practice" to emphasise the existence and significance of shared practices within the profession of sport journalism. Particularly in the case of journalists working for established newspaper and broadcast organisations, these practices and the values attached to them exhibit continuity with a longer history of journalism and news reporting. However, these practices and values are located within a more complex, mobile, uncertain and multi-layered media environment than even a decade ago:

> The basics don't really change. It's about developing contacts and coming up with ideas and being able to write news stories based on breaking news stories or following news stories through contacts. And coming up with original feature ideas and interviews that you can go and do … That aspect of the job hasn't changed. I think what has changed is some of the more nuts and bolts aspects of it, in terms of how much you're writing or what platform you're doing an interview on, and fitting things around the demands to be multi-platform. (Sportswriter and Broadcaster, interview, 9 November 2015)

The ongoing challenge for journalists and editors is to maintain these "basics" in the midst of volatile news and media markets where the fevered pursuit of reliable revenue and funding is paramount. As this article has shown, a conundrum confronted by news media organisations is how to adequately resource engagement with fickle audiences that exist across mutable devices, formats, platforms and networks. The arduous task of consistently attracting the attention of large audiences through different combinations of adaptable content is also having material consequences for those who create reports and stories. A recurring theme for sport journalists—and journalists more generally—is that the security of working for an established news outlet on a full-time basis is a privilege that fewer and fewer enjoy.

In returning to Zelizer (1993), the evidence presented here suggests that the institutionally legitimated interpretive authority of sport journalism is fragmenting. The growth of quasi-news services whose institutional antecedents are in public relations, corporate communications and information technology (e.g. search and social media) have contributed to an erosion of sport news as a coherent textual system. In some cases news is as general as "anything" that citizens are "willing to read", while in others as specific as a "flattened out" format that needs to "sit on the screen of a mobile phone". These developments are resulting in a much needed defence of the journalistic practices that underpin the production of reliable news that, in principle, serves the interests of wider publics. This defence connects to the "double time" now performed by sport journalists, the character of which has changed since Zelizer (1993, 224) described a temporally constituted interpretive process over 20 years ago. The double time of contemporary sport journalism is a fraught affair of adaptive reporting with dwindling resources in the present while thinking forward into a future that promises constant change in communications and media technology, journalistic routines and institutional relations.

ACKNOWLEDGEMENTS

This article was made possible by the support of the Centre for Cultural Policy Research at the University of Glasgow and the Australian Research Council. Thank you to all of the individuals who generously shared their time and insights in the research completed for this paper. Thank you also to Alison Anderson for her assistance in the organisation and coding of the interview data.

DISCLOSURE STATEMENT

No potential conflict of interest was reported by the authors.

FUNDING

This research was supported by an Australian Research Council Future Fellowship [FT130100506; http://artsonline.monash.edu.au/mobilemediasport/].

NOTES

1. Interview data presented in this paper are de-identified in accordance with the conditions of clearance provided by the relevant University Human Research Ethics Committee.
2. The terms "community of practice" and "communities of practice" have also been used in educational theory and business studies to describe "groups of people bound together by shared expertise and passion for a joint enterprise" (Wenger 1999; Wenger and Snyder 2000, 139). While acknowledging previous meanings associated with these terms, our use of "community of practice" developed from a reading of Zelizer (1993) and an attempt to identify values, beliefs and relationships that characterise contemporary sport journalism and news.

3. The "Mobile Media Sport Moment: Markets, Technologies, Power" Project website can be found at http://artsonline.monash.edu.au/mobilemediasport/.

4. Although this does not mean successful technology start-ups have never emerged from Scotland or Australia. The daily fantasy sport service, Fan Duel, began life in Scotland and its headquarters are now in New York. The high-profile wearable technologies and performance analytics company, Catapult, emerged out of sport science research activities at the Australian Institute of Sport and now has a major presence in US, UK and European markets.

REFERENCES

Allan, Stuart, ed. 2012. *Routledge Companion to News and Journalism*. London: Routledge.

Boyle, Raymond. 2006. *Sports Journalism: Context and Issues*. London: Sage.

Boyle, Raymond, and Richard Haynes. 2013. "Sports Journalism and Social Media: A New Conversation?" In *Digital Media Sport: Technology, Power and Culture in the Network Society*, edited by Brett Hutchins and David Rowe, 204–218. New York: Routledge.

Boyle, Raymond, David Rowe, and Garry Whannel. 2010. "'Delight in Trivial Controversy'? Questions for Sports Journalism." In *The Routledge Companion to News and Journalism*, edited by Stuart Allan, 245–255. London: Routledge.

Carey, James W. 1983. "Technology and Ideology: The Case of the Telegraph." *Prospects* 8: 303–325.

Cotter, Colleen. 2010. *News Talk: Investigating the Language of Journalism*. Cambridge, UK: Cambridge University Press.

Couldry, Nick. 2012. *Media, Society, World: Social Theory and Digital Media Practice*. Cambridge, UK: Polity Press.

Crawford, Kate. 2011. "News to Me: Twitter and the Personal Networking of News." In *News Online: Transformations and Continuities*, edited by Graham Meikle and Guy Redden, 115–131. Basingstoke, Hampshire: Palgrave Macmillan.

Curran, James. 2011. *Media and Democracy*. London: Routledge.

Davies, Nick. 2011. *Flat Earth News*. London: Vintage.

English, Peter. 2012. "Caught by the Web: The Case of Guardian News and Media's Sports Desk." *Journal of Sports Media* 7 (1): 133–148.

English, Peter. 2014. *Sports Coverage in Print and Web Newspapers: How Online Journalism Has Changed Sports Journalism*. Unpublished PhD Thesis, University of the Sunshine Coast, Queensland, Australia.

English, Peter. 2016. "Twitter's Diffusion in Sports Journalism: Role Models, Laggards and Followers of Social Media Innovation." *New Media & Society* 18 (3): 484–501.

Goggin, Gerard. 2011. "The Intimate Turn in Mobile News." In *News Online: Transformations and Continuities*, edited by Graham Meikle and Guy Redden, 99–114. Basingstoke, Hampshire: Palgrave Macmillan.

Goggin, Gerard. 2014. "Mobile Video: Spreading Stories with Mobile Media." In *The Routledge Companion to Mobile Media*, edited by Gerard Goggin and Larissa Hjorth, 146–156. New York: Routledge.

Goggin, Gerard, Fiona Martin, and Tim Dwyer. 2015. "Locative News: Mobile Media, Place Informatics, and Digital News." *Journalism Studies* 16 (1): 41–59.

Hanusch, Folker, and Axel Bruns. 2016. "Journalistic Branding on Twitter." *Digital Journalism*. doi:10.1080/21670811.2016.1152161.

Hermida, Alfred. 2012. "Twitter as an Ambient News Network." In *Twitter and Society*, edited by Katrin Weller, Axel Bruns, Jean Burgess, Merja Mahrt, and Cornelius Puschmann, 359–372. New York: Peter Lang.

Hutchins, Brett. 2015. "Tales of the Digital Sublime: Tracing the Relationship between Big Data and Professional Sport." *Convergence* 22 (5): 494–509.

Hutchins, Brett, and David Rowe. 2012. *Sport beyond Television: The Internet, Digital Media and the Rise of Networked Media Sport*. New York: Routledge.

Lewis, Justin. 2013. *Beyond Consumer Capitalism: Media and the Limits to Imagination*. Cambridge, UK: Polity Press.

Ling, Rich. 2012. *Taken for Grantedness: The Embedding of Mobile Communication into Society*. Cambridge, MA: The MIT Press.

Lloyd, John, and Laura Toogood. 2015. *Journalism and PR: News Media and Public Relations in the Digital Age*. Oxford, UK: IB Tauris/Reuters Institute for the Study of Journalism.

MacGregor, Phil. 2007. "Tracking the Online Audience—Metric Data Start a Subtle Revolution." *Journalism Studies* 8 (2): 280–298.

Mandle, William F. 1977. *Going It Alone: Australia's National Identity in the Twentieth Century*. Ringwood, Victoria: Allen Lane.

McEnnis, Simon. 2015. "Following the Action: How Live Bloggers Are Reimagining the Professional Ideology of Sports Journalism." *Journalism Practice*. doi:10.1080/17512786.2015.1068130.

McIlvanney, Hugh. 2016. "After Six Decades of Writing, It's Time for a New Chapter." *The Sunday times*, 28 February. http://www.thesundaytimes.co.uk/sto/sport/Columns/hughmcllvanney/article1672425.ece

McNair, Brian. 2006. *Cultural Chaos: Journalism, News and Power in a Globalised World*. London: Routledge.

Meikle, Graham, and Guy Redden. 2011. "Introduction: Transformation and Continuity." In *News Online: Transformations and Continuities*, edited by Graham Meikle and Guy Redden, 1–19. Basingstoke, Hampshire: Palgrave Macmillan.

Nel, Francois, and Oscar Westlund. 2012. "The 4C's of Mobile News: Channels, Conversation, Content and Commerce." *Journalism Practice* 6 (5-6): 744–753.

Perform, Kantar Media, and Sport Business. 2014. *Know the Fan: The Global Sports Media Consumption Report 2014*. London: Perform, Kantar Media, and Sport Business.

Pew Research Center. 2015. *State of the News Media 2015*. Washington, DC: Pew Research Center.

Reuters Institute for the Study of Journalism. 2015. *Reuters Institute Digital News Report 2015*. Oxford, UK: Reuters Institute for the Study of Journalism.

Revers, Matthias. 2014. "The Twitterization of News Making: Transparency and Journalistic Professionalism." *Journal of Communication* 64 (5): 806–826.

Rogers, Danny. 2016. "From the Editor-in-Chief: Talent Flocks to PR but at a Cost to Journalism." *PR Week*, 10 March. http://www.prweek.com/article/1386751/editor-in-chief-talent-flocks-pr-cost-journalism

Rowe, David. 2016. "Sports Journalism and the FIFA Scandal: Personalization, Co-Optation, and Investigation." *Communication & Sport*. doi:10.1177/2167479516642206.

Rushkoff, Douglas. 2016. *Throwing Rocks at the Google Bus: How Growth Became the Enemy of Prosperity*. New York: Portfolio Penguin.

Schlesinger, Philip, and Gillian Doyle. 2015. "From Organizational Crisis to Multi-Platform Salvation? Creative Destruction and the Recomposition of News Media." *Journalism: Theory, Practice & Criticism* 16 (3): 305–323.

Sherwood, Merryn, and Matthew Nicholson. 2013. "Web 2.0 Platforms and the Work of Newspaper Sport Journalists." *Journalism: Theory, Practice & Criticism* 14 (7): 942–959.

Sherwood, Merryn, Matthew Nicholson, and Timothy Marjoribanks. 2016. "Access, Agenda Building and Information Subsidies: Media Relations in Professional Sport." *International Review for the Sociology of Sport*. doi:10.1177/1012690216637631.

Singer, Jane B., Alfred Hermida, David Domingo, Ari Heinonen, Steve Paulussen, Thorsten Quandt, Zvi Reich, and Maria Vujnovic. 2011. *Participatory Journalism: Guarding Open Gates at Online Newspapers*. Oxford, UK: Wiley-Blackwell.

Tumber, Howard. 2014. "back to the Future? The Sociology of News and Journalism from Black and White to the Digital Age." In *Media Sociology: A Reappraisal*, edited by Silvio Waisbord, 63–78. Cambridge, UK: Polity Press.

Weber, Max. 1991 [1948]. "Technical Advantages of Bureaucratic Organization." In *From Max Weber: Essays in Sociology*, edited by H. H. Gerth and C. Wright Mills, 214–216. London: Routledge.

Weiss, Amy Schmitz, and David Domingo. 2010. "Innovation Processes in Online Newsrooms as Actor-Networks and Communities of Practice." *New Media & Society* 12 (7): 1156–1171.

Wenger, Etienne. 1999. *Communities of Practice: Learning, Meaning, and Identity*. New York: Cambridge University Press.

Wenger, Etienne C., and William M. Snyder. 2000. "Communities of Practice: The Organizational Frontier." *Harvard Business Review* 78 (1): 139-145.

Westlund, Oscar. 2013. "Mobile News: A Review and Model of Journalism in an Age of Mobile Media." *Digital Journalism* 1 (1): 6–26.

Westlund, Oscar. 2014. "The Production and Consumption of News in an Age of Mobile Media." In *The Routledge Companion to Mobile Media*, edited by Gerard Goggin and Larissa Hjorth, 135–145. New York: Routledge.

Whigham, Stuart. 2014. "'Anyone but England'? Exploring Anti-English Sentiment as Part of Scottish National Identity in Sport." *International Review of the Sociology of Sport* 49 (2): 152–174.

Zelizer, Barbie. 1993. "Journalists as Interpretive Communities." *Critical Studies in Mass Communication* 10 (3): 219–237.

CONTROLLING THE MESSAGE AND THE MEDIUM?

The impact of sports organisations' digital and social channels on media access

Merryn Sherwood, Matthew Nicholson and **Timothy Marjoribanks**

Sports organisations' recently acquired ability to deliver their own news—through social and digital platforms—represents a potential paradigm shift in the once symbiotic relationship between sports organisations and the media that cover them. While sports organisations once needed the media to deliver their messages, they now have their own media. This study examined the impact of sports digital and social platforms, such as websites, Twitter and Facebook, on sports journalism through 37 interviews with public relations staff in Australian sports organisations and one targeted case study in a professional Australian Rules Football club competing in the Australian Football League (AFL) in Australia. It found that while public relations staff in Australian sports organisations still value traditional media coverage, they also signalled that their own platforms were increasing in value as distribution channels. The case study of the professional AFL club found that the club selectively chose to distribute some stories on their own platforms instead of through traditional media. These stories were not simply delivered on the club's own platforms, but the public relations staff actively framed the narrative of these stories for strategic benefit. These results have significant implications for sports journalism, as it suggests the rapid development of sports organisations' social and digital media platforms has the potential to irrevocably alter the once symbiotic relationship between sport and media.

Introduction

While sports journalists have traditionally enjoyed close relationships with sports sources (Rowe 2004), recent anecdotal evidence indicates the opposite may now be true. Sports journalists from the United Kingdom (Greenslade 2013), India (Narayanan 2015) and Australia (Hinds 2012; Gaskin 2013) have criticised the lack of access to athletes and coaches and the heightened role of public relations staff in policing this access. Even in the United States, where media access has traditionally been both mandated and open, the gates have started to swing shut. A recent survey of US college football reporters found most now believed their chances of gaining a 10-minute interview with an athlete for a profile were somewhere between "no" to "absolutely no chance this will happen" (Sherman 2015). According to journalists, the reason for this change is that sports organisations are now attempting to compete as media organisations in their own right, delivering their own news direct to their publics (Boyle and Haynes 2006, 2014). In Australia's National Rugby League competition, a high-profile club declined an interview request from Sydney's major newspaper, but later that week the same player appeared in an interview on the club's website (Kent 2014), evidence that club staff made a deliberate choice that preferenced an internally controlled distribution channel.

In a dramatic example of this trend, English third-division football club Swindon Town F.C. banned all media in 2015. Aside from a post-match press conference and approval for one BBC reporter to interview the manager pre-game, which were league broadcast requirements, no interview requests would be granted, no general media opportunities would take place during the week, and no access would be granted to a dedicated press box on match days (Borden 2015; Peck 2015). Instead, the club planned to create its own content and deliver it through its own website and an app, Fanzai. The club described how its "in-house journalist" would conduct interviews with the players, management and staff to "give [fans] more of an insight into how the team and club is run" (Ponsford 2015). Ultimately, Swindon Town's foray into complete control of their media content ended fairly quickly; midway through 2016 there was no reference to the Fanzai app on their website and their media information page encouraged journalists to contact the media manager for requests. The Swindon Town example, despite its failure, is a harbinger of the potential for a sports organisation to cut off outside media access all together, in favour of delivering its own news.

This potential shift to the exclusive delivery of sport-based news via internally controlled distribution channels is significant because professional sport and the media have historically shared a mutually beneficial, symbiotic relationship. In this partnership, media have relied on sport content to provide high ratings or readership, broadcast rights were a major revenue source for sports organisations and sports organisations utilised the media's reach to communicate with fans (Nicholson, Kerr, and Sherwood 2015). Despite the widespread use of communication platforms by sports organisations and their potential to influence sports public relations strategy (Boyle and Haynes 2014), there is a limited amount of research that examines how these new platforms and channels might impact the ability of journalists to access sports sources. Are all sports organisations deliberately aiming to cut off traditional media and become their own content creators, like Swindon Town? This study aimed to answer this question and explore a significant gap in the research field, through qualitative interviews with 37 Australian sports public relations staff and an in-depth case study of public relations practice at a professional Australian Football League (AFL) club in Australia, which examined how digital media platforms are being utilised by Australian sports organisations.

Agenda-building, Sports Media and Sports Public Relations

McCombs' (2005, 2013) model of agenda-building posits that the media agenda consists of three major influences: the norms and traditions of journalism; intermedia agenda-setting; and the continuous interactions of news organisations with numerous sources, including the individual agendas of those sources. However, media scholars have argued that the system of newswork prioritises the role of sources (Carlson 2009), so much so that statements made in landmark news studies in the 1970s, such as "news is, after all, not what journalists think, but what their sources say" (Sigal 1986, 29), are even more applicable in the twenty-first century. The role of sources in the production of sports news is potentially even more influential due to the demand conditions of sports newswork (Marr, Francis, and Randall 1999). Due to the beat system of sports journalism, where journalists must report news every day even if it is not necessarily what would normally be considered newsworthy (Lowes 1999), the reliance on sources is so crucial, some stories may be left untold in order to keep a relationship intact (Boyle, Dinan, and Morrow 2002). It is therefore understandable that sports journalists have long been criticised for their reliance on sports public relations sources (Anderson 2001; Surface 1972; Wulfemeyer 1985). Anderson remarked in his content analysis of Major League Baseball's (MLB's) labour disputes in US newspapers that favourable coverage given to the MLB administration is related to the power of sports organisations:

> As long as the distribution of power is narrow and the decision processes are closed, then journalists will never be free from the small group of public relations experts, official spokespersons, and powerful leaders whose self-serving pronouncements have become firmly established as the bulk of the daily news. (Anderson 2001, 364)

More recent research has indicated sports journalists' reliance on sports public relations practitioners as sources has increased. Interactions between sports journalists and athletes and coaches are restricted to highly managed and controlled group settings, such as media conferences, rather than informal, personal encounters (Howe 2008; Sugden and Tomlinson 2007; Suggs 2015). Sports journalists have also reported that the introduction of sports organisations' own news platforms has impacted on their access (Grimmer and Kian 2013; Sherwood and Nicholson 2013). Coombs and Osborne's (2012, 418) study on English football reporters found that "sports reporters believe football organisations' quests to manage their own branded content has led to prioritizing their own club sites over outlets where they cannot control the message".

This body of work is at odds with most of the research on sports public relations, which establishes that a key function of these staff in sports organisations is to facilitate media access. Various sports public relations textbooks (Moynahan, Hall, and Taylor 2002; Nicholson, Kerr, and Sherwood 2015; Pedersen, Miloch, and Laucella 2007; Schultz, Caskey, and Esherick 2014) and profiles of these staff (Hardin and McClung 2002; McCleneghan 1995) have noted that a key function of sports public relations is servicing the media, most often referred to as media relations. Fortunato's detailed case study of the National Basketball Association (NBA) public relations practice helped explain why facilitating media access is important, quoting Brian McIntyre—then NBA Senior Vice President of Public Relations:

> What a whole lot of players and coaches forget, or conveniently forget, is that the media represent the fans in an ideal perfect world, they are the eyes and the ears so if you are not talking to the media, you are not going to get the word out to your fans. (Fortunato 2000, 488)

More recently, Stoldt, Miller, and Vermillion (2009) examined the roles of staff in both college and professional sports organisations in the United States and found that the main goal of these staff was to offer effective service to the media. While some research indicates that these roles have become more strategic, (e.g. Cleland's [2009] study of staff and fans in four English football clubs listed media relations alongside three other roles, including brand promotion and protection, fan communication and crisis management), there is a gap on the detailed work undertaken by sports public relations practitioners. In the twenty-first century this is in need of further exploration, as the introduction of new digital platforms has meant that sports organisations now have multiple ways to communicate, including through channels that they can now control. This has potentially impacted on sports media relations practice, and in turn caused conflict in the symbiotic sport and media relationship.

Sports Public Relations and Digital Platforms

Hutchins and Rowe (2010) highlighted the potential for digital platforms to change the nature of sports media, and the potential for conflict, as sport content shifted between traditional rights-holding broadcasters to new online platforms. The new media sport content economy involved moving from a broadcast model, characterised by scarcity and high barriers of access, to a new online model defined by "digital plentitude" (Hutchins and Rowe 2009, 354), or:

> Significantly lower barriers of access and cost have multiplied the number of media companies, sports organisations, clubs, and even individual athletes who can produce and distribute content for online consumption and allowed large numbers of users to appropriate, modify, and share digital sports footage through web sites. (Hutchins and Rowe 2009, 356)

The volume of scholarly work on social media use in sports confirms how quickly sports organisations have become a major content creator. One recent analysis of the field found 70 articles in sport management journals on social media uses and applications in sport (Filo, Lock, and Karg 2015). Other work established that social media is being used by sports public relations practitioners in their work (Gibbs and Haynes 2013; Stoldt 2012), but there is far less that examines how sports organisations' channels potentially influence media access.

Work that has explored the management of these channels, mostly blogs and websites, indicated staff have found it complicated to manage. The case study of Mikosza and Hutchins (2010) of digital and social media use at the Beijing 2008 Olympic Games detailed how public relations staff were struggling to use these platforms within the strict guidelines that were allowed. A media manager for a national sporting organisation described how creating content for an athlete blog, at face value a relatively easy task, was made extremely difficult by IOC (International Olympic Committee) media rights rules and restrictions. They noted, "It was a 'rather difficult' exercise when you are allowed to write a blog entry, but at the same time are forbidden from mentioning your team members or opposition" (Mikosza and Hutchins 2010, 286). Scherer and Jackson's (2008) study of the All Blacks (New Zealand's national rugby union men's team) website noted that staff wanted the site to be the number one source of news on the team, but also stated these staff saw allblacks.com as a "controlled and managed" way for players to record their thoughts and experiences and connect with fans directly, rather than the "unknown" experience of communicating through a newspaper reporter that they do not trust (Scherer and Jackson 2008, 198). Yanity's (2013) ethnographic study of a journalist's new employment within a college athletic department also indicated the difficulty of this space. While the staff member self-identified as a journalist, his work was driven by a promotional agenda, and he was restricted from telling certain stories or even asking certain questions. For example, the coach had told him to stop asking about injuries, even in a general press conference. These important case studies indicate that sports organisations' platforms are not "news" sites in the traditional definition. They cannot report all news, and are likely to maintain a certain narrative that benefits the club. In light of the increasing importance of sports public relations practitioners in facilitating sports news, combined with the fact that sports organisations are now attempting to create their own news, this study aims to explore the impact of digital platforms on traditional public relations roles within sports organisations. The key question that this paper aims to explore, building on the questions noted in the introduction, is:

RQ1: How does the introduction of a professional sports team's digital platforms influence sports public relations practice?

Method

In order to explore the impact of digital platforms on sports public relations practice, this study employed a mixed-method approach, using interviews with sports public relations staff and a qualitative case study with a professional AFL club. Interview participants were recruited from a survey of Australian sports public relations practitioners. The initial sampling framework for this survey was designed to include all staff working in public relations and communications roles in Australian sports organisations. It included organisations that were defined by the Australian Sports Commission—the Australian government body responsible for sport—as a sports organisation and funded within the 2012/13 financial year. In addition to the national sporting organisations or national sporting organisations for athletes with a disability included in these definitions, the sample was widened to all Australian professional and semi-professional sports leagues, all Australian racing clubs and professional sport circuits with regular ongoing events in Australia (such as the WTA, ATP and Grand Slam tennis events or ASP surfing events). Furthermore, the sample was also widened to include the state sporting bodies of the Coalition of Major Professional and Participation Sports, which included the state associations of Football Federation Australia (FFA), the Australian Rugby Union (ARU), Tennis Australia (TA), Netball Australia (NA), the Australian Football League (AFL), Cricket Australia (CA) and the National Rugby League (NRL). The sample was then refined to only include sports organisations that employed a staff member responsible for sports public relations, through a combination of online organisational research and follow-up phone calls. This led to a sample of 166 sports organisations, which were identified as having at least one staff member dedicated to public relations, media relations or communications. Individual participants, totalling 261, were then identified using publicly available contact details via their websites. Participants were asked in the survey whether they would be interested in participating in an interview, and 49 respondents indicated they would. During the time between the survey completion and the interview stage, five of these respondents had left their jobs. A further six interviews could not be conducted due to scheduling constraints. Thirty-seven interviews were conducted, in 2014 and 2015. Interviews and observation notes were transcribed and entered into NVivo for further analysis, where a two-step process of coding, using methods set out by Saldaña (2013), was applied. In brief, this coding process involved initial descriptive coding, followed by process coding.

The professional case study employed a case study framework articulated by Yin (2013). It involved the researcher undertaking observational and interview research for a week in 2015 at a professional AFL club in Australia, based on the sampling logic provided by Yin (2013), that a case study should be selected on its ability for replication of theory. Based on the anecdotal and scholarly evidence that sports organisations are using digital media platforms for certain purposes (Scherer and Jackson 2008; Yanity 2013) and that sports organisations are limiting access with an aim to publish content on those platforms (Coombs and Osborne 2012; Grimmer and Kian 2013; Suggs 2015), a professional AFL club in Australia was deemed an appropriate place to explore the research question. The AFL is Australia's leading major sports code based on broadcast rights figures; its latest deal was worth AUD$2.5 billion—the highest price ever recorded for an Australian market (Stensholt and Mason 2015). The AFL, which consists of 18 teams located in five Australian states, generated AUD$458 million in revenue in 2014, with individual club revenues between AUD$30 million and 70 million (Baker 2014; King 2015). In 2015 the league's average crowd attendance was 32,436, which was the fourth highest in the world, behind only the NFL, Bundesliga and English Premier League (AAP 2015). A benefit of Yin's (2013) case study approach was that it advises including multiple methods of data collection, such as documents, observations and interviews. In order to answer the research question, whether or not digital platforms were impacting on public relations practice, this paper combines a content analysis of the club's Twitter and Facebook posts and content on their website, in-depth interviews with public relations staff and observations. Data on the club's content production was captured and analysed for particular trends or patterns relating to communication and sports public relations practice. Interviews and observation notes were transcribed and entered into NVivo for further analysis, where the same two-step process of coding that was used for the interviews was applied. The major ethics issue for both the interviews and case studies related to maintaining the confidentiality of participants and their organisations. For that reason, actual individual and organisational names are not used. A benefit of this multi-method approach is that this case study is able to offer not only a presentation of the club's content during the week of analysis, but also explore how it is managed, as well as the underlying reasons for a particular media strategy and whether or not media access was being affected by the use of digital and social platforms.

Results

Use of Social and Digital Platforms—Interviews

The demographic characteristics of the 37 interviewees are summarised in Table 1. The average interview participant was between 30 and 39 years old (40.5 per cent), was slightly more likely to be male than female (56.3 per cent male, 43.2 per cent female) and had an undergraduate degree (64.9 per cent). The participants mostly worked at professional sports leagues, professional clubs and major events (37.8 per cent), national sporting organisations (24.3 per cent) and state sporting organisations (18.9 per cent). The age range of the respondents was from 25 to 61, with 72.9 per cent of respondents aged 39 years or less.

Interviewees were asked to discuss how their organisations used digital and social channels, such as websites and social media channels, and all noted they used these platforms regularly to communicate information externally. However, none had reached the level of Swindon Town, cutting off media access entirely. Instead, many noted that the addition of new platforms had meant deciding where stories should be placed—i.e. traditional media or on their own platforms—was made on a case by case basis, as this quote from Interviewee 21 illustrates:

> It's not just a matter of black and white, to hold content for ourselves or saying "our website gets no traffic so let's just give everything to the papers". Or, "hey, that journo is a really good bloke, well, let's just give him stuff". It's got to be bigger and better than that.

TABLE 1
Descriptive statistics of interview participants

Variable	Value	Frequency	%
Gender	Female	16	43.2
	Male	21	56.3
Education level	High school	5	13.5
	Advanced diploma or TAFE (technical and further education)	3	8.1
	Undergraduate degree	24	64.9
	Postgraduate degree	5	13.5
Age	20–29	12	32.4
	30–39	15	40.5
	40–49	7	18.9
	50–59	2	5.4
	60+	1	2.7
Place of employment	National sporting organisation	9	24.3
	Professional sport club, league or event	14	37.8
	State sporting organisation	7	18.9
	Professional sport player association	2	5.4
	National representative organisation (i.e. Australian Olympic Committee)	1	2.7
	Professional sport and state sporting organisation	3	8.1
	Other	1	2.7

N = 37.

However, when asked to describe why they would place a story on their own platforms, and which media they would engage with, the answers revealed two distinct approaches to media management and justifications. The first relating to maintaining an engagement with mainstream media, and the second relating to a preference for sports organisations to use their own channels. The first justification was that their organisations would rarely attempt to put anything newsworthy through their own channels, and they would still use traditional media as the best way to distribute these stories. For those that noted traditional media was still valuable, the most common reason was that it still had more reach than their own channels (15 of 37 responses), which is illustrated in the following quote from Interviewee 1:

> I think we would get better coverage in the newspaper. [Own website] might work for AFL, but for us, for brand awareness, having it in the newspaper is more valuable than having it on the website. It's just [our sport] fans that go to the website, it's people that love [our sport] and know about the players and the teams, whereas if I'm getting access to a few hundred thousand more people flicking through the newspaper, it's much more valuable.

Another reason for electing to place content in traditional media was that sponsors still valued traditional media (five responses); Interviewee 11, from a professional sports club, noted that a prominent sponsor placed a dollar value on every story that appeared in the Sydney-based *Daily Telegraph* newspaper and because of this "we definitely would never go to a position where we don't do anything with the mainstream media". These comments, stated in similar ways by other participants, illustrate that many sports organisations in Australia still value media coverage and would not use their own channels to break news.

For those interviewees who noted that they would, on occasion, preference their own channels over legacy media, there were three main reasons. First, interviewees from sports governing bodies (whose sports were more likely to lack a high public profile) were likely to say they used their own channels to communicate to their stakeholders as they struggled to gain mainstream media coverage (seven responses), as explained by Interviewee 28:

> We can't communicate through mainstream media, the option's not there. So social media obviously takes more and more precedence I think for small sports than it does for your NRL club or your AFL club. Sure they need social and they need to converse with their people in social and listen to their people, but if they didn't use social they're still going to get enough mainstream media to go 80 per cent of the way.

Second, interviewees noted that they wanted the ability to communicate directly with members (eight responses). Interviewee 11, from a professional club, noted that for a player re-signing they would give the news to their members first:

> They are the people that are stakeholders in the club: they put in the money in to support the team, so we believe that they do have a right to be the first to know when it comes to big information surrounding the club.

Third, the interviews identified that choosing internal channels was an opportunity to build the value of these platforms, so that in the future they would potentially have the audience to use them extensively (11 responses). In the main these were interviewees who worked in professional sport. Interviewee 15, who worked at a professional

AFL club, discussed an instance where the club had announced a player's new contact on its own platforms. The fact that they announced it through their own platforms, rather than the actual contract news, was reported on the back page of a major Melbourne paper the next day. While Interviewee 15 acknowledged there was a balancing act to be performed, as providing media access was still an important part of their role at the organisation, they admitted that their digital platforms were becoming the primary vehicle to deliver news:

> That's the way the way the industry's going and I think the media are probably a little bit scared because it makes them a bit redundant. We kind of have to advocate to the media as well, so we're in a real balancing act to try and decide what we give to the media, what we give to our digital guys. But the thing is in the end we're communicating to our supporters, and the digital channels are the easiest way to do that. (Interviewee 15)

The interviews with sports public relations professionals clearly demonstrated that for many Australian sports organisations, stories in legacy media were valuable and they would actively facilitate this coverage. However, a significant proportion of the interviewees also acknowledged that more sports organisations, particularly professional sports organisations, were strategically choosing to develop in-house digital platforms and use them to deliver news. In order to explore this issue in greater depth, a professional AFL club was chosen for the second stage of research, a qualitative case study.

Use of Social and Digital Platforms—Case Study

In order to explore whether or not the introduction of digital platforms had influenced the media relations practice of the professional AFL club, the first stage of the research was to establish how the club was utilising its digital platforms in the week of the case study, in particular the club's social media channels and website. The analysis aimed to investigate whether or not content with particular players was made available on the digital channel but was not being provided to other media outlets.

Social media. The club used social media platforms to distribute content to fans, but it was not often content exclusive to those platforms. Throughout the week of the case study, the club made 21 posts on its Facebook page and sent 116 tweets on Twitter. The club posted most frequently on match day during the week of the study. There were eight posts on Facebook on Saturday, which was a match-day for both the senior AFL team and their reserves team in the Victorian Football League competition. Of the tweets, 47 were across the six non-match days within the week of the case study, with the remaining 69 tweets delivered on Saturday, match-day. During the week, the posts on both channels were most often promoting content, either written, video or both, on the club's website. There was little unique content posted to these channels during the week. On match-day, there was unique content in the form of photos; for example, there were photos of the players inside the changing rooms after the match, posted on Twitter and Facebook. Most of the pictures were of the players singing the team song (an AFL tradition after each game), which is a photographic opportunity open to accredited broadcasters and photographers. But, there were also two photographs that appeared to be of players in areas that were not accessible to all media covering the game. This analysis indicated that there was very little unique or exclusive content being produced for those social media channels, particularly in which club sources were being interviewed. The club used their social media channels to cover general media opportunities, such as live tweeting each official press conference held that week, but club sources did not appear exclusively through their social channels.

Website. The club delivered 57 pieces of content on its website, which are represented in Table 2. The majority of the content related to matches, either the previous week's match and follow-up content from that, or previews, reviews and highlights. These included the club's press conferences that week, one with a coach—which is a mandatory League requirement—and one with a player who was preparing to play a milestone match. The next most common category was history, which focused mostly on historical flashbacks and facts and figures features, with topics such as "10 moments from the last time we played this club". Player-specific pieces included those that were in the style of player profiles, in which a single player was typically the focus.

More than half the website content (52.6 per cent) was produced internally, while external sources of content included fans, journalists, television publicity releases and AFL Media. Fans provided regular weekly pieces, such as match previews and historical facts and figures stories. AFL Media is perhaps a unique case in sport, as the governing body has created its own media company to cover the league, but with a mandate of objectivity (Hayes 2015). One of the benefits of this approach is that all clubs can access AFL Media's content for their website, and in this week the club used nine pieces of content from AFL Media. Media within the club did not need to produce content on events where AFL Media were in attendance, which included the two press

TABLE 2
A week of website content at an AFL club

Digital content breakdown	Value	%
Topic		
Match related	22	38.6
History/flashback	11	19.3
Player specific	7	12.3
Victorian Football League	6	10.5
Media coverage	5	8.8
Fan information	4	7.0
Press conference	1	1.8
Other	1	1.8
Content creator		
Internal	30	52.6
External	26	45.6
Combination	1	1.8
Content type		
Text only	14	24.5
Video only	23	40.4
Text and video	20	35.1
Quotes		
Quotes or interview	12	21.1
No quotes	45	78.9

N = 57.

conferences held each week—one a coach and one a player celebrating a milestone game. They also did not need to write a match report, or produce any written content from the match—as this was instead prepared by AFL Media. However, this content was not tailored from the club's point of view; for example, a match report where the team lost was likely to be critical.

One of the most intriguing results in exploring the impact of digital platforms on media relations is that the overwhelming majority of pieces did not include quotes or interviews with club sources. Excluding AFL Media pieces—which included quotes or interviews from press conferences—there were only five items of content that week that included interviews, where the players had spoken to the club's media production staff. All these pieces of content were videos; they included an injury update video and a selection news video with the head of football operations, one of the senior players interviewing other members of the team about the player about to complete his milestone match, an extended video piece on an up-and-coming player in the Victorian Football League team, and a shorter piece on two young players who had become senior team regulars. The last two of these were produced specifically for an extended video piece to be broadcast on the club's online video platforms. However, this did not always indicate that the talent available in these opportunities was not available to other media, as one of the younger players profiled completed post-match broadcast media commitments.

Overall, based on the analysis of content published by the club on its digital platforms during the week of the case study, this research found minimal evidence to support the claim that the professional AFL club was withholding media access to publish exclusive content direct to fans through social and digital channels. However, observation and interviews with the media management staff revealed that there were certain cases where they would prioritise the use of their own channels to tell a story, and aim to set the media agenda by doing so, which is now discussed in greater detail.

Management of social and digital platforms. At this professional sports club in Australia, there are three staff members who are primarily engaged with media management, who will be referred to as Media Manager 1, Media Manager 2 and Media Manager 3. Day-to-day content production and management of the club's digital and social platforms is undertaken by different members of staff, including a content manager, multiple video producers and editors, and also a number of external or voluntary staff that provide written content. The overall management of the club's digital and social platforms sits within the media department, overseen by Media Manager 1.

The key roles of the media management team, in their words, were to facilitate access to media, but facilitate it strategically. All of the media management team noted that mainstream media were still important stakeholders, and that they would continue to service them; for example, Media Manager 2 noted "my opinion might change over time but I still think there has to be a place for traditional media. At the moment that's where the club's main income is and that's where all the eyeballs are". But they noted that the club's own platforms had become a useful way to direct the narrative of some stories. Media Manager 3 described a case in the previous year where they had produced an extended feature on a particular player, which had significantly shifted public perceptions, and argued that:

> simply because of our proximity and understanding to the person, we are best placed to do it. You can't trust the mass media that they are going to understand the same complexities and treat it in that manner when they don't know the person.

The same media manager also noted that the internal platforms would be used for "anything particularly sensitive, it's already the case that we will address it through our internal platforms". The media relations staff at this professional AFL club therefore see the potential in utilising the club's own digital platforms to deliver a particular narrative. During the week of the case study, one key observation of the researcher was that the content on the club's website was mostly not an attempt to set the media agenda, in that it did not seek to be *news*. Much of the content was fan focused, and the pieces featuring players were mostly fun and irreverent. The club did not attempt to break news stories, or even use their website to report news angles. For example, the biggest story from the club that week was a senior player's form—or lack of it. It was addressed significantly in the coaches press conference that week and in subsequent stories across both print and broadcast media, but that particular angle did not appear on the club's own channels.

However, there was one specific story during the week of the case study that did provide an insight into how the club might manage these platforms more strategically in the future. This story created tension internally within the media department and between the club and external news organisations. The story, of a sick child visiting the club, had been planned to be exclusively covered by the club's own in-house media staff. On the day of the event two external broadcast news crews arrived at the club, alerted to the story by a radio station report. Media Manager 1 initially asked the broadcast crews to leave, describing a confrontational encounter where he said it was "off limits to them". However, the television crew ended up going over the media manager's head to a senior executive in the club and gained access to the story. Both broadcast crews present then recorded vision of the visit, interviews with some staff and the child's family. That story was then broadcast on the two major commercial networks in Melbourne that day.

This example illustrated that there is tension not only within the overall organisation about the role of the club's own platforms, but also within the media department itself. One member of the media management team felt strongly that the opportunity should have been available to media, while the other two gave preference to the club's own channels. However, the general opinion of the media management staff was that this particular story illustrated the potential of their media channels, as Media Manager 1 noted:

> So you can argue about what the right approach was. Should we just have opened it and let everyone in and said "bugger the club?", which is an old way of doing it I think. We want ours to be a full-scale production house … we're a million miles away, but in order to get there we have to do things that are counter-intuitive I think … They aren't going to make sense in the traditional way. Why would you lock people out from something that's only going to benefit [the club]?

Media Manager 2 disagreed with the approach taken:

> I felt like this week was really the first time where I thought we were doing the wrong thing. I've never felt that before … But I've always thought it was to be the right story,

> this was a bit of a sensitive one … for me I thought "who are we to say that only [our fans] could see that story?" It is an interesting one because I think we should be growing our own channels, but I don't think it should be to the detriment to all our supporters and all our other media … At this stage, it needs to be a fine balance.

Media Manager 3 explained that they saw the use of internal channels as a way to control the organisation's message effectively without the filter of the media. But the right balance had not yet been reached:

> The global trend is to seize control of the news because news has economic value. By eliminating the middleman, the megaphone that is the press, we are able to tell the story in the way that we want without any filter or interpretation. Because we are in this process of evolution at the moment, by no means have we come to terms with some of the challenges. So, we need to reconcile these conflicting pressures. We have the demands of broadcasters which is a non-negotiable … Broadcasters are separate to this equation. But in terms of your mainstream press versus in house media, well you can challenge what you have. As you saw yesterday we haven't arrived at a solution yet, so we need to know, what is the key imperative here? Is it to furnish the value of our internal assets we hope to sort of transform into a 24-hour network, or is it content that we can then on-sell, content we can sell to broadcasters? And the best way to do that and increase the value is by acting as the first call for all [club] content … But we also have to understand that the habits of the general public when it comes to consuming news haven't moved there yet and the mainstream media still has an incredibly significant role to play in shaping perceptions and in communicating to a mass audience. So the challenge is, there is not set formula for this, so the challenge is to determine on a case-to-case basis what would be the best platform to disseminate this particular information.

This particular story, where the club attempted to seize control of content and then failed to hold on to the story, is an empirically revealing case in the context of the changing sports media nexus. It illustrated that the club was attempting to create some content exclusively for its own channels, but also that there was significant disagreement within the media staff about whether this was the correct or appropriate strategy. This case study demonstrated that while the club was using their social and digital media platforms extensively, their exact role in the organisation was still yet to be finalised; it was still subject to internal organisational contest and conflict. However, it is clear that this club expected these platforms to play a more important role in the future, particularly to tell stories in which they wanted to control the narrative completely.

Discussion

The main aim of this study has been to explore whether or not the introduction of sports organisations' own social and digital platforms had affected their public relations practice; or more bluntly, to answer the question: were Australian sports organisations cutting off media access in order to publish stories on their own platforms? The interviews clearly demonstrated that sports organisations in Australia are using these platforms to communicate with stakeholders, but generally, most organisations still value traditional media coverage and aim to facilitate this first, supporting traditional models of sports public relations (Fortunato 2000). This research also found that smaller sports organisations used their social and digital media platforms to communicate with stakeholders because they could not gain mainstream and commercial media attention.

The interviewees from professional sports organisations, however, were using digital platforms more strategically. Granting media access was now not the default position of their roles, but instead these staff weighed up the best outlet for their stories on a case-by-case basis—and sometimes their own platforms won. The results of the case study confirmed this strategic narrative and indicated that at a professional AFL club in Australia, the public relations staff were attempting to grow their digital and social channels, maybe not to become a direct news competitor, but as a way to influence the media agenda. The analysis of a week's worth of content found minimal evidence to indicate that this strategy had been fully implemented, given only a small amount of the content shared on these channels included access to sources within the sports organisation. However, what this case study did uncover was that the professional club had selectively chosen to distribute some stories on their own platforms instead of through traditional media. While acknowledging that traditional media was still valued, and that achieving mainstream media coverage was a key component of their role, media management staff within the club noted the power of using their in-house channels to present "sensitive" stories. The staff extolled the virtue of being able to tell a *better* story than a journalist, because of their knowledge of the source, and because they could control the content and its distribution. Media Manager 3 noted that they could not "trust" the mass media to understand a story as well as an athlete's own organisation, which echoes the quotes of an allblacks.com staff member in Scherer and Jackson's (2008) study. This is an interesting thread, which indicates that from the perspective of the managers within this sports organisation, traditional media are not to be trusted with the ability to tell stories, their core business, and again highlights an ongoing thread of conflict between the sports media and sports organisations (Hinds 2012; Hutchins and Rowe 2009).

While introduction of in-house media channels is still an emerging issue within professional AFL clubs and the best strategic location of material is still being negotiated, the club had started to use their own social and digital media to present particular stories in frames of the club's making. This supports work that found that sports organisations' websites are highly framed (Scherer and Jackson 2008; Yanity 2013), not simply charged with delivering news, but delivering stories with a narrative that benefits the club. More broadly, this study supports previous work that has examined the highly structured nature of the contact sports journalists have with sources (Howe 2008; Sugden and Tomlinson 2007; Suggs 2015), and in doing so confirms the fears of sports journalists that professional sports organisations are moving towards a model where more content may be delivered on their own platforms (Coombs and Osborne 2012; Grimmer and Kian 2013; Sherwood and Nicholson 2013). Sports public relations practitioners have already been criticised for having too much power in building the media agenda (Anderson 2001; Surface 1972; Wulfemeyer 1985), and the introduction of in-house digital platforms, through which they can completely control the narrative, is likely to further enhance their power, as well as the concomitant criticism.

Finally, this research highlights that conflict between media and sports organisations, articulated by Hutchins and Rowe (2009), is developing rather than receding.

Unlike early exchanges in this area though, which resulted in a federal government inquiry in Australia (Hutchins and Rowe 2010), these tensions are less likely to be played out in public. Instead, small everyday negotiations within the media departments of sports organisations, and between those departments and the rest of the organisation, are likely to determine what stories appear on the sports media agenda, through what channels and how those stories are framed. As sports organisations attempt to enter the space that was once the exclusive preserve of news organisations, conflict and tension rather than symbiosis are increasingly likely to characterise the relationship between sport and the media.

Conclusion

This research argues, via the analysis of interviews with public relations staff at Australian sports organisations and a case study of public relations practice at a professional AFL club in Australia, that the addition of social and digital platforms has not dramatically altered the practice of sports public relations, *yet*. The public relations staff at the professional sports club interviewed as part of the case study still facilitated media access to their club, but they utilised their own platforms to communicate "sensitive" stories in which they wished to control the narrative. These results have significant implications for sports journalism, as they suggest that the addition of a sports organisation's social and digital media platforms has, in this case, irrevocably altered the once symbiotic relationship between sport and media. Where sports journalists previously relied on close relationships with sports sources to complete their work, this research indicates the addition of sports organisations' own platforms has the potential to limit journalists' access to sports sources further. In one sense, this is unsurprising looking at the wider context of public relations sources and journalism. In political journalism, access has increasingly become more strategic and managed (Davis 2000), and politicians are also using social media to communicate directly with constituents and construct their own narratives (Ekman and Widholm 2014). Sports organisations' adoption of these tactics therefore reflects issues in the broader field of news construction.

There are several limitations which restrict the generalisability of this research. First, it offers an insight into the public relations practice in Australian sports organisations and may not be applicable to other major contexts. The US sports market, with four major codes that all fight for media attention, may mean that the media access first strategy presented in Fortunato's (2000) study of the NBA may still be prevalent. Also, while a single case study presents a valuable yet unique view of media relations practice, the findings might not apply to other professional clubs, either within the same league or within the same country. An additional limitation of this study is that it does not include the voices of sports journalists and their opinions about the ways in which their access to athletes is changing. While this perspective has been covered in the literature previously (Coombs and Osborne 2012; Grimmer and Kian 2013; Sherwood and Nicholson 2013), and this study aimed to research a gap in public relations research, research that includes the additional perspective of sports journalists would be a valuable further contribution to the field. In addition, research that examines fan responses (such as Cleland 2011) to changes in sport media production would also be valuable. As the failed Swindon Town F.C.

example perhaps indicates, while sports organisations move towards delivering news directly to the fans, there are questions to be asked concerning whether or not this is the fans preference.

DISCLOSURE STATEMENT

No potential conflict of interest was reported by the author(s).

FUNDING

This research received no specific grant from any funding agency in the public, commercial or not-for-profit sectors.

REFERENCES

AAP. 2015. "AFL Maintains Crowd-pulling Status." *The Australian*, May 21. http://www.theaustralian.com.au/sport/afl/afl-maintains-crowdpulling-status/news-story/b4ca1cc859749bc22ec27169094e4b1c.

Anderson, William B. 2001. "Does the Cheerleading Ever Stop? Major League Baseball and Sports Journalism." *Journalism and Mass Communication Quarterly* 78 (2): 355–382.

Baker, Grant. 2014. "The Spending Gap between the AFL's Rich and Poor Has Ballooned to $5.6 Million." *Herald Sun*, January 24. http://www.heraldsun.com.au/sport/afl/the-spending-gap-between-the-afls-rich-and-poor-has-ballooned-to-56-million/story-fni5ezdm-1226811508363.

Borden, Sam. 2015. "English Club Shuts out Journalists with New Kind of Defense." *The New York times*. http://www.nytimes.com/2015/08/05/sports/soccer/english-soccer-club-sets-up-tight-defense-but-this-one-repels-journalists.html?_r=0.

Boyle, Raymond, and Richard Haynes. 2006. "The Football Industry and Public Relations." In *Public Relations. Critical Debates and Contemporary Practice*, edited by Jacquie L'Etang and Magda Pieczka, 221–240. Mahwah, NJ: Lawrence Elbaum Associates.

Boyle, Raymond, and Richard Haynes. 2014. "Sport, Public Relations and Social Media." In *Routledge Handbook of Sport and New Media*, edited by Andrew C. Billings and Hardin Marie, 133–143. Abingdon, Oxon: Routledge.

Boyle, Raymond, William Dinan, and Stephen Morrow. 2002. "Doing the Business?: Newspaper Reporting of the Business of Football." *Journalism* 3 (2): 161–181.

Carlson, Matt. 2009. "Dueling, Dancing or Dominating? Journalists and Their Sources." *Sociology Compass* 3 (4): 526–542.

Cleland, Jamie A. 2009. "The Changing Organizational Structure of Football Clubs and Their Relationship with the External Media." *International Journal of Sport Communication* 2: 417–431.

Cleland, Jamie A. 2011. "The Media and Football Supporters: A Changing Relationship." *Media, Culture & Society* 33 (2): 299–315.

Coombs, Danielle S., and Anne Osborne. 2012. "Sports Journalists and England's Barclays Premier League: A Case Study Examining Reporters'Takes on Modern Football." *International Journal of Sport Communication* 5: 413–425.

Davis, Aeron. 2000. "Public Relations, News Production and Changing Patterns of Source Access in the British National Media." *Media, Culture & Society* 22 (1): 39–59.

Ekman, Mattias, and Andreas Widholm. 2014. "Politicians as Media Producers." *Journalism Practice* 9 (1): 78–91.

Filo, Kevin, Daniel Lock, and Adam Karg. 2015. "Sport and Social Media Research: A Review." *Sport Management Review* 18 (2): 166–181.

Fortunato, John A. 2000. "Public Relations Strategies for Creating Mass Media Content: A Case Study of the National Basketball Association." *Journal Article. Public Relations Review* 26 (4): 481–497.

Gaskin, Lee. 2013. "Bogut, Cambage Slam Hideaway Camp." *The Canberra times*, January 26. http://www.smh.com.au/sport/basketball/bogut-cambage-slam-hideaway-camp-20130725-2qnld.html.

Gibbs, Chris, and Richard Haynes. 2013. "A Phenomenological Investigation into How Twitter Has Changed the Nature of Sport Media Relations." *International Journal of Sport Communication* 6: 394–408.

Greenslade, Roy. 2013. "MPs Condemn Football Clubs for Banning Journalists." *The Guardian*, December 13. https://www.theguardian.com/media/greenslade/2013/dec/10/nationalunionofjournalists-newcastleunited.

Grimmer, Christoph G., and Edward M. Kian. 2013. "Reflections of German Football Journalists on Their Relationships with Bundesliga Club Public Relations Practitioners." *International Journal of Sport Communication* 6 (4): 446–463.

Hardin, Robin, and Steven McClung. 2002. "Collegiate Sports Information: A Profile of the Profession." *Public Relations Quartely* 47 (2): 35–39.

Hayes, Alex. 2015. "How AFL Media Became Australia's Biggest Sports Platform." *Mumbrella*. http://mumbrella.com.au/how-afl-media-became-australias-biggest-sports-platform-285062.

Hinds, Richard. 2012. "All Action, No Talk in Code of Silence." *The Sydney Morning Herald*, September 1. http://www.smh.com.au/sport/all-action-no-talk-in-code-of-silence-20120831-255eo.html?skin=text-onl.

Howe, P. David. 2008. "Paralympic Media and the 'Production' of Elite Disability." *International Review for the Sociology of Sport* 43 (2): 135–150.

Hutchins, Brett, and David Rowe. 2009. "From Broadcast Scarcity to Digital Plenitude: The Changing Dynamics of the Media Sport Content Economy." *Television & New Media* 10 (4): 354–370.

Hutchins, Brett, and David Rowe. 2010. "Reconfiguring Media Sport for the Online World: An Inquiry into 'Sports News and Digital Media'." *International Journal of Communication* 4 (2010): 696–718.

Kent, Paul. 2014. "Round One Has Revealed the NRL's Advertising Campaign as Nothing More than a Lie, Writes Paul Kent." *The Daily Telegraph*, March 12. http://www.foxsports.com.au/nrl/round-one-has-revealed-the-nrls-advertising-campaign-as-nothing-more-than-a-lie-writes-paul-kent/story-e6frf3ou-1226851831605.

King, Travis. 2015. "Demetriou, McLachlan Earn Combined $3.3 Million Salary." *Afl.Com.Au*, March 4. http://www.afl.com.au/news/2015-03-04/afl-reveals-financial-results.

Lowes, Mark Douglas. 1999. *Inside the Sport Pages: Work Routines. Professional Ideologies and the Manufacture of Sports News*. Toronto: University of Toronto Press.

Marr, Liz, Dave Francis, and Dave Randall. 1999. "'The Soccer Game' as Journalistic Work: Managing the Production of Stories about a Football Club." In *Media Studies: Ethnomethodological Approaches*, edited by Paul L. Jalbert, 111–134. Maryland, USA: University Press of America.

McCleneghan, J. Sean. 1995. "The Sports Information Director - No Attention, No Respect, and a PR Practitioner in Trouble." *Public Relations Quartely*, No. 40: 28–32.

McCombs, Maxwell. 2005. "A Look at Agenda-Setting: Past, Present and Future." *Journalism Studies* 6 (4): 543–557. doi:10.1080/14616700500250438.

McCombs, Maxwell. 2013. *Setting the Agenda: The Mass Media and Public Opinion*. Hoboken: Wiley.

Mikosza, Janine, and Brett Hutchins. 2010. "The Web 2.0 Olympics: Athlete Blogging, Social Networking and Policy Contradictions at the 2008 Beijing Games." *Convergence* 16 (3): 279–297.

Moynahan, Patrick, Allan Hall, and Janis Taylor. 2002. *Media Relations in Sport*. Morgantown, WV: Fitness Information Technology.

Narayanan, Chandresh. 2015. "Time to Bring Media, Indian Cricket Team Closer." *The Indian Express*, March 12. http://indianexpress.com/article/sports/cricket-world-cup/2315205/time-to-bring-media-indian-cricket-team-closer/.

Nicholson, Matthew, Anthony Kerr, and Merryn Sherwood. 2015. *Sport and the Media: Managing the Nexus*. 2nd ed. Abingdon, Oxon: Routledge.

Peck, Tom. 2015. "Tom Peck: Swindon's Media Ban Might Seem Comic but the Fanzai App is Serious about Selling." *The Independent*, July 18. http://www.independent.co.uk/sport/football/news-and-comment/tom-peck-swindon-s-media-ban-might-seem-comic-but-the-fanzai-app-is-serious-about-selling-10398068.html.

Pedersen, Paul M., Kimberley S. Miloch, and Pamela. C. Laucella. 2007. *Strategic Sport Communication*. Champaign, IL: Human Kinetics.

Ponsford, Dominic. 2015. "Swindon Town FC Extends Local Press Ban to All Media as It Signs up to Fanzai Smartphone App." *Press Gazzette*. http://www.pressgazette.co.uk/swindon-town-fc-extends-local-press-ban-all-media-it-signs-fanzai-app.

Rowe, David. 2004. *Sport, Culture and the Media: The Unruly Trinity*. Buckingham: Open University Press.

Saldaña, Johnny. 2013. *The Coding Manual for Qualitative Researchers*. 2nd ed. London: SAGE Publications.

Scherer, Jay, and Steven J. Jackson. 2008. "Producing Allblacks.Com: Cultural Intermediaries and the Policing of Electronic Spaces of Sporting Consumption." *Sociology of Sport Journal, No.* 25: 187–205.

Schultz, Brad, Philip H. Caskey, and Craig Esherick. 2014. *Media Relations in Sport*. Morgantown, WV: Fitness Information Technology.

Sherman, ed. 2015. "The Problem with the Dwindling Media Access to College Athletes." *Poynter*, December 3. http://www.poynter.org/2015/the-problem-with-the-dwindling-media-access-to-college-athletes/387726/.

Sherwood, Merryn, and Matthew Nicholson. 2013. "Web 2.0 Platforms and the Work of Newspaper Sport Journalists." *Journalism* 14 (7): 942–959.

Sigal, Leon V. 1986. "Sources Make the News." In *Reading the News*, edited by Robert Karl Manoff and Michael Schudson, 9–37. New York: Pantheon Books.

Stensholt, John, and Max Mason. 2015. "AFL Signs $2.5 Billion Broadcast Deal." *The Sydney Morning Herald*, August 18. http://www.smh.com.au/business/media-and-marketing/afl-to-announce-2b-broadcast-deal-20150818-gj1ppz.html.

Stoldt, G. Clayton. 2012. "The Impact of Social Media on College Athletics Communications."http://cosida.com/media/documents/2012/7/Social_media_im pact_2012_Stoldt_study.pdf.

Stoldt, G. Clayton, Lori K. Miller, and Mark Vermillion. 2009. "Public Relations Evaluation in Sport: Views from the Field." *International Journal of Sport Communication* 2: 223–239.

Sugden, John, and Alan Tomlinson. 2007. "Stories from Planet Football and Sportsw orld." *Journalism Practice* 1 (1): 44–61.

Suggs, David Welch. 2015. "Tensions in the Press Box: Understanding Relationships among Sports Media and Source Organizations." *Communication & Sport*, 1–21.

Surface, Bill. 1972. "The Shame of the Sports Beat." *Columbia Journalism Review* 10 (5): 48–55.

Wulfemeyer, K Tim. 1985. "Ethics in Sports Journalism: Tightening up the Code." *Journal of Mass Media Ethics* 1 (1). Routledge: 57–67.

Yanity, Molly. 2013. "Publishing for Paydirt: A Case Study of an Athletic Department Writer." *International Journal of Sport Communication* 6: 478–489.

Yin, Robert K. 2013. *Case Study Reseach: Design and Methods*. 5th ed. SAGE Publications.

CHEERLEADERS OR CRITICS?

Australian and Indian sports journalists in the contemporary age

Peter English

Sports journalists have often been criticised for their casual approach to work and cheerleading content in stories. This style of journalism contrasts with the traditional norms of objectivity employed in other areas of newsrooms. It is also opposed to the critical watchdog role considered essential to objective reporting. To examine how sports journalists operate in relation to being cheerleaders or critical watchdogs, this study utilises the Australia–India Test cricket series of 2014–15 as a platform to investigate sports journalists' views, and the content they produce. It employs in-depth interviews with 18 sports journalists from Australian and Indian newspaper organisations in conjunction with a content analysis of 1265 articles from eight Australian and Indian publications. This allows a comparison of the perceptions of the sports journalists with what they are producing in their stories. Selecting a major international event with historical importance, such as the Australia–India Test series, is important in providing an example for analysis of whether contemporary sports journalists have confused the roles of reporter and supporter. An important finding in this study, given the long-standing criticism of sports journalists, was a considerably higher proportion of critical reports about the series in both nations than of cheerleading. Overall, this was consistent with the perceptions of the sports journalists in the in-depth interviews.

Introduction

Sports journalists have often been criticised for the subjective content in their stories and their approach to the profession. Operating in "a fairly cosy world" (Rowe 2007, 399), they are known for "cheering for the home team" and "serving as a source of scrapbook material for the stars" (Garrison and Salwen 1989, 57). They have been described as cheerleaders, hero worshippers, fans, homers and sycophants; they are biased and responsible for boosterism of athletes, teams, organisations and the sports industry (Anderson 2001; Boyle, Rowe, and Whannel 2012; Hardin 2005; Hardin, Zhong, and Whiteside 2009; McEnnis 2015; Rowe 2004; Schultz-Jørgensen 2005; Steen 2011). This approach to journalism contrasts with the traditional norms of objectivity considered essential to other areas of newsrooms (Hardin 2005; Schudson 2001; Tuchman 1972). It is also opposed to the critical watchdog, Fourth Estate or crusader roles considered essential to objective sports reporting (Boyle, Rowe, and Whannel 2012; Hardin,

Zhong, and Whiteside 2009; Rowe 2004). In fact, Boyle, Rowe, and Whannel (2012) question whether sports journalists have confused the roles of reporter and fan. This issue is significant, for both the producers and consumers of news, and provides a foundation for an empirical analysis into perceptions and practices in contemporary sports journalism.

To examine how sports journalists operate in relation to being cheerleaders or critical watchdogs, this study utilises the Australia–India Test cricket series of 2014–15 as a base to analyse sports journalists' views alongside the content they produce. In-depth interviews with 18 sports journalists from Australian and Indian newspaper organisations have been conducted and, to ensure a comprehensive overview of the issue, a content analysis of 1265 articles from eight news organisations has been undertaken. This allows a comparison of the perceptions of the journalists' roles with what they are producing in their pages. Selecting a major international event with historical importance was important in providing a platform for analysis to examine whether contemporary sports journalists have confused the role of reporter and supporter (see Boyle, Rowe, and Whannel 2012). Previous research has often avoided comparative studies in relation to issues of cheerleading and critical reporting. Further, specific focus on sporting events has generally involved the Olympics (Billings 2008; Billings, Angelini, and Dan 2011; Steen 2011), leaving a gap for analysis of a bilateral sporting contest involving nations and reporting from differing media systems.

India and Australia have had a long sporting rivalry, having opposed each other in Test cricket since 1947–48. In Australia, cricket is considered the national game while in India it has been described as religion (Majumdar 2008). The contests between these nations, which have a following of more than a billion people, have gained a reputation for being fractious and portraying nationalistic attitudes, particularly since the "Monkeygate" series of 2007–08 in Australia (see Rowe 2011). In fact, the rivalry has become so intense that senior cricket administrator John Harnden (as quoted in Ali 2014) said it has "matched—and even bettered" the long-running Ashes contests between Australia and England. The 2014–15 series was played over four Tests between December 9 and January 10, with Australia winning 2–0 with two Tests drawn. With international sports reporting able to highlight nationalistic elements in media (Billings, Angelini, and Dan 2011), this major international cricket series is a valuable contest for examining the role of sports journalists as cheerleaders or critics.

Literature Review

Criticism of sports journalism and the roles and responsibilities of its practitioners has come from many sources, including in newsrooms and academic research. Historically, Anderson (2001, 355) notes how a baseball journalist crying during a New York Giants defeat in the 1911 World Series "illustrates the nature of baseball reporting", with the reporters viewed as cheerleaders and even considered "part of the team". More recently, there was criticism of an Australian sports journalist during the 2014 Commonwealth Games for taking a "selfie" with Usain Bolt at a press conference (Tomarchio 2014). As the Australian sports journalist Richard Hinds (as quoted in Tomarchio 2014) tweeted: "Embarrassing sycophancy 1, sports journalism 0. I hope they supplied buckets for real reporters." At sports matches, there is often a "no cheering in the press box" rule. Australian reporters watching a San Francisco 49ers pre-season American football game involving the rugby league convert Jarryd Hayne discovered this when "a hearty cheer" after a Hayne run was followed by a reminder they were breaking NFL etiquette (Wilson 2015). *Wisden* editor Lawrence Booth (2013, 5) argues the greatest insult for a sports journalist is to be described as a "fan with a laptop" (for an example, see Keating 2001). As Booth (2013, 7) states, sports journalists want to be taken seriously because "we reside, we know, in the toy department. Yet we aspire to adulthood". These newsroom examples help to highlight the divide between sports journalists as cheerleaders and watchdogs.

Boyle, Rowe, and Whannel (2012) argue this positioning is one of the major issues involving sports journalists, and exposes the conflict with the traditional role of objective, detached and emotion-free journalism (see Schudson 2001; Tuchman 1972). Hardin (2005) notes professionalism in sports journalism means objective reporting, and that injecting bias into reports compromises journalistic integrity. However, she argues boosterism occurs when reporters themselves are fans, or develop close relationships with sources. These relationships can be compromised—or ended—by stories perceived as negative, and can also result in backlash from supporters and employers (Anderson 2001; English 2015b; Hardin, Zhong, and Whiteside 2009; Rowe 2004; Steen 2015). This can be problematic for sports journalists when organisations focus on meeting their athlete and team needs ahead of reporters seeking access or information (Sherwood, Nicholson, and Marjoribanks 2016). In this situation, there is potential for journalists to comply with the organisational restrictions to avoid being cut off. Hardin (2005, 66) notes how sports journalists are regarded as utilising dubious ethical techniques by writing from a "biased perspective". She found 39 per cent of editors "believe sports pages should cheer home teams" (70). Hardin, Zhong, and Whiteside (2009, 335) conclude "boosterism, even among reporters who seem to value public-service journalism, persists". Consequently, Rowe (2007, 399) argues sports journalists are likely to avoid "sustained, intensive critical inquiry into sport and its relationship with other major areas of society and culture". This also relates to a significantly reduced focus on investigative journalism (see Boyle and Haynes 2009; Henningham 1995; Rowe 2004; Steen 2011). However, it is important to recognise the value of sports journalists who operate to keep institutions and individuals accountable, and perform roles that lead to critical debate (Boyle, Rowe, and Whannel 2012; Hardin 2005; Hardin, Zhong, and Whiteside 2009). Recent examples of investigative journalism include David Walsh exposing Lance Armstrong's drug taking, Andrew Jennings highlighting corruption in FIFA, and the German broadcaster ARD's documentary into systemic doping in Russian athletics. Sports journalists themselves say they want to be able to investigate (Hardin, Zhong, and Whiteside 2009; Henningham 1995; Nicholson, Zion, and Lowden 2011; Steen 2011), although it is more difficult in the contemporary era due to commercial and economic restrictions. Henningham (1995, 17) concludes sports journalists have a "'participant' concept of journalism", while Boyle (2006, 117) discusses how they are involved in "compromise or journalistic complicity" with those in the sports industry (see also Boyle and Haynes 2009). Billings, Angelini, and Dan (2011) examined national biases in television coverage of the Olympics, noting how reporting can fall into home versus other nation portrayals, even though companies such as NBC have polices against "nationalistic cheerleading". In live blogging, McEnnis (2015) found sports journalists in the

United Kingdom alternated between subjective and objective approaches in their descriptions, which placed them in neither cheerleading nor crusading roles.

Promotion of the athletes, teams and sports is also viewed as problematic, particularly with the increasing commercialisation of media (Boyle 2006; Boyle, Rowe, and Whannel 2012; English 2015a; Rowe 2007; Schultz-Jørgensen 2005). As Boyle (2006, 125) states, "promoting the game is simply not what sports journalism is about", and it is "winning and success on the field of play that remains the most important driver in shaping journalistic opinion and comment". This comment is particularly valuable in an examination of cheerleading and critics because it suggests that when dealing with victory, praise of athletes or teams is legitimate and justified. In this context, it is helpful to consider what Boyle and Haynes (2009) argue is the requirement for sports journalists. "In short, sports journalism should be about reporting, enquiring, explaining and at times holding to account sports on behalf of fans" (Boyle and Haynes 2009, 183; see also Boyle, Rowe, and Whannel 2012). This explanation allows sports journalists space both to compliment and critique athletes, contests and events.

Previous research has focused on a range of media and topics, utilising various research methods. Surveys have been a popular approach (see Garrison and Salwen 1989; Hardin 2005; Hardin, Zhong, and Whiteside 2009), along with interviews (see Boyle 2006; Boyle and Haynes 2009; McEnnis 2015; Rowe 2004) and analysis of content (Anderson 2001; Schultz-Jørgensen 2005). Research employing multiple methods has not been utilised in depth, providing scope for a study employing qualitative interviews with content analysis. While previous research has examined the Olympics (Billings 2008; Billings, Angelini, and Dan 2011; Steen 2011) and baseball (Anderson 2001), there is an absence of specific studies into cricket coverage. Hardin, Zhong, and Whiteside (2009) have suggested future research focusing on the content of everyday stories written by sports journalists, as well as looking outside the United States. Further, Billings, Angelini, and Dan (2011) have called for work in sportscasts examining differences in discourse and choices at gatekeeping levels. While this relates to television, it is also relevant to investigate among newspaper sports journalists from two nations. Finally, Boyle, Rowe, and Whannel (2012) question the confusion of sports journalists' roles, making it an important issue to investigative in a contemporary context. The combination of these aspects and the absence of sustained mixed-methods research into cheerleading and critical watchdog reporting provide a gap for research that adds to the broad field of sports media research.

Method

The main aim of the study was to examine the prevalence of cheerleading and critical reporting in a contemporary sports journalism context, focusing on the Australia–India Test cricket series of 2014–15. The study's research questions were:

RQ1: To what extent do Australian and Indian sports journalists consider themselves cheerleaders, supporters of the home team or critical watchdogs?

RQ2: To what extent does cheerleading and critical watchdog content appear in the sports reporting of Australian and Indian newspapers?

A mixed-method approach was employed combining 18 in-depth interviews with a content analysis of 1265 newspaper articles. The interviews were utilised in order to answer RQ1, and the content analysis for RQ2. In this comparative research, sports reporting in two nations is examined to highlight similarities and differences in news-gathering and publishing approaches. Australia and India were selected in this study due to: the common sporting interest of cricket as part of their Commonwealth histories; they are situated in different media systems; one is considered a Western nation and the other a developing nation; and there is widespread publication of English newspapers (English 2015a; Hanitzsch et al. 2010; Yin 2011).

In-depth Interviews

In order to understand the perceptions of sports journalists in relation to cheerleading and critical reporting, in-depth interviews were conducted with 18 journalists, including nine each from the Australian and India press corps during the Test cricket series. The face-to-face interviews occurred between December 15, 2014 and January 6, 2015 in Brisbane and Sydney, before and during the second and fourth Test matches. This allowed interviewees to discuss these issues at the same time they were reporting on the series, which also fell within the date range of the content analysis. Respondents were recruited from the series' accreditation lists of newspaper journalists. Due to the nature of touring, there were more Australian journalists to select from than Indian journalists. However, the sample of 18 represented more than half of the print journalists who appeared on the two accreditation lists in Brisbane and Sydney. While the results are not representative of all sports journalists in these nations, the sample provides a valuable overview of the perceptions of the cricket reporters and columnists involved in chronicling the series.

Respondents were asked in the interviews to consider whether they felt like a fan or supporter when writing about this major event; whether they were expected to promote the national team; and the importance of keeping key figures accountable as critical watchdog journalists. The interviews, which averaged 25 minutes, were anonymous and responses were placed into themes for analysis. Each respondent was given a code, for example, A1 or I7. There were 11 sports journalists from broadsheet/quality publications from the two nations and seven from tabloid titles. The average age of the sports journalists was 42.8 years. They had spent on average 18.3 years in sports journalism, and 14.8 years writing about cricket.

Content Analysis

The content analysis examined eight newspapers, with four each from Australia and India, and totalled 1265 articles. Equivalence is an essential aspect in comparative research (Rössler 2012) and similar newspaper titles were selected for analysis. The sample included two national broadsheets (*The Australian* and *The Times of India*); the nations' largest-selling tabloids (*Herald Sun* and *Mumbai Mirror*); large-selling, state-based broadsheet/quality titles (*The Sydney Morning Herald* and *Hindustan Times*); and a region-based tabloid (*The West Australian* in Perth and *Mid-day* in Mumbai). The sample ensured publications were selected that had influence and widespread distributions (see Rössler 2012). Print editions were collected through subscriptions to the organisations or the Press Reader newspaper service.

Rössler (2012) outlined the importance of procedural equivalency in content analysis and a codebook was constructed for application by the single coder. The sample started on Monday, December 8, 2014, two days before the first Test match, and finished on January 10, 2015 at the conclusion of the series. Articles were collected over this timeframe from Monday to Saturday, excluding Christmas Day, to ensure consistency of the data collection. Each story was coded for details such as headline, date, organisation, nation of organisation and author, before addressing the key questions for analysis. These were: Is cheerleading or fan behaviour evident? Which nation is the cheerleading for? Is critical watchdog reporting evident? Which nation is the story being critical of? Articles selected in the sample had to include elements about the Test series, and did not include items focusing on one-day or domestic games or issues.

Results

The results from the 18 sports journalists and the 1265 newspaper articles reflected a variety of responses to the presence of cheerleading and critical watchdog reporting during the Australia–India Test cricket series. The in-depth interview data will be examined first, followed by the content analysis. This allows a comparison of the sports journalists' perceptions of their work before an examination of the content they produce. In order to answer RQ1, issues focusing on attitudes towards cheerleading, promoting the home team and keeping key figures in the game accountable are presented.

"You're Supposed to Be Neutral"

To determine whether the sports journalists considered themselves cheerleaders, they were asked whether they felt like "fans" or supporters. It is important to note the definition of a fan can be broad and contain differing levels of commitment or obsession, as well as more passive support. In this study, the definition of fans and cheerleading is based on the journalistic aspects previously outlined. This includes reporters operating as "fans with laptops", injecting bias or excessively promoting a team (Booth 2013; Boyle 2006; Boyle, Rowe, and Whannel 2012; Keating 2001). Eleven of the respondents said they did not operate as fans, while three—all from India—admitted they did. Four outlined mixed views on the issue. In national terms, seven of the Australian respondents did not consider themselves cheerleaders, while four in India felt the same way. Most of the sports journalists who rejected the tags of cheerleaders or fans did so vehemently. As A4 said, "No. No. No!" A5 said he never felt like that, a view supported by I2. The importance of being neutral was outlined in particular by interviewees from India. As I5 said, "You're supposed to be neutral and you are paid good money to be neutral." The passionate and definite responses in this category were summed up by I6 who said:

> I always try to maintain objectivity. I don't clap, I don't stand up … I constantly look through a lens of objectivity otherwise I am not able to do justice to my work, because that would amount to a fan reporting for his team.

A3 said he had never actively hoped Australia would win a match while A7 agreed there was "not a great deal of fan-ism" in the nation's cricket media. This was supported by A9 who said: "I don't see much cheerleading in the box."

The respondents were critical of other sports journalists who acted as cheerleaders, either in their work, or in the press box. There was general agreement that this type of behaviour was not appropriate. However, other respondents in both nations noted the difference between writing as a professional cheerleader, and being a fan of the sport. I5 said it was important to "love" the game, an emotion which was considered essential by multiple respondents as a way to describe and interpret the contest to the audience. This aspect was also present in the responses from the four respondents—two from each nation—who outlined a mixed approach to being fans. For example, A1 discussed how he was swept away by moments in matches, a view which was supported by I4 who said: "There's a joy of watching, there's a joy of writing. That's why we all love sport, because we appreciate the finer points." Three respondents said this not as a way of justifying celebrating a team or its players, but to pass on this enthusiasm through stories to entertain the audience, which would often be passionate about the result. A2 noted it was acceptable for journalists to be fans because "fans can be immensely discriminating and well-informed".

The three Indian journalists who considered themselves fans also discussed the passion for the game influencing their responses. Interestingly, there was no sense of covering up their feelings. As I8 said, "Absolutely, absolutely, from day one I've always felt like a fan." Respondent I1 said there was nothing wrong with sports journalists taking this position. "If I'm not a fan about the Indian team, I wouldn't be doing sports journalism. As a fan if I feel bad I will criticise them, but if I'm indifferent I won't criticise them." This feeling of being able to cheer for a team and scrutinise it as a fan was also supported by I3.

It's Not "We" or "Us"

A key element of writing as a fan is promoting the local side and, to explore this aspect of cheerleading further, the sports journalists were asked if they were ever expected to support their national team. Interestingly, the themed responses were the same in both nations. Eight respondents from each country said they were never required to do this; one in each indicated they were. In comparison with the question about operating as fans, responses were often delivered succinctly and directly. The replies from I9—"No, no, no, never, never"—and A9—"No. Absolutely not!"—were reflective of the overall answers in the no category. Multiple respondents talked about being objective, neutral or balanced in their reports. Telling the truth and giving credit to whichever side was playing better was also considered important, as noted by I9, who said it was not his role to "be beating their drums". Attempting to be detached from the result was mentioned by multiple respondents. A1 looked to the example of Richie Benaud, the late commentator, who "never referred to Australia as 'we' or 'us'.

You know it's just 'Australia'. So I find after a while you get pretty, not dispassionate about it, but a story's a story and you just go for it". I3 stated he considered Indian sports writers to be "some of the most neutral". One interviewee discussed how the desire not to be a cheerleader actually led him to be more critical.

The sports journalists were also asked if their readers expected them to support their national team. Respondents in the no category outlined how audience requirements could lead to a greater focus on what the home team was doing well or badly. A6 said he would like to be less home-team focused in selecting what to write about. "Look, there's always going to be more interest in Australia. So you'll tend to write about Australia first because you know that's what the readership is more interested in." Due to the knowledge of the readers, many of the reporters noted they would not be allowed by the audience, through its feedback, to cheerlead on a day when the side had done badly anyway. I2 summed up the situation by saying: "If the team is not doing well, they [the readers] definitely expect that I should write a critical piece." This was considered, in particular, in regard to the knowledge of India's cricket supporters. In Australia, it was suggested by A8 that defeat would be covered more emotionally than a victory:

> If Australia loses the Test or the series, it's a disaster for everyone. If they lose Tests at home with everyone watching, I think we're expected to hit them over the head. To demand answers on behalf of the millions of fans around the country because they feel they own the team.

The two respondents who indicated they were expected to support their national team argued it was to satisfy the requirements of the readers. A4 stressed he was not there to "promote" the Australian side, but outlined he was responsible for writing for the audience.

> They're not wanting to read about the Indian team at great depth, they're wanting to read about the Australian team, so there's no question that my coverage is slanted in that direction ... I do think that you are biased in the sense that you are looking at things through Australian eyes.

I8 was the only respondent to say he operated both as a fan and was required to support the national team. He stated he was responsible for supporting India in his stories because the audience was so passionate. This in turn influenced his own attitude to the team and matches. As he said, "I have no qualms admitting it, that I feel like a fan."

"Every Stakeholder Has to Be Accountable"

There was an overwhelming response from the sports journalists in support of critical watchdog-style reporting. This did not mean that the reporters were undertaking long-form investigations to expose corruption or match-fixing, because economic and staffing issues within newsrooms often prevented this from occurring. Respondents noted staff cutbacks and increased workloads—since the global financial crisis in Australia and more recently in India—as reasons for being tied to their daily duties focused on match reporting and press conferences, rather than searching more widely for unique content (for an example, see Conn 2010). However, their support of watchdog reporting involved them viewing the players, teams and matches from a critical standpoint in their day-to-day dealings and on-field performances. In this way, they were operating as critics as opposed to cheerleaders. As Boyle and Haynes (2009) state, sports journalism involves enquiring and holding those involved in the contests or decisions to account. When asked whether it was important in their work to keep players and officials accountable, 15 of the 18 respondents indicated it was a vital aspect. Eight of the nine interviewees from India felt this way, with the other respondent, I6, saying it was important for administrators but not the players. In Australia, seven agreed it was a vital approach, with two columnists considering their roles to be more about interpreting play than scrutinising key figures. A1 said keeping people accountable was "the essence of the job", while A4 stated it was the reporter's role to critique the players' performances. In support, A8 felt accountability was "fundamental". The view was shared among the Indian journalists. As I1 said, "Every stakeholder has to be accountable for what he does and what he doesn't." I2 stated it was "the most important thing", while I3 noted it was "very important".

Despite the desire to pursue this line, respondents outlined difficulties in finding out key elements of information about players, officials or events due to suffocating media management. A3 gave the example of the then Australian captain, Michael Clarke, injuring his hamstring but the media having to wait five days to discover—or be told—the exact problem.

> So that's a high-profile injury to the country's most prominent cricketer, and it's impossible to get a result. You can say you can hold them to account but it's hard to hold people to account if no one opens the doors.

I4 also noted the inaccessibility of information from the team in relation to India. In contrast, A6 recognised the criticism that contemporary sports reporting was less "dogged" or "energised" in the pursuit of breaking stories than previous generations.

Cheerleading and Critical Watchdog Content

The results from the content analysis varied from the general responses of the in-depth interviews. In relation to RQ2, there were some notable differences in the amounts of cheerleading and critical reports produced by journalists in Australia and India, through the eight news organisations. Overall, 244 articles, or 19.3 per cent, contained elements of cheerleading out of the 1265 story units for analysis (see Table 1). Stories were considered to include aspects of cheerleading if they included descriptions promoting the home side; contained exaggerated praise; or utilised "we" or "I" in relation to team performance. Examples from the analysis coded in this way included: a *Hindustan Times* (December 8) column from a former India captain finishing by saying "Good luck India"; a report about Virat Kohli in *The Times of India* under the headline "Take That, Australia" (January 9) saying: "The next legend of Indian batting has arrived ... combative, feisty, masterful, refreshing"; the *Herald Sun* reported on December 26: "The MCG [Melbourne Cricket Ground] will erupt today as new skipper Steve Smith aims to lead the Aussies to a series-clinching win"; and a sports journalist's column in *The Sydney Morning Herald* (December 19) about the wicket-keeper Brad Haddin said, "Let's hope he stays in the middle for as long possible."

TABLE 1
Instances of articles including cheerleading or critical watchdog elements

	Cheerleading evident		Critical watchdog evident		
	N	% of total stories	*N*	% of total stories	Total stories
The Australian	52	31.9	60	36.8	163
The Sydney Morning Herald	44	18.3	92	38.2	241
Herald Sun	53	24.4	65	30.0	217
The West Australian	15	19.0	23	29.1	79
Australian total	164	23.4	240	34.3	700
The Times of India	30	16.8	64	35.8	179
Hindustan Times	22	13.4	62	37.8	164
Mumbai Mirror	5	6.8	10	13.7	73
Mid-day	23	15.4	32	21.5	149
Indian total	80	14.2	168	29.7	565
Overall total	244	19.3	408	32.3	1265

At a cross-national level: $\chi^2(2, N = 1265) = 12.14$, $p < 0.05$, with a Cramer's V of 0.08, suggesting a weak relationship.

There was a considerably higher percentage of stories containing elements of cheerleading in Australia (23.4 per cent) than in India (14.2 per cent). In terms of individual news organisations in Australia, this ranged from 31.9 per cent of stories in *The Australian* to 18.3 per cent in *The Sydney Morning Herald*, another broadsheet/quality title. All of the Indian titles contained a smaller proportion of cheerleading aspects in stories than Australia, with the largest percentage occurring in *The Times of India* (16.8 per cent) and the smallest in the *Mumbai Mirror* (6.8 per cent). It is important to note the *Mumbai Mirror* utilised news agency bylines for almost half of its stories on the series, with agency copy recognised as being "straight", or unbiased, and a less likely space for cheerleading.

A greater proportion of stories were coded as containing elements of critical watchdog reporting in each nation and news organisation. This totalled 408 of the 1265 articles for analysis. Interestingly, Australia also had the highest amount in this category, with 34.3 per cent of all stories compared with India's 29.7 per cent. Items in which the author was critical of a player, team, official or selections in parts of the story were coded in this category. These aspects were considered to be holding those involved to account (see Boyle and Haynes 2009). Examples included: a *Mumbai Mirror* (January 7) report describing India's bowling as "toothless" and a "pathetic display"; a *Mid-day* (December 13) story criticising the bowling plans as "dumb" and saying the players should not get involved with Australia's sledging; *The Australian* (December 27) reporting Haddin "has forgotten everything about the art of batting"; and *The West Australian* (December 18) stating Australia was suffering its "worst day at home since the 2010–11 Ashes campaign". In Australia, the highest percentage of articles with critical elements appeared in *The Sydney Morning Herald* (38.2 per cent), while the smallest amount was published in *The West Australian* (29.1 per cent). *Hindustan Times* (37.8 per cent) and *The Times of India* (35.8 per cent) were considerably higher than India's two tabloid publications, with the *Mumbai Mirror* again having the smallest figures with 13.7 per cent due to its heavy reliance on news agency copy.

It is also important to note 63 stories were coded as having both cheerleading and critical watchdog elements in the same story, highlighting balance in the pieces. This occurred 38 times in the Australian titles, led by the *Herald Sun* (14) and *The Australian* (13); of India's 25 items in this category, 9 were from *The Times of India*, and *Hindustan Times* and *Mid-day* both had 8. The rest of the articles in the overall sample were coded as neutral reporting.

Further analysis of the data allowed an examination of which nation the cheerleading and critical reporting was focused on. Elements of cheerleading in articles in this category were primarily about the nation of the publication. In the 80 stories in which this was evident in the Indian publications, 87.5 per cent focused on India. Of the 164 items in the Australian sample, 76.2 per cent included aspects coded as cheerleading for Australia. *Mid-day* had the largest proportion of cheerleading for India at 91.3 per cent (21 of 23 items), ahead of *Hindustan Times* at 90.9 per cent. *The Times of India* and the *Mumbai Mirror* were at 80 per cent or above. In Australia, the *Herald Sun* had the highest amount at 84.9 per cent (45 out of 53 items), followed by *The Australian* (78.8 per cent), *The West Australian* (73.3 per cent) and *The Sydney Morning Herald* (63.6 per cent). While cheerleading for the opposition nation was rare, occurring on no more than two occasions in any publication, the Australian titles employed a form of cheerleading through "attacking" the India team or its players in 36 instances. An example of a story coded in this way appeared in *The Australian* (December 26) and included phrases such as "India's tour of the sub subcontinent is headed for the usual disappointing denouement", with the players having the choice to "get on with it and win friends … or throw a tantrum". *The Sydney Morning Herald* published 34.1 per cent, or 15 of 44 stories, with elements attacking the opposition in a cheerleading fashion, while the other three Australian publications were between 15.1 and 20.0 per cent. *The Times of India* was the only Indian title to attack Australia in this way, doing so on five occasions.

Stories employing elements of critical watchdog reporting focused even more heavily on the publication's own nation at the national level. In India, 94.6 per cent, or 159 of 168, articles concentrated on their own nation's issues, in comparison with Australia's 88.3 per cent, or 212 of 240 items. All of the individual Indian titles were at 90 per cent or above, with all 10 of the *Mumbai Mirror*'s stories appearing in this category. The *Herald Sun* had the highest proportion of the four Australian media outlets at 90.8 per cent, while *The West Australian* and *The Sydney Morning Herald* were the lowest at 87.0 per cent. Twelve of *The Sydney Morning Herald*'s items contained elements of critical watchdog reporting about India, while there were seven in *The Australian*, six in the *Herald Sun* and three in *The West Australian*.

Discussion

The mixed-methods employed in this study have revealed some important similarities and differences between Australian and Indian sports journalism. Sports journalists have often been accused of being cheerleaders or fans, sitting in the press box and turning off their critical eyes (for examples, see Anderson 2001; Boyle, Rowe, and Whannel 2012; Hardin 2005). What this study has found in the contemporary environment is that sports journalists say they are not generally confused about their roles as individual journalists (see Boyle, Rowe, and Whannel 2012). However, as a group there was not unanimity in the in-depth interview responses, which at times conflicted with the data from the content analysis. For example, while an overall majority of the journalists rejected being fans or home-team supporters in the interviews, there was still a considerable number of stories containing elements of cheerleading in the content analysis. This can indicate that what the journalists perceived they were doing was different to the material actually produced in their stories, and that they may have been cheerleading more than they realised. In Australia, almost a quarter of stories included aspects of cheerleading, which was in contrast to the interview responses. No Australian journalist said they considered themselves cheerleaders or fans, with two outlining mixed views; only one said he was expected to support the home team. Yet the amount of stories with cheerleading aspects was considerably higher than the 14.2 per cent of articles in India, where only four respondents said they did not feel like fans. It is important to note these articles were not always dominated by cheerleading, but were coded as including aspects of boosterism, worship, sycophancy, cheering and bias (see Anderson 2001; Boyle, Rowe, and Whannel 2012; Hardin 2005; Hardin, Zhong, and Whiteside 2009; McEnnis 2015; Rowe 2004; Steen 2011). Reporting in this way conflicts with the traditional journalistic approach of objectivity, which is detached, emotion-free and critical watchdog in style (Boyle, Rowe, and Whannel 2012; Hardin 2005; Hardin, Zhong, and Whiteside 2009; Rowe 2004; Schudson 2001; Tuchman 1972). However, it is also important to note praising athletes and teams for their achievements is not unethical and can be a legitimate reporting tool in a range of scenarios. Boyle (2006, 125) argues winning and success in sport are "the most important" elements in "shaping journalistic opinion and comment". A similar point was made by I6 during the interviews. "It is a sport and largely it's about wins and celebrations. You write a little glowingly but not necessarily as a fan." In the sporting contest being examined, Australia won the first two matches and claimed the series 2–0, therefore giving the home side's media more to "cheer" about than the touring reporters, who were required to interpret defeat. This could be a reason for the reduced amounts of cheerleading in the Indian publications, particularly given the more prevalent view of the respondents in perceiving themselves as fans.

In this study, the issue of bias was acknowledged by two reporters, who felt they were expected to support the home team in their work. This figure contrasts with Hardin (2005), who found 39 per cent of editors believed their publications should cheer for the local side. Further, in the current research project, 16 of the 18 sports journalists did not consider that they operated as boosters, as previous research of sports journalists has found (see Hardin 2005; Hardin, Zhong, and Whiteside 2009). Billings, Angelini, and Dan (2011) called for more work examining these types of news choices at gatekeeping levels, and this finding suggests there are differences in the perceptions of journalists operating at the individual level compared with the organisational view, in which figures such as sports editors are responsible for instilling company policy. In rejecting the cheerleading approach, multiple respondents mentioned the importance of neutrality and objectivity in their reporting (see Schudson 2001; Tuchman 1972). As A9 said, "I think that's the worst area you can get into, the cheerleading aspect of it. I'm very careful not to do that … I think most reporters do the same thing." Clapping and cheerleading in the press box were discouraged by the respondents, who in most instances did not perceive themselves as "fans with laptops" (see Booth 2013; Keating 2001). However, some respondents did note their passion for cricket, and believed this was important in passing on the context of the game to the readers. Importantly, they considered these feelings were separate from their professional views of the players or teams they were reporting on. These examples reflect the broad nature of being a fan, and highlight differences between personal and work influences. The respondents said they appreciated the game but did not watch with the same intensity as if they were members of the crowd, and applied journalistic standards to their reports.

Critical watchdog-style reporting was evident in the perceptions of the journalists through the interviews, and the nations' publications. Given the long-standing criticism and scepticism of sports journalists as professionals (for examples, see Garrison and Salwen 1989; Rowe 2007), an important finding was that in both nations there were considerably more critical reports about the series in the content analysis than those involving excessive praise or cheerleading. In Australia, more than a third of stories had critical elements, compared with less than a quarter containing cheerleading, while in India there were 29.7 per cent of critical articles compared with 14.2 per cent of cheerleading. These results reflected the views of the 15 sports journalists who outlined the importance of keeping players and officials accountable. The findings from both methods highlight that sports journalists are capable of operating within the traditional journalistic norm of objective, detached and critical watchdog-style news gathering (Boyle, Rowe, and Whannel 2012; Hardin 2005; Hardin, Zhong, and Whiteside 2009; Rowe 2004; Schudson 2001; Tuchman 1972). However, it is important to note that this does not mean the journalists were undertaking "sustained" long-form investigations or acting as crusaders (Rowe 2004, 399; see also Rowe 2007). During the content analysis, no article was coded as being investigative in the traditional sense. However, in day-to-day reporting, critical analysis of issues was being employed, and at higher rates in relation to coverage containing elements of cheerleading. The general feeling of respondents towards watchdog reporting was summed up by A3: "Decisions get made in the shadows and they've got to be put in the light to be examined." As a result, critical enquiry was not being avoided by the sports journalists writing for these publications during the study (see Rowe 2007). Another relevant aspect in relation to watchdog reporting was the difficulty over access to players and key sources. This trend has been recognised in other sports in Australia (Sherwood, Nicholson, and Marjoribanks 2016), and highlights the difficulties of investigative or watchdog reporting in an environment where complicity is encouraged and sometimes rewarded. These elements, which challenge objective reporting, are faced by sports journalists in both of these nations, who operate in a heavily media-managed environment.

Finally, it is important to note there was a home-team bias in the selection of stories to cheerlead or be critical about. Almost 88 per cent of stories in the cheerleading category in India focused on the publications' nation, while slightly more than three-quarters in the Australian titles were about the home team. The result in Australia was reduced by the category highlighting how often cheerleading occurred through "attacking" the other nation's players or play. This is a form of nationalistic cheerleading described by Billings, Angelini, and Dan (2011), in which the portrayal can take on "us versus them" characteristics. In stories that utilised elements of critical reporting, the home nation was the focus in all but nine of 168 articles in this category in the India publications, and in all but 28 of the 240 stories in the Australian titles. The other nation was barely a focus in both cheerleading and critical categories. In this aspect, there was not necessarily boosting and promoting the success of the home team (Anderson 2001; Hardin 2005; Steen 2011), but writing about it in significantly more depth to satisfy their audience. While individual journalists were often defiant in pointing out their neutrality or absence of fan-like feelings, they were operating as gatekeepers with an eye on the home side in their news selection—even if this did not mean they were writing about them in a complimentary way.

Conclusion

The professionalism of sports journalists has often come under scrutiny from both researchers and other sections of the newsroom. As previously noted, Boyle, Rowe, and Whannel (2012) have questioned whether sports journalists have confused the roles of reporter and fan. In this one example in the contemporary sports journalism environment, it was apparent that individual journalists were clear-thinking about their reporting responsibilities. This did not mean that there was universal agreement about what the role of a sports journalist was in relation to cheerleading, supporting the home side or keeping key figures accountable. Clearly, cheerleading and local support exists in the newspaper coverage in this study, and there is a dominant focus on the home team in news selection. However, in relation to RQ1, the majority of journalists in Australia did not consider themselves fans, while four in India also answered in this way. In both nations, the majority felt they were not expected to write in support of the home team, and considered keeping key figures to account as a vital factor in their work. The content analysis results utilised to answer RQ2 generally supported these findings in revealing a noticeably larger proportion of stories incorporating critical watchdog elements than cheerleading. This study does not argue that sports journalists are as objective as other areas of the newsroom, or that cheerleading is a thing of the past. In fact, examples have been presented to justify some of the criticism directed at this corner of the newsroom. Through this analysis, it is evident that there are both cheerleading and critical elements in the sports journalists' coverage of this cricket series. However, it is important to recognise there are many sports journalists in this sample who want—and are responsible for providing significant amounts of—reporting that is "enquiring, explaining and at times holding to account sports on behalf of fans" (Boyle and Haynes 2009, 183; see also Boyle, Rowe, and Whannel 2012). Of course, their coverage is often driven by winning and success (Boyle 2006), but also a desire to inform the audience with news, facts, figures and flourishes.

There are limitations in this study, which focused on only two nations playing one sport over a five-week period. The interview sample was limited by the relatively small number of Indian journalists on this particular tour but it provided a valuable overview of cricket journalists involved in the series. However, it is important to note it is not representative of sports journalists in both nations. In future research, examining entire tournaments, such as the one-day or Twenty20 World Cups, could reveal more detail about the nationalistic cheerleading described by Billings, Angelini, and Dan (2011). Elements of critical reporting and cheerleading in sport could also be compared with other areas of media publications, such as general news, the arts and lifestyle sections. A comprehensive analysis of investigative reporting into sports topics, particularly in relation to uncovering recent corruption in football, athletics and cycling, would also be advantageous. Research into this critical watchdog area has the potential to help boost sports journalism's often ailing reputation as the toy department of the newsroom.

DISCLOSURE STATEMENT

No potential conflict of interest was reported by the author.

REFERENCES

Ali, Amin. 2014. "Australia-India Cricket Rivalry Has Even Bettered Ashes: John Harnden." *The times of India*, June 30. http://timesofindia.indiatimes.com/interviews/Australia-India-cricket-rivalry-has-even-bettered-Ashes-John-Harnden/articleshow/37477233.cms.

Anderson, William. 2001. "Does the Cheerleading Ever Stop? Major League Baseball and Sports Journalism." *Journalism and Mass Communication Quarterly* 78 (2): 355–382.

Billings, Andrew. 2008. "Clocking Gender Differences: Televised Olympic Clock Time in the 1996–2006 Summer and Winter Olympics." *Television & New Media* 9 (5): 429–441.

Billings, Andrew, James Angelini, and Wu Dan. 2011. "Nationalistic Notions of the Superpowers: Comparative Analyses of the American and Chinese Telecasts in the 2008 Beijing Olympiad." *Journal of Broadcasting & Electronic Media* 55 (2): 251–266.

Booth, Lawrence. 2013. "Boxing Clever." *The Nightwatchman*: 4-9, summer. http://www.thenightwatchman.net/wp-content/uploads/2013/06/The%20Nightwatchman%20-%20Issue%202%20-%20Sample%20edition.pdf.

Boyle, Raymond. 2006. *Sports Journalism: Context and Issues*. London: Sage.

Boyle, Raymond, and Richard Haynes. 2009. *Power Play: Sport, the Media and Popular Culture*. 2nd ed. Edinburgh: Edinburgh University Press.

Boyle, Raymond, David Rowe, and Garry Whannel. 2012. "'Delight in Trivial Controversy'? Questions for Sports Journalism." In *The Routledge Companion to News and Journalism*, edited by Stuart Allan, 245–255. Abingdon, Oxfordshire: Routledge.

Conn, Malcolm. 2010. "Live from the Warne-Waugh Affair." *ESPNCricinfo*, June 24. http://www.espncricinfo.com/match-fixing-anniversary/content/story/463242.html.

English, Peter. 2015a. "Mapping the Sports Journalism Field: Bourdieu and Broadsheet Newsrooms." *Journalism*: 1–17. doi: 10.1177/1464884915576728.

English, Peter. 2015b. "New Rules of the Game: Sports Journalism and Profiles." In *Profile Pieces and the 'Human Interest' Bias*, edited by Sue Joseph and Richard Keeble, 195–208. London: Routledge.

Garrison, Bruce, and Michael Salwen. 1989. "Newspaper Sports Journalists: A Profile of the 'Profession'." *Journal of Sport and Social Issues* 13 (2): 57–68.

Hanitzsch, Thomas, Folker Hanusch, Claudia Mellado, Maria Anikina, Rosa Berganza, Incilay Cangoz, Mihai Coman, et al. 2010. "Mapping Journalistic Cultures across Nations." *Journalism Studies* 12 (3): 273–293.

Hardin, Marie. 2005. "Survey Finds Boosterism, Freebies Remain Problem for Newspaper Sports Departments." *Newspaper Research Journal* 26 (1): 66–72.

Hardin, Marie, Bu Zhong, and Erin Whiteside. 2009. "Sports Coverage: 'Toy Department' or Public-Service Journalism? The Relationship between Reporters' Ethics and Attitudes toward the Profession." *International Journal of Sport Communication* 2: 319–339.

Henningham, John. 1995. "A Profile of Australian Sports Journalists." *The ACHPER Healthy Lifestyles Journal* 42 (3): 13–17.

Keating, Frank. 2001. "These Australians the Best Ever? Stark Raving Lunacy." *The Guardian*, July 29. http://www.theguardian.com/sport/2001/jul/30/comment.

Majumdar, Boria. 2008. "Soaps, Serials and the CPI(M), Cricket Beats Them All." In *Television in India*, edited by Nalin Mehta, 124–139. Abingdon, Oxfordshire: Routledge.

McEnnis, Simon. 2015. "Following the Action: How Live Bloggers Are Reimagining the Professional Ideology of Sports Journalism." *Journalism Practice*. doi:10.1080/17512786.2015.1068130.

Nicholson, Matthew, Lawrie Zion, and David Lowden. 2011. "A Profile of Australian Sport Journalists (Revisited)." *Media International Australia* 140: 84–96.

Rössler, Patrick. 2012. "Comparative Content Analysis." In *The Handbook of Comparative Communication Research*, edited by Frank Esser and Thomas Hanitzsch, 459–468. New York: Routledge.

Rowe, David. 2004. *Sport, Culture and the Media*. 2nd ed. Maidenhead: Open University Press.

Rowe, David. 2007. "Still the 'Toy Department' of the News Media?" *Journalism* 8 (4): 385–405.

Rowe, David. 2011. "The Televised Sport 'Monkey Trial': 'Race' and the Politics of Post-Colonial Cricket." *Sport in Society* 14 (6): 792–804. doi:10.1080/17430437.2011.587294.

Schudson, Michael. 2001. "The Objectivity Norm in American Journalism." *Journalism* 2 (2): 149–170.

Schultz-Jørgensen, Søren. 2005. "The World's Best Advertising Agency: The Sports Press." *The House of Monday Morning*, October 31. http://www.playthegame.org/upload//Sport_Press_Survey_English.pdf.

Sherwood, Merryn, Matthew, Nicholson, and Tim Marjoribanks. 2016. "Access, Agenda Building and Information Subsidies: Media Relations in Professional Sport." *International Review for the Sociology of Sport*: 1–16. doi: 10.1177/1012690216637631.

Steen, Rob. 2011. "Rose-Tinted Spectacle? The View from the Pressbox." In *Watching the Olympics: Politics, Power and Representation*, edited by John Sudgen and Alan Tomlinson, 213–227. London: Routledge.

Steen, Rob. 2015. *Sports Journalism: A Multimedia Primer*. 2nd ed. London: Routledge.

Tomarchio, Cameron. 2014. "Commonwealth Games Press Conference Was Insane." *News.Com.Au*, July 27. http://www.news.com.au/sport/commonwealth-games/usain-bolts-commonwealth-games-press-conference-was-insane/story-fnnx3zsr-1227003036202.

Tuchman, Gaye. 1972. "Objectivity as Strategic Ritual: An Examination of Newsmen's Notions of Objectivity." *American Journal of Sociology* 77 (4): 660–679.

Wilson, Aaron. 2015. "No Cheering in the Press Box Reminder Issued as 49ers' Jarryd Hayne Draws Applause." *Houston Chronicle*, August 15. http://blog.chron.com/ultimatetexans/2015/08/no-cheering-in-the-press-box-as-49ers-jarryd-hayne-draws-applause/#34970101=0.

Yin, Jiafei. 2011. "Growing Pains in the Development of a Free Press in Africa and Asia: A Comparative Analysis - South Africa and India." *Ecquid Novi: African Journalism Studies* 32 (2): 20–35.

PLAYING ON THE SAME PITCH
Attitudes of sports journalists towards fan bloggers

Simon McEnnis

Sports journalism's perceived proximity to fandom has posed professional problems relating to status, prestige and standards. Sports journalists are now seeing performative aspects of their occupational practice appropriated by fans using digital platforms. This paper outlines a study that involved in-depth semi-structured interviews with UK print sports journalists to explore what fan blogging has meant for their occupational identity. This study found sports journalists did not consider fan bloggers to be a threat to their professional distinctiveness. Bloggers seeking to emulate sports journalism's daily beat routines were seen as conflictive. However, participants considered the occupation to be safeguarded by privileged accreditation to professional sport and access to resources. The study also discovered sports journalists held nuanced attitudes towards bloggers and did not necessarily see them as inferior. Sports journalists saw a value in bloggers with niche, writer-driven interests providing complementary content to mainstream media. Sports journalists could legitimise blogs through acceptance and adoption while asserting their own cultural dominance. There were positive indications this expansion and diversification of the sports section of print media websites could lead to a range of perspectives and exposure of marginal voices. Participants also indicated blogging had become an entry route into the occupation.

Introduction

Sports journalists have a rather dubious reputation as "cheerleaders", "fans with typewriters" and the "toy department" (Boyle 2006; Rowe 2004). Previous research has claimed that core journalistic principles of objectivity and neutrality give way on the sports desk to subjectivity and partisanship on matters considered to be of trivial interest (Boyle 2006; Hutchins and Rowe 2012; Rowe 2004; Rudin and Ibbotson 2003). Furthermore, sports journalists are considered to take an uncritical and unquestioning stance towards the professional sports environment while building a collusive and complicit relationship with sources (Boyle 2006; Rowe 2004; Sugden and Tomlinson 2007).

Sports journalists' proximity to fandom can be considered to be increasingly problematic in the twenty-first century as "fans with typewriters" in the literal sense are a common feature of the sport communication process through blogs. Print sports journalists are considered to still be "key cultural narrators" despite declining newspaper circulations and the economic primacy of broadcast media (Boyle, Rowe, and Whannel 2009, 252). Historically, journalists have experienced a dominant and hegemonic position in sports culture that derives from the mass media's monopoly control over communication channels. However, external agents such as clubs, organisations, athletes and fans are all now producers and distributors of sports content (Hutchins and Rowe 2012). Blogging is an example of "digital plenitude" around sports information that has contributed to journalism becoming a "leaking craft" (Hutchins and Rowe 2009, 2012). How sports journalists make sense of these shifts can provide insight into how mainstream, legacy media attempts to sustain its hegemonic dominance in a digital environment.

Blogging has involved an adoption of performative norms and codes that have been the domain of the professional culture of sports journalism (Kian, Burden, and Shaw 2011; McCarthy 2012, 2014). Fans, the traditional consumers of sports texts, are also "playing on the same pitch" as journalists through shared use of platforms across digital and social media. Fan bloggers engage in journalistic activity yet do not consider themselves to be journalists. They "appear to take their communicative cues from print sports journalism" (McCarthy 2012, 429) while self-identifying as non-mainstream journalists (Kian, Burden, and Shaw 2011). A growing research culture into sports blogs has emerged (Dart 2009; Kian, Burden, and Shaw 2011; McCarthy 2012, 2014) but there is scant in-depth analysis of the perspective of traditional media gatekeepers, specifically print sports journalists.

Sports journalists, along with the wider newsroom, have experienced considerable upheaval to working practices in the transition of newspapers from analogue to digital platforms (Ketterer, McGuire, and Murray 2014; McGuire and Murray 2013; Sherwood and Nicholson 2012). However, these shifts also pose questions for identity (McEnnis 2013; Reed 2013). Journalists, as a dominant group, are forced to make sense of not only the presence of subordinate agencies such as clubs, fans and organisations in sports communication but also the fact their professional values, norms and practices have been adopted by "outsiders" to the occupational group. This article outlines a study that focused on how UK journalists in mainstream media are making sense of fan-led interventions in sports communication through blogging. Hutchins and Rowe (2012, 150) state that sports journalism's "once relatively robust habitus … has turned fragile and permeable" as the difference between professionals and amateurs has become increasingly problematic.

This research sought to provide clarity on how sports journalists are making sense of these complexities and what they mean for their occupational identity. Particular consideration was given to how sports journalists interpret their distinctiveness and whether they seek to assert hegemonic dominance in their responses, relationships and interactions with bloggers. The study used in-depth semi-structured interviews with a small sample of seven sports journalists working for national, mainstream print media in the United Kingdom to facilitate concentrated and detailed insight into the research problem.

Sports Journalists and Occupational Identity

The problematic relationship that sports journalists have with their occupational identity and the inherent contradictions within the profession need unpacking. Sports journalism is considered to belong to the print tradition despite the emergence of the broadcast sports journalist in the late twentieth century (Boyle 2006; Rowe 2004). Journalism does not conform to standard notions of professionalism based around training and certification as requirements of entry (Reed 2013). Sports journalists may be hired for their backgrounds in training, work with fanzines, level of sporting knowledge, access to contacts and previous careers as professional sportspeople (Boyle 2006; Rowe 2004). Boyle (2006) also notes a growing "graduatisation" of the profession due to the emergence of sports journalism degree courses in the United Kingdom. Rowe (2004) argues sports journalism's difficulty in establishing a clearly defined entry route, allied to the internal battles for legitimacy and authority that have ensued, have contributed to its lowly prestige and status.

Paradoxically, sports journalists wield considerable economic power because they attract considerable audiences to media products yet suffer from low cultural power (Boyle 2006; Rowe 2004). Sports journalists' failure to meet expected standards of professionalism is a primary source of anxiety among them (Salwen and Garrison 1998). Sports journalists are beholden to similar expectations to the wider newsroom largely due to its historically entwined relationship. Sports journalism was absorbed into generalist newspapers in the nineteenth century and a specialist sports press struggled to sustain itself in the United Kingdom (Boyle and Haynes 2009).

Sports journalism's privileged position in society has stemmed from its accreditation to the wider professional sports environment. The beat system is an essential feature of sports journalism's professional culture built around the "myth of access to the inside story" (Boyle 2013, 95). Reporters are expected to be able to develop and cultivate contacts within the wider sports environment for the purpose of uncovering information (Lowes 1999). This organisation of news work leads to a favouring of official sources (Lowes 1999; McChesney 2008). The beat system serves an ideological function in that it ensures interest in sport as a commodity by audiences/consumers is maintained on a daily basis (Lowes 1999).

Sports journalists' source relations within this promotional culture are considered to lack professional distance and be defined by collusive activity. Here, reporters' loyalties reside with insiders rather than the public (Sugden and Tomlinson 2007). Sports journalists also form a curious "press pack" whereby they are colleagues and rivals so therefore both camaraderie and competition exist (Boyle 2006; Sugden and Tomlinson 2007). Favourable access is granted to either those who own rights, such as broadcasters, and those journalists who provide positive coverage or self-censor (Salwen and Garrison 1998; Sugden and Tomlinson 2007). The beat system also operates as a closed shop based around accreditation controlled by media managers. Access is biased towards traditional media, although there are signs newer outlets are starting to gain entry to the wider sports environment (Suggs Jr 2015).

Sports journalism saw its function of describing the sports event usurped by the advent of broadcast media which led to a schism towards either more reflective, contextual writing or gossip and celebrity "churnalism" (Boyle 2006; Boyle and Haynes

2009; Hutchins and Rowe 2012). Generalisations around sports journalism principles and practice are therefore problematic because of internal struggles for legitimacy.

The print tradition can be divided into two typologies—the "quality" broadsheet with its emphasis on sports writing and the "hack" tabloid with its focus on sports reporting (Boyle 2006; Rowe 2004). These two distinctions are sites of tension over journalistic values. Tabloid reporters value speed and economy, and believe that broadsheet writers consider them inferior. On the other hand, the broadsheet writer strives for stories of literary merit and that contextualise sport's relationship with society. These typologies are evidenced in the broadsheet emphasis on cricket and rugby union and the tabloid obsession with football. Rowe (2004, 61) notes "the assertion of the quality writing function over and against that of 'hack' journalism is constantly made by those who wish to elevate media sports texts … to the status of art".

Sports journalists' occupational status is further impacted by the increasing shift towards what Eco (1986) describes as "sports chatter" at a time when there has never been a greater need to scrutinise a highly commercialised wider sports environment (Boyle 2013). Sugden and Tomlinson (2010) note increased comment and opinion as one of the consequences of a 24-hour rolling news culture. There can also be a discrepancy between sports journalists' perception of their work routines and what appears in their output. Sheffer and Schultz's (2010a, 2010b) content analysis revealed that sports journalists primarily use Twitter for commentary and opinion despite the self-perception that they mainly posted breaking news and promotion on the social media site.

Sports Blogging

Sports blogs are part of a wider internet phenomenon that encompasses other subject areas such as business and politics. Blogging is considered to have become a common activity by the turn of the twenty-first century (Kian, Burden, and Shaw 2011). Barriers of entry to media production have been lifted by access to cheap technology and digital networks facilitated by the user-friendliness of blog-creation sites including blogger.com (Walker Rettberg 2014). Hendrickson (2007, 188) advises that "some defining characteristics should be identified if analysis is to be of any use". Blogs share basic, structural commonalities such as postings in reverse chronological order, hyperlinks and a facility for reader comments (Herring et al. 2005; Lenhart and Fox 2006).

The number of blogs worldwide was reported to have risen from 36 million in 2006 to 181 million in 2011 (Nielsen Wire 2012). Sysomos' (2010) analysis of 100 million blog posts found the United Kingdom (6.75 per cent) to be the second most populated country within the blogosphere behind the United States (29.2 per cent). Blogs are difficult to quantify through their existence across disparate online spaces and a lack of a central repository, while being constantly created, abandoned and used for spamming purposes (Walker Rettberg 2014). Rampton's (2012) survey of 1000 US bloggers discovered Wordpress (43 per cent) was the most popular platform followed by Blogger (35 per cent), Tumblr/TypePad/Posterous (16 per cent) and other (6 per cent). Rampton also found that 329 million people in the United States view a blog and 25 billion pages were viewed per month.

Directories and aggregators for sports blogs tend to rely on submissions for inclusion (footballblogdirectory.co.uk, sportsblogsdirectory.com) or use the website operator's discretion (soccerblogs.net) rather than strive for completism. Further, the process of filtering fan blogs from other types of sports blogs, such as athlete and journalist, as well as by country of origin is problematic in internet searches. Little is known about the history and scale of sports blogging in the United Kingdom. US studies, however, can give an indication of popularity and demography around sports blogs. Sports bloggers are considered to be overwhelmingly male and mainly under the age of 30 in the United States (Kian, Burden, and Shaw 2011), when the overall blogosphere is reported to contain balanced gender distribution (Sysomos 2010). Thirteen per cent of hobbyist bloggers concentrate on sport as subject matter (Technorati 2011) while the research of Lenhart and Fox (2006) into US bloggers found sports (6 per cent) was the fourth most popular type behind life and experiences (37 per cent), politics/government (11 per cent) and entertainment (7 per cent). Limited attempts have been made by the mainstream media to accommodate fan blogs in their output. *The Guardian* has a revenue-sharing model, called the *Guardian Sports Network*, whereby 25 selected fan bloggers contribute posts to the website. The blogger therefore has the potential to reach *The Guardian*'s mass readership while the media organisation is provided with content. However, the *Guardian Sports Network* model is unique within the UK print media market.

Sports blogging has attracted scholarly interest in terms of the questions that it poses for mainstream media (Hardin and Ash 2011; Kian, Burden, and Shaw 2011; McCarthy 2012, 2014). These key issues can be described as in what ways sports blogging constitutes journalism and whether bloggers can be considered as belonging to the occupational group of sports journalism. Questions also involve whether sports blogging contests or complements mainstream media.

Blogs can be interpreted as constituting a form of journalism in frequently adopting its normative and performative features including news, opinion and commentary (Hendrickson 2007). In the context of sports, bloggers adopt journalistic conventions, forms and styles such as match reports, analysis, opinion, previews, headlines and photos (McCarthy 2012). However, this similarity does not mean bloggers share the same professional concerns or self-identify with sports journalists as an occupational group even though they consider their work to be a form of sports journalism (Kian, Burden, and Shaw 2011; McCarthy 2014). Furthermore, bloggers may be motivated by a desire to interact socially with other like-minded bloggers and connect knowledge rather than strive for inclusion and acceptance in the mainstream media (McCarthy 2012; Singer 2006).

Other research has considered in what way bloggers provide competition to journalists. Journalists can view blogs as lacking rigour in terms of accuracy and fact-checking (Lowrey and Burleson Mackay 2008). Hardin and Ash (2011), using a content analysis, compared standards and found sports journalists are more likely to place their stories in social context compared to bloggers. However, bloggers can potentially spur the mainstream media to improve its professional standards (Lowrey 2006; Wall 2005). Sports bloggers can also contest mainstream media by offering a dissenting voice (McCarthy 2014; Sanderson 2009). In this context, blogging must be seen as a political act concerned with fans reclaiming sport from the media–sport nexus that drives narratives and determines what is visible and invisible (McCarthy 2014).

Blogging has also been interpreted as a complementary sports communication process to mainstream media. Motivations can stem from dissatisfaction with the coverage of a particular sport or issue and blogs may be used to fill a gap in the sparse coverage of niche sports such as gymnastics (McCarthy 2012). Bloggers can also present news information that has been overlooked by journalists (Lowrey 2006). Singer (2006) argues that journalism and blogging co-exist and have developed an interdependent relationship. Bloggers can provide journalists with a source for stories but also formulate their opinions based on stories that appear in the mainstream media. Furthermore, bloggers rely on journalists to give them publicity to generate both awareness and audiences. However, Lowrey (2006, 491) points out "the argument that blogging and journalism are not in conflict but should rather complement each other serves journalism".

Sports blogging can be considered to have its antecedents in fanzines. Like blogging, the growth of fanzine culture in 1970s and 1980s arose out of technological shifts. The fanzine sub-culture, of producing underground, subversive publications, exploded in the 1980s because of access to printing technology such as word processors and home computers (Haynes 1995). Many fanzines were driven by enthusiasm and passion for football but also expressed dissatisfaction with mainstream media as they "railed against … the irresponsibility and sensationalism of the press" (Haynes 1995, 36). Fanzine culture can also be interpreted as a response to the perceived promotional culture of mainstream media (Rowe 1992, 1995). Research into journalist attitudes towards fanzines found a more positive reception from editors, who commission material, than reporters, who saw them as competition and cheaper entry routes into mainstream media (Rowe 1995).

Sports journalists occupy a self-perception of having superior knowledge to fans (Sherwood and Nicholson 2012) but also need to "raise their game" in the digital age because "advances in digital technology make it easy for anyone to exercise many of the functions of the journalist from their own PC" (Lambert 2012, 33). McEnnis (2013) notes that sports journalists recognise the difficulty in asserting authority because fans are increasingly better informed due to greater and easier access to information over the internet. Sports journalists are reflecting on what constitutes professional distinction and worthiness because of the challenge of sharing content and publishing platforms with users (McEnnis 2013).

The blogosphere—and indeed the distinction between amateur and professional—is further complicated and obscured by the fact that journalists can also be bloggers. Schultz and Sheffer (2007) discovered that sports journalists are reluctant bloggers, as they do not recognise its value, apply traditional attitudes and blog because they are told to do so by managers. Dart (2009) found the sports–media complex appropriated blogging with its alternative format providing appeal. Journalists posed as fan bloggers at the 2006 football World Cup finals to ensure that dominant narratives were sustained and alternative voices restricted to the margins (Dart 2009). Lowrey (2006) argues that journalism as a dominant occupational group is showing signs of absorbing blogging as a subordinate practice.

The terms "blogging" and "blogger" can also be used as distancing labels from journalism that serves commercial interests. The labels suggest an alternative and edgy sports journalism that carries with it a cultural cool and cache (Vogan and Dowling 2016). However, they can also be conveniently described as forms of personal expression by sports organisations and leagues as a means of protecting the exclusivity of content and therefore maintain the high value of rights deals with mainstream media (Hutchins and Mikosza 2010).

Methodology

This study analysed the attitudes of print sports journalists towards bloggers and formed part of a wider project that investigated challenges for the occupational group in the digital age. Eligible participants for the study were sports journalists working for national print organisations in the United Kingdom. The term "print" alludes to titles that were traditional newspapers but now either partly or, in the case of *The Independent*, wholly publishes content on digital platforms. Sports journalists employed on either a permanent staff contract or regular freelance basis were invited to take part in the study. Previous research has shown that using interviews can prove effective in providing detailed and rich insight into the attitudes and experiences of sports journalists (Billings 2009; Boyle 2006; Cramer 1994; Hardin and Shain 2005, 2006; Hutchins 2011; Kian 2007; Rowe 2004).

The following research questions were determined:

RQ1: What are the mainstream sports journalists' experiences of bloggers in their work routines?

RQ2: How do mainstream sports journalists perceive blogging in relation to their own professional principles and occupational practices?

RQ3: In what ways do sports journalists utilise blogs and bloggers in the mainstream media?

The following seven sports journalists took part in the study:

- Sean Ingle, senior sports writer, *The Guardian*. Athletics correspondent and former sports editor of *guardian.co.uk*. Sean is also a regular contributor to the *Guardian Football Weekly* podcast. Started his career with magazine publisher EMAP. Aged 40. Interview took place on 19 January 2016.
- Justin Allen, sports reporter, *The Sun*. General reporting duties covering football. Started journalism career on local newspapers at the *Kent Messenger*. Aged 39. Interview took place on 18 January 2016.
- Paul Campbell, sport community co-ordinator editor, *The Guardian*. Mainly an editorial decision maker but role also includes writing, maintaining social media accounts and overseeing user engagement on the sports section of *guardian.co.uk*. Formerly worked for the leading fanzine *When Saturday Comes*. Aged 32. Interview took place on 13 May 2016.
- Nick Szczepanik, freelance sports writer, *The Independent*, *Daily Telegraph* and *The Times*. General reporting duties covering football, tennis and gridiron. Former staff sports writer for *The Times* between 1999 and 2010. Started career as a teacher before moving into sports journalism in 1994. Aged 62. Interview took place on 25 May 2016.
- Dave Bromage, deputy sports editor, *The Sun*. Duties include editorial decision making and managing production. Started on local newspapers in Hertfordshire before joining *The Sun* early in his career. Aged 37. Interview took place on 9 June 2016.

- Tom Hopkinson, football reporter, *Sunday People*. General reporting duties. Also contributes to BT Sport's *Football Writers* podcast. Previously worked for *Sunday Express*, *Daily Express* and the *London Evening Standard*. Aged 39. Interview took place on 20 July 2016.
- Jonathan Wilson, freelance sports journalist, *The Guardian* and *The Independent*. General reporting duties covering football while specialising in tactics. Former football correspondent for the *Financial Times*. Has authored five books including *Inverting the Pyramid*, which won the Football Book of the Year award in 2009. Also runs a journal called *The Blizzard*, which publishes long-form sports journalism. Aged 39. Interview took place on 19 January 2016.

A small sample was selected to enable an in-depth analysis of the perceptions and attitudes of print sports journalists. The sample contained a mixture of "beat" reporters and editorial decision makers within mainstream media organisations. These two dimensions to the sports desk are common to previous studies that have involved in-depth interviews with sports journalists (Boyle 2006; Hutchins and Rowe 2012; Sugden and Tomlinson 2007, 2010).

A purposive sampling method was initially employed which transitioned to a snowballing technique based on recommendations from initial participants. The typologies of sports journalism were reflected in the final sample with four participants coming from the broadsheet tradition and three interviewees attached to the tabloid, popular press. The final sample was indicative of sports journalism's status as a male-dominated profession (Boyle 2006; Franks and O'Neill 2016). Sports blogging is considered to be an activity more popular among males than females (Lenhart and Fox 2006). Kian, Burden, and Shaw's (2011) study into sports bloggers contained a sample of eight participants, of whom seven were male.

The researcher and author of this article is a former sports journalist who worked for a tabloid, national newspaper for nine years. The researcher's sports journalism experience informed the interpretive approach and helped to guide participants in reflecting on their occupational principles and practices. Four of the participants were already known in a professional context (Justin Allen, Dave Bromage, Sean Ingle and Tom Hopkinson), one participant contributed to a previous study (Nick Szczepanik), and contributors recommended two further participants (Paul Campbell and Jonathan Wilson).

Interviews took place between January and July 2016 in person in either staff canteens, bars, restaurants or cafes, and lasted between 45 minutes and 1 hour and 15 minutes. Participants were presented with the opportunity to be anonymous but all gave consent to be named. Interviews were recorded with a digital audio device and manually transcribed.

Findings and Discussion

Two broad themes emerged from the findings that represented the different aspects of participants' attitudes towards bloggers. These categories were labelled as *competitive* and *complementary* and reflected the key thematic areas that emerged in the interviews and which conveniently linked back to the issues identified in the literature review. *Competitive* related to discussions on situations where bloggers were seen as clashing with sports journalists' occupational practice. *Complementary* was reflective of conditions in which participants were accepting and accommodating of blogging activity.

Competitive

Participants spoke about bloggers who focused on newsgathering, opinion and gossip around the professional sports environment in competitive terms. Here, discussions were concentrated on the importance of privileged access to the inside sports environment in distinguishing between professional journalists and fan bloggers. Interviewees considered that their privileged access to sports insiders, for example athletes and coaches, led to knowledge production that was not generally available to fan bloggers. This ideological outlook reinforced the value that journalists place on official sources and commercial, professional sport (Lowes 1999; McChesney 2008). However, this finding also highlighted the sense of ownership of controlled spaces such as press conferences and mixed zones. Reporters may experience difficult relationships with media managers yet this collusive dynamic helps the print media to safeguard its occupational base.

Respondents considered the availability of resources—specifically time and money—as also leading to the generation of knowledge that was not usually accessible to fan bloggers. Nick Szczepanik, freelance journalist with *The Independent*, *Daily Telegraph* and *The Times*, said:

> That's not to say that online journalists can't get things right and sometimes there are people out there who know more than we do. Some people are really solidly into their club and do have their contacts and can get a better story than a Fleet Street journalist. Generally speaking, I know whom my money is on because that's the way it works. The more time you give to something and the more you are paid to get it right, the more incentive you have.

Sean Ingle, senior sports writer with *The Guardian*, referred to athletics bloggers when he stated, "some are knowledgeable and others think everyone is on drugs. I know a lot more than them. I'm speaking to agents and I know more stuff". Tom Hopkinson, football writer with the *Sunday People*, pointed to experience when he said, "when you've been a reporter for 10, 15, 20 years, you've got better contacts".

Participants found that bloggers were not usually present on the "beat" because of the difficulties in securing accreditation from media managers. Jonathan Wilson, freelance sports journalist for *The Guardian* and *The Independent*, indicated that, "they just don't get in. Data cards are hard to get which is a good thing on the inside". Bloggers who were able to gain access could be considered an undesirable presence. Justin Allen, sports reporter with *The Sun*, was referring to both bloggers and journalists from non-mainstream media when he stated, "they really mess up your press conferences. They come up with an absolutely ridiculous question. A question that's maybe been answered already, or something that's not in relation to anything".

This sports journalist attributed the lack of interviewing skills as being due to either lack of professional training or experience. However, this intervention could also disrupt the "press pack's" attempts to work together in gaining newsworthy information from the media briefing (Sugden and Tomlinson 2007). Justin Allen also said, "it breaks up the flow of the press conference and the manager might be thinking for a minute about that stupid question they've had and you're trying to ask a proper question". Justin Allen pointed out bloggers were more than likely to sit in the corner of the press conference room and be content to take notes from answers deriving from questions posed by journalists working for mainstream media.

One sports journalist reported a general suspicion among the "press pack" towards unfamiliar faces at conferences and briefings. However, acceptance could be gained if bloggers abide by what Sugden and Tomlinson (2007) refer to as "reciprocal relations" between reporters covering the same beat. Sports journalists work in a paradoxical environment of collaboration and competition with each other. Sugden and Tomlinson (2007) noted that reporters working for rival publications share information and, here, this practice was linked to acceptance within the beat environment. A culture of co-operation linked to acceptance was indicated by Nick Szczepanik who said, "people are always willing to give everyone a chance as long as they are prepared to muck in and share transcribing of quotes".

Participants were sceptical of bloggers who derived their information from the mediated sporting spectacle because they were not able to gain access to the professional sports environment. Nick Szczepanik stated:

> I was talking to someone who went to an awards ceremony and he met someone who was up for an award as online journalist of the year. He said "I'm sorry, I don't know your name?" He was just a blogger. He said "I only write about Manchester United, I never go to press conferences". Somehow it makes your thoughts impure. Well, is that journalism or is it stream of consciousness, off-the-top-of-your-head stuff? With press conferences—it's not always what you get taking notes down. It's also being at training grounds, security people at the gates, gossip chat, a few indiscreet remarks and talking to other journalists.

Another sports journalist reinforced this sense of a hierarchy of knowledge delineated by access/non-access by stating, "it's really easy to underestimate how regularly being at matches—how much extra knowledge and perspective that gives you. The little details you glean, hearing questions other people ask. If you're at home watching telly, you don't get that" (Wilson). Tom Hopkinson, of the *Sunday People*, said, "they [bloggers] are not necessarily at games, they're just watching it [sport] on telly or just reading everything they can and giving their opinions on it without having built those relationships". Tom Hopkinson also pointed to bloggers' lack of accountability because they are not answerable to sports insiders if their stories or claims are inaccurate,

> If I write something, I have to be mindful that I could be sitting in the front row of their press conference ... I'm in the firing line. With bloggers, there's no right of reply. None of us on the road will mind if we get picked out in a mixed zone and told "you wrote this about me, it's not true". We give it so we have to take it.

Participants recognised that bloggers could access the professional sports environment, particularly outside football, but these were exceptions rather than the norm. Dave Bromage, assistant sports editor with *The Sun*, said, "I know a few athletics bloggers and they don't have a wide reach but they know what they are talking about".

Tom Hopkinson said, "you might be lucky, your uncle might be a manager somewhere".

Interviewees also pointed out that blogs could be a useful journalistic tool or contact (Singer 2006). Dave Bromage perceived bloggers as a useful source of stories by saying about his reporting staff, "most of them follow blogs. Blogs are essentially a tweet times 100—social media can be described as journalism in some perverse way. Journalists need to be across blogs in the same way as social media". Justin Allen said, "If they've got a good interview, you're thinking 'yeah, it would be good to talk to that bloke'. You've got to look at all avenues in gaining access".

One sports journalist connected blogging to the general uncertainty around the future of journalism. Fears were expressed that a decline in sports journalists and rise in blogging could lead to lack of critical enquiry. Nick Szczepanik added:

> The danger is as newspapers and "professional" operations fade away or go under, given the tide of free content—is it going to be more and more bloggers who give you their opinion? Or are swallowing club lines because they haven't got the resources or the experience to go out there and spend the whole day outside Carrington[1], chasing up contacts and leads to get the real story.

Complementary

Participants also spoke of bloggers who had developed specialist, focused and sometimes offbeat interests that supplemented rather than competed with print sports journalism's core professional routines. These blogs tended to involve in-depth analysis of niche issues that were considered by the print media to be able to attract and drive audiences. Respondents clearly identified how fan bloggers could complement rather than conflict with professional journalism. Sean Ingle said:

> In the UK we think much more about stories, news and inevitably the people with contacts and access are going to have those stories. The bloggers are on a smaller niche—talking to other fans, talking about stats or things the mainstream media isn't doing.

Tom Hopkinson made a clear separation between niche bloggers and newspaper journalists by saying, "they're looking for the tactics, whereas we're looking for the mud on boots stories—transfers, training-ground bust-ups, behind-the-scenes stuff". One participant thought there was an appetite among audiences for, "the slightly quirkier often longer stuff that is in some way attached to the news agenda but also not" (Campbell).

Participants pointed to specific examples of fan bloggers and the nature of these niche blogs. One participant explained, "one of the trends more recently is stats/data journalism" (Ingle). Michael Caley, who provides analytics[2], and Michael Cox, who writes on tactics[3], were cited as examples here. Sean Ingle also argued that it was not just mainstream media who were recruiting more statistics-orientated bloggers but that "some of them have been signed by clubs—they can see it's interesting and bring it into their organisation. The best ones have found paid work with another media company or a specialist football blog". One participant described this genre of sports content as "hipster" (Hopkinson). Sean Ingle thought that UK media organisations were less likely to use bloggers than in the United States. These views reflected Boyle's work on sports journalism which describes the US tradition as being more expansive, literary and "fixated with statistics" than in the United Kingdom (Boyle 2006, 34). Ingle said:

> We haven't really got a British Grantland.[4] America's much better at taking people who are bloggers. They are much more datacentric over there because they have sports that lend themselves to it. Also, there is more of a tradition of longer-form journalism. A lovely piece of writing is easier if you are a magazine or US longer-form site that recognises it as part of the genre.

Participants spoke about the selection process involved in admitting fan bloggers into the mainstream media. Three participants referred in particular to the *Guardian Sport Network*. The rationale is for mainstream media to benefit from the audiences and advertising that the blogs attract while the blogger increases their profile by accessing the readership of an established brand.

One participant (Paul Campbell) oversaw the *Guardian Sport Network* as part of his duties as sport community co-ordinator editor of *The Guardian*, while another (Sean Ingle) played a significant role in establishing the concept in 2011. Paul Campbell indicated that he was looking for blogs that offered something different to *The Guardian*'s beat journalists. He said, "sometimes you think 'that's a version of this, on the website, it's already being done better'. Sometimes people want to write about Premier League football and there's enough of that out there". Campbell indicated that the adoption of bloggers by mainstream media could create a complexity around identity by stating, "I'd say writer rather than blogger. The term blogger—it's not that it's a dirty word, it's just not a word that I would use. I see them as sports writers, perhaps not professionally". Furthermore, Campbell described the bloggers as offering a fan's perspective that supplemented the perceived unbiased views of *The Guardian*'s own sports journalists. He explained:

> If we sent a reporter to Manchester United, he has to be objective because that's his job. A while ago we published a piece written by an Aston Villa fan about their season. We already have a Midlands correspondent but it's a different perspective. I want both —the professional journalist—who is the neutral guy—and the fan. Some people will read the reporter, some people will read fan, some will read both. If you can provide both these services and they are clearly marked as "an Aston Villa fan writes about their relegation fight", I think there's a value in that.

However, this expansion of sports content could also give a voice to more alternative discourses. Paul Campbell remarked that, for instance, the *Guardian Sport Network* had used a volunteer's perspective from the Street Child Games.[5]

One participant presented a view of the *Guardian Sport Network* that indicated traditional media was maintaining its dominance over more subordinate groups (Dart 2009). He described the contributors as "usually fairly trustworthy people, quality is proven. If you can't beat them, employ them. You bring them in-house or you make them your blogger" (Szczepanik). Sean Ingle indicated that the increasing maturity of blogging as an online practice had meant the mainstream media had now selected the best bloggers. He said, "I honestly think blogs aren't as big as they were. The best ones have been incorporated into the mainstream". Another sports journalist working in the tabloid press indicated that this supplementary content would always be less valuable than core newsgathering practices because, "if you want to really drive your website and get those thousands of clicks then it's the breaking news stories" (Hopkinson).

Participants also spoke about bloggers as entrants to the occupational group. One participant stated, "It is another entry route—you're putting yourself out there. I've never heard of a sports journalist applying for a job by sending in a CV—it's all there under your byline. People can see what you can do" (Szczepanik). Tom Hopkinson said, "your talent will shine through if you're insightful or you're breaking news". Sean Ingle suggested that more traditional opportunities within the occupational group are in decline and that blogging has emerged to replace them. He said:

> There are fewer staff and freelance opportunities now—therefore it's understandable that if you are young and you want to write then why not have a blog. It's also understandable that the very best ones, or the ones which have a niche, may be picked up.

Participants also told of their own blogging activities, which reinforced previous studies that have found writing blogs has become part of a journalist's work routines (Hermida 2009; Schultz and Sheffer 2007; Singer 2005). Tom Hopkinson spoke about blogging for his newspaper's website as an integral part of his work routines while Dave Bromage told of regular blogging activity with his local newspaper. Freelance sports journalists also saw blogging as another employment opportunity for them. Jonathan Wilson stated that he contributed to non-mainstream media websites including whoscored.com, a predominantly football statistics service.

Conclusion

This study examined print sports journalists' attitudes towards fan bloggers in relation to their occupational identity. The findings provide greater clarity to how a culturally significant and dominant occupational group is navigating the complexities posed by its norms, values and practices becoming diffuse and porous (Hutchins and Rowe 2012). The study also offers insight into how traditional, mainstream media seek to assert hegemonic dominance of the digital environment. This study focused on fan bloggers because of the key questions posed for sports journalists relating to their perceived low professional standards and proximity to fandom.

The two core findings to this study reflected nuanced attitudes from print sports journalists towards fan bloggers—in competitive and complementary terms—that pointed to the complexity, diversity, size and scale of the blogosphere. This outcome indicates that professional journalists do not necessarily see bloggers as inferior around issues of fact-checking and accuracy (Lowrey and Burleson Mackay 2008) while recognising that they can co-exist alongside mainstream media (Singer 2006).

The study found that sports journalists considered their occupational distinctiveness to be intact despite the emergence of fans appropriating their performative norms and practices through blogging on digital platforms. Participants perceived bloggers who emulated the daily beat routines of sports journalists to be problematic. These working practices generally related to newsgathering, opinion and gossip around the commercialised professional sports environment, with football's Premier League a prime example. However, sports journalists' privileged access to insiders and the availability of resources, such as time and money, maintained their professional distinctiveness because it led to sites of knowledge production not generally available to fan bloggers.

Participants considered privileged access to professional sports as helping to provide a valuable distinction from fan bloggers despite often tense and fraught relationships with media managers (Sherwood, Nicholson, and Marjoribanks 2016). Sports journalism's ability to continue to negotiate privileged access with media managers is therefore important to the continued cultural dominance of the occupational group. Fan bloggers who pursued similar work routines to sports journalists were considered competition because they were impinging upon core occupational and ideological practices that news organisations devote considerable labour and financial resources towards (Boyle and Haynes 2009).

The study also found sports journalists recognised certain types of blogs—specifically those with niche, writer-driven interests in areas including statistics or tactics—could complement mainstream media and enhance the sports provision of traditional print organisations. Bloggers with specialised interests enable media organisations to expand and add variation to their sports coverage, thus improving the attractiveness of the website to audiences. The *Guardian Sport Network* applied broadsheet principles of quality writing to their selection of blogs. Print organisations can offer different perspectives in a digital environment that has no spatial restrictions and a seemingly insatiable appetite for sports information from audiences.

Here, sports journalists act as gatekeepers and apply their professional values in determining which blogs are legitimised through acceptance by the mainstream media. This process also helps sports journalists to assert their cultural dominance. This finding can also be interpreted as further evidence that sports journalism is resilient and adaptable to technological developments (Boyle 2006; Rowe 2004). There was, however, evidence in this study that alternative, marginalised discourses were being brought into this arena (specifically, the *Guardian Sport Network* featuring an article about the Street Child Games).

Blogging, like fanzine writing before it, was seen as a valid entry route into a profession that is not credentialised and has a history of recruiting staff through informal recruitment processes such as casualisation rather than formal application procedures. Therefore, blogs can provide a useful "shop window" for mainstream media. Furthermore, the recruitment of bloggers by mainstream media could encourage future activity to be more conformist than contentious.

The research project provides an in-depth insight into how sports journalists are reacting to the challenges posed by fan blogging. However, this study cannot be generalised to all UK sports journalists due to its small sample and focus on a very specific source of blogs. Furthermore, fan blogging is only one professional issue confronted by sports journalists in the digital age.

Sports journalists' perspectives tended to relate to bloggers who have actively come into contact with mainstream media either by being physically present in the wider sports environment, providing serious competition in the generation of significant audiences, harbouring ambitions to become a sports journalist, or wishing to have their work published by mainstream media with the attendant financial and/or promotional benefits. Bloggers who act as networked communities and do not seek the attention of mainstream media were not among the discussions with participants.

A small sample was selected to generate rich and comprehensive data that enabled detailed exploration of the sports journalist perspective and encourage participants to be fully reflective of their experiences. The study's data were mainly generated from mid-career journalists with participants predominantly aged between 30 and 40. This demographic was the result of a methodological approach that involved purposive and snowball sampling. Future research could make use of a more stratified approach to explore potential generational differences in attitudes among sports journalists towards bloggers.

This study focused on fan bloggers but there is additional scope to explore the potential disruption that non-mainstream, alternative sports journalism websites are causing traditional, legacy media in the United Kingdom. The findings also offer further potential future direction for research that includes how bloggers are employed by organisations beyond the print media. A "sister" study that reverses this study and explores the experiences of bloggers who provide content for print media would offer further insight into this subject area.

ACKNOWLEDGEMENTS

Many thanks to the participants for taking part in this study. Thanks also to the anonymous reviewers for their time and comments. Further thanks to Alan Tomlinson for his wisdom, and Mark Doidge and Daniel Burdsey for the conversations and suggestions.

DISCLOSURE STATEMENT

I have not gained any financial interest or benefit arising from the direct application of this research.

NOTES

1. Manchester United's training ground near the village of Carrington in Greater Manchester.
2. Michael Caley is analytics editor for *Howler Magazine*, a US publication on football (soccer) and also writes for espnfc.com. His Twitter bio describes him as "bringing baseball stat nerdiness to football".
3. Michael Cox writes about tactics under the moniker of Zonal Marking and regularly contributes to *The Guardian* and *FourFourTwo* magazine. The "About" section of www.zonalmarking.net cites the 2008 book *Inverting the Pyramid: The History of Football Tactics* as a key influence. This book was written by Jonathan Wilson, who was a participant in this study.
4. Grantland was a US sports website specialising in long-form journalism launched by ESPN in 2011 and was edited by blogger Bill Simmons. The site was named after Grantland Rice, a prominent figure in the American sports writing literary tradition. ESPN closed the site in October 2015. See Vogan and Dowling (2016).
5. The Street Child Games took place from 14 to 20 March 2016 in Rio, Brazil, and served as an Olympics equivalent for homeless children from nine countries.

REFERENCES

Billings, Andrew. 2009. "Conveying the Olympic Message: NBC Producer and Sportscaster Interviews regarding the Role of Identity." *Journal of Sports Media* 4 (1): 1–23.

Boyle, Raymond. 2006. *Sports Journalism: Context and Issues*. London: Sage.

Boyle, Raymond. 2013. "Reflections on Communication and Sport: On Journalism and Digital Culture." *Communication & Sport* 1 (1-2): 88–99.

Boyle, Raymond, and Richard Haynes. 2009. *Power Play*. 2nd ed. Edinburgh: Edinburgh University Press.

Boyle, Raymond, David Rowe, and Garry Whannel. 2009. "Delight in Trivial Controversy? Questions for Sports Journalism." In *The Routledge Companion to News and Journalism*, edited by Stuart Allan, 245–254. London: Routledge.

Cramer, Judith, A. 1994. "Conversations with Women Sports Journalists." In *Women, Media and Sport: Challenging Gender Values*, edited by Pamela Creedon, 159–180. Thousand Oaks, CA: Sage.

Dart, Jon. 2009. "Blogging the 2006 World Cup Finals." *Sociology of Sport Journal* 26: 107–126.

Eco, Umberto. 1986. *Faith in Fakes: Travels in Hyperreality*. London: Secker & Warburg.

Franks, Suzanne, and Deidre O'Neill. 2016. "Women Reporting Sport? Still a Man's Game?" *Journalism* 17 (4): 474–492.

Hardin, Marie, and Erin Ash. 2011. "Journalists Provide Social Context Missing from Sports Blogs." *Newspaper Research Journal* 32 (2): 20–35.

Hardin, Marie, and Stacie Shain. 2005. "Female Sports Journalists. Are We There Yet? 'No'." *Newspaper Research Journal* 26 (4): 22–35.

Hardin, Marie, and Stacie Shain. 2006. "Feeling Much Smaller than You Know You Are. the Fragmented Professional Identity of Female Sports Journalists." *Critical Studies in Mass Communication* 23 (4): 332–358.

Haynes, Richard. 1995. *The Football Imagination: Rise of Football Fanzine Culture*. Farnham: Ashgate Publishing.

Hendrickson, Laura. 2007. "Press Protection in the Blogosphere: Applying a Functional Definition of Press to News Web Logs." In *Blogging, Citizenship and the Future of Media*, edited by Mark Tremayne, 187–205. Abingdon: Routledge.

Hermida, Alfred. 2009. "The Blogging BBC: Journalism Blogs at 'the World's Most Trusted News Organisation'." *Journalism Practice* 3 (3): 268–284.

Herring, Susan C., Lois Anne Scheidt, Sabrina Bonus, and Elijah Wright. 2005. "Weblogs as a Bridging Genre." *Information, Technology & People* 18 (2): 142–171.

Hutchins, Brett. 2011. "The Acceleration of Media Sport Culture: Twitter, Telepresence and Online Messaging." *Information, Communication and Society* 14 (2): 237–257.

Hutchins, Brett, and Janine Mikosza. 2010. "The Web 2.0 Olympics: Athlete Blogging, Social Networking and Policy Contradictions at the 2008 Beijing Games." *Convergence* 16 (3): 279–297.

Hutchins, Brett, and David Rowe. 2009. "From Broadcast Scarcity to Digital Plenitude: The Changing Dynamics of the Media Sport Content Economy." *Television & New Media* 10 (4): 354–370.

Hutchins, Brett, and David Rowe. 2012. *Sport beyond Television: The Internet, Digital Media and the Rise of Networked Sport*. London: Routledge.

Ketterer, Stan, John McGuire, and Ray Murray. 2014. "Contrasting Desired Sports Journalism Skills in a Convergent Media Environment." *Communication & Sport* 2 (3): 282–298.

Kian, Edward M. 2007. "Gender in Sports Writing by the Print Media: An Exploratory Examination of Writers' Experiences and Attitudes." *The SMART Journal* 4 (1): 5–26.

Kian, Edward M., Joe W. Burden Jnr, and Stephanie D Shaw. 2011. "Internet Sport Bloggers: Who Are These People and Where Do They Come from?" *Journal of Sport Administration and Supervision* 3 (1): 30–43.

Lambert, Charlie. 2012. "Why the Press Pack Must Raise Its Game." *British Journalism Review* 23: 32–37.

Lenhart, Amanda, and Susannah Fox. 2006. "Bloggers: A Portrait of the Internet's New Storytellers." Accessed July 19. http://www.pewinternet.org/2006/07/19/bloggers/

Lowes, Mark Douglas. 1999. *Inside the Sports Pages: Work Routines, Professional Ideologies, and the Manufacture of Sports News*. Toronto: University of Toronto Press.

Lowrey, Wilson. 2006. "Mapping the Journalism-Blogging Relationship." *Journalism* 7 (4): 477–500.

Lowrey, Wilson, and Jenn Burleson Mackay. 2008. "Journalism and Blogging: A Test of Occupational Competition." *Journalism Practice* 2 (1): 64–81.

McCarthy, Brigid. 2012. "Consuming Sports Media, Producing Sports Media: An Analysis of Two Fan Sports Blogospheres." *International Review for the Sociology of Sport* 48 (4): 421–434.

McCarthy, Brigid. 2014. "A Sports Journalism of Their Own: An Investigation into the Motivations, Behaviours, and Media Attitudes of Fan Sports Bloggers." *Communication & Sport* 2 (1): 65–79.

McChesney, Robert. 2008. *The Political Economy of Media: Enduring Issues, Emerging Dilemmas*. New York: Monthly Review Press.

McEnnis, Simon. 2013. "Raising Our Game: Effects of Citizen Journalism on Twitter for Professional Identity and Working Practices of British Sport Journalists." *International Journal of Sport Communication* 6 (4): 423–433.

McGuire, John P., and Ray Murray. 2013. "Attitudes of Sport Print Journalists about Developing Electronic Media Skills: A Case Study of Two Major Newspapers." *International Journal of Sport Communication* 6 (4): 464–477.

Nielsen Wire. 2012. "Buzz in the Blogosphere: Millions More Bloggers and Blog Readers." Accessed September 15. http://www.nielsen.com/us/en/insights/news/2012/buzz-in-the-blogosphere-millions-more-bloggers-and-blog-readers.html

Rampton, John. 2012. "Blogging Stats 2012 (Infographic)." Accessed September 15. https://blogging.org/blog/blogging-stats-2012-infographic/

Reed, Sada. 2013. "American Sports Writers' Social Media Use and Its Influence on Professionalism." *Journalism Practice* 7 (5): 555–571.

Walker Rettberg, Jill. 2014. *Blogging*. 2nd ed. Cambridge: Polity Press.

Rowe, David. 1992. "Modes of Sports Writing." In *Journalism and Popular Culture*, edited by Peter Dahlgren and Colin Sparks, 96–113. London: Sage.

Rowe, David. 1995. *Popular Cultures: Rock Music, Sport and the Politics of Pleasure*. London: Sage.

Rowe, David. 2004. *Sport, Culture and the Media*. 2nd ed. Buckingham: Open University Press.

Rudin, Richard, and Trevor Ibbotson. 2003. *Introduction to Journalism: Essential Techniques and Background Knowledge*. Abingdon: Focal Press.

Salwen, Michael, and Bruce Garrison. 1998. "Finding Their Place in Journalism: Newspaper Sports Journalists' Professional 'Problems'." *Journal of Sport & Social Issues* 22 (1): 88–102.

Sanderson, Jimmy. 2009. "'Thanks for Fighting the Good Fight': Cultivating Dissent on Blogmaverick.Com." *Southern Communication Journal* 74 (4): 390–405.

Schultz, Brad, and Mary Lou Sheffer. 2007. "Sports Journalists Who Blog Cling to Traditional Values." *Newspaper Research Journal* 28 (4): 62–76.

Sheffer, Mary Lou, and Brad Schultz. 2010a. "An Exploratory Study of How Twitter is Affecting Sports Journalism." *International Journal of Sport Communication* 3 (2): 226–239.

Sheffer, Mary Lou, and Brad Schultz. 2010b. "Paradigm Shift or Passing Fad? Twitter and Sports Journalism." *International Journal of Sport Communication* 3 (4): 472–484.

Sherwood, Merryn, and Matthew Nicholson. 2012. "Web 2.0 Platforms and the Work of Newspaper Sport Journalists." *Journalism* 14 (7): 942–959.

Sherwood, Merryn, Matthew Nicholson, and Timothy Marjoribanks. 2016. "Access, Agenda Building and Information Subsidies: Media Relations in Professional Sport." *International Review for the Sociology of Sport*. doi:10.1177/1012690216637631.

Singer, Jane B. 2005. "The Political J-Blogger: 'Normalizing' a New Media Form to Fit Old Norms and Practices." *Journalism* 6 (2): 173–198.

Singer, Jane B. 2006. "Journalists and News Bloggers: Complements, Contradictions and Challenges." In *Uses of Blogs*, edited by Axel Bruns and Joanne Jacobs, 27–33. Oxford: Peter Lang.

Sugden, John, and Alan Tomlinson. 2007. "Stories from Planet Football and Sportsworld: Source Relations and Collusion in Sport Journalism." *Journalism Practice* 1 (1): 44–61.

Sugden, John, and Alan Tomlinson. 2010. "What Beckham Had for Breakfast: The Rolling Menu of 24/7 Sports News." In *The Rise of 24-Hour News Television: Global Perspectives*, edited by Justin Lewis and Stephen Cushion, 151–166. Oxford: Peter Lang.

Suggs Jr, David Welch. 2015. "Tensions in the Press Box: Understanding Relationships among Sports Media and Source Organizations." *Communication & Sport*. doi:10.1177/2167479515577191.

Sysomos. 2010. "Inside Blogger Demographics: Data by Gender, Age, Etc." Accessed September 15. https://sysomos.com/reports/blogger-demographics

Technorati. 2011. "The State of the Blogosphere." Accessed October 3. http://technorati.com/state-of-the-blogosphere-2011/

Vogan, Travis, and David Dowling. 2016. "Bill Simmons, Grantland.Com, and ESPN's Corporate Re-Invention of Literary Sports Writing Online." *Convergence* 22 (1): 18–34.

Wall, Melissa. 2005. "'Blogs of War': Weblogs as News." *Journalism* 6 (2): 153–172.

SPORTS JOURNALISM, SUPPORTERS AND NEW TECHNOLOGIES

Challenging the usual complicity between media and football institutions

Ana Carolina Vimieiro

Grounded on the analysis of the campaign #ForaRicardoTeixeira (Get Out Ricardo Teixeira), this article investigates how supporters have used new technologies to challenge controversial decisions of media outlets that hold sports broadcast rights in not covering or under-reporting the severity of scandals involving sports governing bodies and leaders. Adopting a combination of political economy and discursive analysis, this work explores how the interplay between media system and football industry in Brazil led to the perpetuation of a complicity relationship between the Brazilian Football Confederation (CBF) and Grupo Globo, broadcast rights holder of the main football events since the 1970s in Brazil. Such complicity guaranteed that many corruption allegations against Teixeira during his 23 years running CBF received little attention in the news programming of Globo. In 2011, when the company decided not to cover the ISL case (at that time a still ongoing Swiss investigation that implicated Teixeira in an extensive scheme of corruption and bribery), Brazilian supporters organised themselves to create the campaign, which for many observers was indeed one of the factors that pressed Teixeira to resign from his post in 2012. The campaign had several merits, including its effective use of decentralised media production tools. However, its main pitfall was its personalised focus on Teixeira, which prevented a broader thematisation of the structural problems of football.

Introduction

Sports journalism is not an area that enjoys a great reputation, having already being referred to as "the toy department of the news media" (Rowe 2007). Rowe (1992) has pointed out that there is certainly, in such criticism, a social stigma and cultural snobbery derived from the popular representation of sports' ethos as non- or anti-intellectual. On the other side, other works have stressed the failure of sports journalism to engage systematically and critically in the "watchdog" and investigative roles that are crucial to the profession (Boyle 2006; Rowe 2005, 2007, 2016). The lack of prestige and the low quality of the work conducted in this area have also been associated with sports journalists being not specially well trained, tending to have more limited occupational experiences than their colleagues in other departments, and a lower class of origin and level of education (Hargreaves 1986; Rowe 1992).

This article contributes to a better understanding of the reasons underlying such failure and the responses that contemporary audiences have given to it, particularly in the context of media sports scandals. Adopting a combination of political economy analysis and discursive analysis of the online fan-based campaign #ForaRicardoTeixeira (Get Out Ricardo Teixeira), this work explores how the interplay between the media system and football industry in Brazil led to the perpetuation of an exchange of favours policy and a complicity relationship between the Brazilian Football Confederation (CBF) and Grupo Globo, the largest media network in the country and broadcast rights holder of the Brazilian Football Championship (or Brasileirão, as it is commonly referred to) for the last 30 years and of the FIFA World Cup since it started to be live televised in Brazil, in 1970. Such complicity guaranteed that many corruption allegations against Teixeira during his 23 years running CBF were not reported or received very little attention in the news programming of Globo's free TV channel, Rede Globo. In 2011, when Globo once more omitted to talk on its nightly newscast *Jornal Nacional* about the International Sports and Leisure (ISL) case—at that time a still ongoing Swiss investigation that implicated Teixeira in an extensive scheme of corruption and bribery—Brazilian supporters organised themselves to create the online campaign, which for many observers was indeed one of the determining factors that pressed Teixeira to resign from his post in 2012.

The analysis of the campaign provides elements to consider the ways that social media and decentralised media production tools are reconfiguring the relations between sports journalism and its audiences. Historically not used to be demanded to hold football authorities publicly accountable for their wrongdoings in Brazil, Globo has been challenged by a changing media environment and transgressive and articulated supporters who have refused to go with the regular "cheer leader" vibe of sports journalism and wish for a more politically engaged type of sports reporting.

The article is organised as follows: first, a brief introduction to the political economy of Brazilian football is provided, with a focus on the historical mutual dependency established between the football industry and Rede Globo; second, the paper presents the ISL case and discusses the past corruption stories involving Teixeira; third, I introduce the #ForaRicardoTeixeira campaign, giving details about its actions and communication strategies; fourth, I analyse the unfolding conversations on Twitter that followed Teixeira's resignation in March 2012, presenting both a quantitative and a qualitative exploration of the messages and, particularly, of how Globo's coverage of his departure, extensively criticised and ridiculed by users, once more revealed its compliance with the sports leader; finally, I analyse the merits and pitfalls of the campaign, stressing that its personalised focus on Teixeira made it successful in publicising the scandal to a larger audience and in gathering support for its actions. On the other side, it also prevented a broader thematisation of the structural problems of sports institutions and the obscure schemes of negotiation of sports broadcasting rights.

The Complicity Between Rede Globo and CBF: A Brief Introduction to the Political Economy of Brazilian Football

Media systems and sports institutions have developed a somewhat "symbiotic relationship", with the staggering popularity of sports being the result of the enormous amount of attention it receives from media companies and with media companies profiting extensively from the advertising and increased audience that the treatment of sports generates (Mcchesney 2008). This interplay became even more structural in the twentieth century with the advent of TV and the establishment of a buying/selling business relation for the live broadcasting of matches (Boyle and Haynes 2004). This financial interdependency was later advanced by pay-TV and pay-per-view packages, with broadcasting revenues becoming the major pillar of sports finance today and the acquisition of sports events rights a core marketing strategy of large media corporations to reach audiences in an increasingly fragmented and saturated media environment.

In Brazil, the football industry and the largest TV network, Rede Globo, have an interrelationship of mutual dependency that was built through the business agreements established between them over the years for the commercialisation of broadcasting rights of football matches. Since football matches started to be live televised in the country, in the 1970s, Globo has broadcast the major national and international events of the sport: the Brazilian Championship and the FIFA World Cups.

Regarding Brasileirão, the main sporting product in Brazil in terms of TV broadcasting, matches and money paid to the clubs (Santos 2013a), Globo has broadcast it since 1987, when the competition started to be live televised. Globo signed at the time a five-year contract in which it pledged to pay US$3.4 million per season for the rights (Santos 2013a). Globo kept the broadcasting rights of Brasileirão for another five years and, in 1997, the company made a new deal with Club of the 13, the clubs' association in Brazil, in a contract that remained practically the same until 2011. In this period, the network held the rights of all media, including the pay-per-view services, which started to be commercialised in 1997. Over the years, Rede Globo sub-licensed its rights to different stations—Rede Bandeirantes (1997–1999 and 2007–2010) and Rede Record (2002–2006)—but always with the decision-making power on whether it would be the exclusive broadcaster and what the other networks could broadcast (Santos 2013a).

Regarding the FIFA World Cup, Globo has also broadcast it since the event was first televised live in Brazil, in 1970. From the 1970s to the late 1990s, the station did not hold exclusive rights for the events. From the 2002 World Cup, however, the business relationship between Globo and the FIFA event intensified, with the company purchasing the rights of all media of the editions since then and sub-licensing, when convenient, the broadcasting to other stations. Globo also purchased, in 2012, the broadcasting rights of all media for the 2018 and 2022 tournaments. Once again, the agreement allows Globo to sub-license, if convenient, the rights to other stations.

Such a structural connection between broadcast rights holders and sports institutions is not unique to Brazil and has created a variety of economic, political and ethical challenges in many countries around the globe. For instance, in economic terms, in Europe, anti-trust agencies and other legal decisions have condemned the exclusive broadcasting of championship matches by a single TV broadcaster or defined that TV rights should be fairly distributed (Andreff and Bourg 2006). In political and ethical terms, in the recent 2015 FIFA scandal, media rights were in the centre of a bribery, fraud and money-laundering scheme involving primarily football bodies and sports marketing executives.

In Brazil, the centralisation of the rights with Globo for so long (47 years in the FIFA World Cup case and 30 years when it comes to Brasileirão) has given the network overwhelming market powers, imposed on the other media companies, with precedence advantages that are translated into access to audiences, political power, and privileged relationships with publicity agencies and advertisers (Santos 2013a). These privileges in Brazil are intensified because football centralises all sporting attention in the country, with virtually no rival sport: according to the Brazilian Institute of Public Opinion and Statistics (Ibope), among Brazilians who follow any type of sport via TV, 92 per cent watch football-related content, with volleyball coming in second with a mere 24 per cent (Brazilian Institute of Public Opinion and Statistics 2011).

As questionable as the long permanence of the TV rights with the same network, are the strategies that the station has adopted to preserve its position as the broadcaster of the FIFA World Cup and Brasileirão over the years. For instance, recently, a series of critiques and suspicions have been raised about the debatable preferences granted to Globo by football institutions in the negotiations of TV rights, and about tax evasion and possible corruption crimes involving the company and its contracts with the same associations.

Concerning the contracts for the broadcasting of Brasileirão, in 2010, the Brazilian antitrust agency Conselho Administrativo de Defesa Econômica (often referred to as CADE) considered the advantages that the company has historically received economic violations that breached the antitrust legislation of the country. The agency also required the removal of any preference clause in the next agreements for the broadcasting of Brasileirão. The decision was related to a complaint, recorded in 1997 by Sistema Brasileiro de Televisão (another media company popularly known as SBT), against Rede Globo, Club of the 13 and other institutions. As Santos (2013a) elucidates, in 1997, SBT made a higher bid than Globo for the broadcasting rights of Brasileirão, but Club of the 13 rejected its offer and once more closed a deal with Globo. The reason was a preference clause included in the agreements that gave Globo access to other competitors' proposals and the decision-making power to match them or not. However, even more controversial than the historical preference was Globo's strategy at the time to enforce its political and institutional restraints and retain the broadcasting rights of Brasileirão. Instead of respecting CADE's decision concerning the joint negotiation with Club of the 13, the network decided to turn the table and deal with each club in a decentralised way in 2011.

That year, during the negotiations for the 2012–2014 period, Globo offered seductive amounts of money to the clubs in the hope that they would give up trading *en bloc*. Globo effectively achieved its aim when it closed a deal with Corinthians, one of the most popular clubs in Brazil, which was soon followed by all other top clubs. The decentralisation, Santos (2013a, 2013b) asserts, has created a gap between small and big clubs in terms of revenues, which is similar to the situation faced in Spain, for instance, with Real Madrid and Barcelona. According to Santos (2013a), it is clear, from the amounts offered to the clubs by Rede Globo in 2011 and the following deal to extend the contracts (until 2018) with even larger figures in the succeeding year (2012), that Globo was already positioning itself for the entry of Fox Sports to the Brazilian market in 2012. In practical terms, the strategy of the network also caused the virtual extinction of Club of the 13, with the company strengthening even more the political and institutional power that it already possessed.

In relation to the controversies about the contracts for the FIFA events, Globo was fined in 2006 by the Brazilian taxation authority, Receita Federal, for tax irregularities in the purchase transaction of the exclusive rights to broadcast the 2002 World

Cup. According to the process of the taxation office against Globo, the company used an intricate system to disguise the transaction and get away with the Brazilian taxes. The scheme involved several offshore corporations owned directly or indirectly by Globo in tax havens such as the British Virgin Islands, Cayman Islands and the former Netherlands Antilles. In total, the trick resulted in the evasion of R$183.14 million in values of the time. The sum of the tax evaded plus interest and fine reached R$615 million in 2006. The case gained notoriety in 2013, when bloggers denounced that the process had not yet been closed in Receita Federal and that, possibly, Rede Globo had still not paid the debt, which in 2013 values already exceeded R$1 billion (Rosário 2013). The station publicly replied to the complaint, asserting that they had already settled the case, but Receita's system insisted on contradicting the company (Feltrin 2013; Rosário 2013). At the end, the system finally showcased that the debt had been paid off (although it was not clear when), but for months a campaign organised by progressive Brazilian bloggers, that later received support from the larger public, asked the station to show the Darf (the document that proves the payment of debts with the federal government).

Lastly, another controversy about the agreements between Globo and FIFA involved the future events of 2018 and 2022. In 2012, after Globo and FIFA announced they had extended the contract between them for the commercialisation of broadcasting rights for Russia's and Qatar's events, Record, the station that has today the second-largest TV audience share in the country, complained about the non-existence of any bidding process in Brazil, as would be expected in negotiations of this kind. At that time, Record criticised FIFA which supposedly had committed itself to making a public, transparent and open bidding, in a similar way as is done in other markets, for the 2018 and 2022 events, and asserted that they would appeal to the Justice in Switzerland and in Brazil to defend their interests ("Record protesta contra acordo" 2012). Globo, on the other hand, replied to its competitor, stressing that a private institution like FIFA did not have any legal obligation to promote a competition, and that the decision of the association in preserving Globo as the broadcaster holder of the events, without a bidding, was taken in recognition of the value of the successful partnership between them (Farina 2012).

In all this intricate historical scheme of preferences given to Globo, the suspicion is that Teixeira was the facilitator during his tenure as head of CBF (1989–2012). In 2015, the Brazilian federal police began indeed to investigate the relationship between Teixeira and Globo. The past agreements between CBF and the station are being analysed in an action that is part of the Brazilian collaborations with the US Justice in the 2015 FIFA corruption case investigations (Feltrin 2015).

More important for the purposes of this study is that, even if Globo and Teixeira have not committed criminal acts together (which is up to the Justice to establish), we cannot exempt the station from scrutiny regarding the journalistic role that the company should have played concerning football in Brazil and it has evaded for years. First, it is important to stress that the company, which discursively presents itself as holding exemplary standards of quality (above all, through its famous "Globo's quality standard" slogan), has never done any investigative work related to CBF and its executives despite the suspicions surrounding them for years in the country. On the contrary, historically, Globo has been criticised for sparing Teixeira and the institution in the news (sports and, above all, in *Jornal Nacional*) when these were investigated by the Justice or other media companies.

Second, the suspicions about how much Globo's business relations have influenced its editorial decisions increase when we consider the rare moments when such regular complacency was broken. Santos (2013a) explains that during the 2011 Brazilian Championship, CBF decided to change the starting time of the Saturday matches to 9 pm.[1] without consulting with Rede Globo. The new schedule was defined as a test to increase the pay-per-view revenues because the match would have an isolated airing. Supposedly, as a "payback", in August, *Jornal Nacional* reported a brief note about the suspicions concerning the friendly game between Brazil and Portugal, disputed in Brasília in 2008, which was under investigation by the Federal Police. As Santos explains, Globo had not broadcast complaints against CBF since 2001, when it dedicated a whole episode of *Globo Repórter*, Globo's weekly documentary TV show, to talking about the corruption accusations against the institution. That time, football insiders have conjectured, the report was produced amid an imbroglio involving the TV rights for the 2002 and 2006 World Cups (Mello and Bombig 2001). The programme would have been produced as a notice to Teixeira, who, in return, soon after, changed the schedule of a Brazil versus Argentina match to 7:45 pm (Pinheiro 2011). With the shift, Globo was forced to change its prime-time programming, suffering as a consequence great losses in terms of advertising. After the scuffle, the two historical partners seem to have made peace, since two months later the station announced it had closed a deal for the broadcasting of the events (Mello and Bombig 2001).

Yet, it is important to stress that in the Brazilian context the business relations of TV networks have contributed not only to a certain degree of complacency by Globo with the football institutions but also it has instigated Record, Globo's greatest rival, to adopt an adversarial attitude in relation to these same institutions and leaders. In 2011, when the ISL case gained notoriety in Brazil and Globo refused to cover it (a point discussed below in greater detail), Record did a series of long news reports denouncing Texeira, CBF and its known partners, such as Corinthians and the Media Sports Investment fund, which were aired day-after-day for a week in June in Record's nightly newscast *Jornal da Record* (Feltrin 2011). Football insiders believe that the offensive had been prepared as a payback for the collusion among Globo, CBF and Corinthians to undermine the bidding for Brasileirão's TV rights for the 2012–2014 period (Feltrin 2011). As mentioned earlier, Corinthians had a fundamental role in the episode, being the first club that closed a deal with Globo, which consequently imploded Club of the 13 and decentralised the negotiation system in Brazil.

The ISL Case and Teixeira's Past

The ISL case was not the first time that Teixeira's name was associated with corruption. In 1994, Teixeira was involved in a controversy related to the Brazilian Customs when coming back from the successful campaign in the US FIFA World Cup. When the Brazilian team arrived in Brazil, Teixeira refused to pass through Customs and later it was discovered that he and many players indeed had many undeclared goods. The case, which is known in Brazil as the "Voo da Muamba" (Contraband Flight), ended up with Teixeira being obliged by the Brazilian Justice to pay back the due taxes and fines —17 tonnes of baggage were not declared on arrival (Kelso 2009; Pinheiro 2011). In another case, this time in 2000, Teixeira was investigated by Parliamentary Committees of Inquiry in the Brazilian Congress regarding suspicious relations between him and the American sportswear firm Nike. The case was controversially dropped, but the allegations included embezzlement, money laundering and tax evasion. It is also relevant to note that Teixeira made his way into the football world through João Havelange, his former father-in-law and president of FIFA from 1974 to 1998. Havelange held an honorary presidency at FIFA until 2013, when he resigned from his position to escape a probable punishment related to the ISL case.

The #ForaRicardoTeixeira campaign followed allegations of corruption and bribery involving Teixeira reported by the BBC TV programme *Panorama*, in November 2010—the ISL case. ISL, established by former Adidas boss Horst Dassler, was responsible for the commercialisation of broadcasting rights to FIFA events such as the World Cup, and, in 2008, an investigation in Switzerland revealed that the company had paid at least 138 million Swiss francs to senior officials to secure broadcasting contracts worth several billion US dollars (Play The Game 2015). The names of the executives were not revealed at the time, but the *Panorama* programme, presented by the investigative reporter Andrew Jennings, suggested Teixeira was one of them.

The case also gained attention around May/June 2011 because of the FIFA elections, which occurred on 1 June. FIFA was criticised at that time for trying to prevent the release of ISL case documents, which were being held in secrecy and would prove FIFA members' involvement (including Teixeira and Havelange) in embezzlement and omission (Conn 2012). Yet, in May 2011, the former Football Association chairman, Lord Triesman, claimed that four FIFA members had sought bribes in return for a vote for England in the 2018 World Cup bid—one of them was Teixeira. Teixeira's controversial interview with the Brazilian magazine *Piauí*, published in July 2011, was the last straw that triggered a huge popular uprising against him in Brazil.

Most TV channels and online multimedia portals covered those stories[2] at that time, but Globo[3] ignored them, and its lack of action was significant in triggering the protests. In the interview with *Piauí*, Teixeira himself stressed the importance of Globo's nightly TV newscast, *Jornal Nacional*, in the country. In an obnoxious tone, Teixeira stated that he "couldn't give a shit" about the corruption allegations being covered by other channels and that he would "only start sweating" when he saw the accusations on Globo's nightly news (Pinheiro 2011). Even though the case did not receive attention from Globo, the hashtag and the coverage by other media companies kept the case alive, with other bribery allegations emerging some months later from an investigation made by *Folha de São Paulo*, a traditional Brazilian newspaper.

The Campaign #ForaRicardoTeixeira

The #ForaRicardoTeixeira campaign was launched on 21 July 2011, shortly after the controversial interview that Teixeira gave to *Piauí*. The first "Twitterstorm" was organised soon after, on 27 July. According to information from the organisers of the action, their website had 117,000 visits in the first 10 days of the campaign, including users from more than 87 countries. The distinct hashtags used were tweeted 180,000 times in the beginning and the profiles assigned on Twitter and Facebook accumulated 3699 followers and 9775 friends, respectively. On Facebook, the posts had a total of 887,885 views in this first period. Just on the day of the first Twitterstorm, the hashtag

#ForaRicardoTeixeira was tweeted 50,839 times (Fora Ricardo Teixeira 2012). The campaign also gained an "offline" expression, with street parades and stadium demonstrations being organised through collaborations between the creators of the online campaign and associations of sports fans, such as the Supporters National Front and the Popular Committee for the World Cup and Olympic Games.

The distinct hashtags related to the protest made the Trending Topics list in Brazil, Portugal and worldwide multiple times. Mainstream-media outlets covered the online campaign as well as the street and stadium demonstrations ("O Rio vai às ruas contra Teixeira" 2011, "Manifestação '#ForaRicardoTeixeira' ganha força" 2011; Leal 2011). On the website of the campaign[4], there was a meter that registered the two hashtags most widely used by the protesters. On 25 July 2012, the counter had registered 229,350 mentions of #ForaRicardoTeixeira and 94,467 of #CaiForaRicardoTeixeira. Notwithstanding the imperative tone of the hashtags, on the website, the campaign adopted a more comic approach, saying that the initiative "did not intend for Mr. Ricardo Terra Teixeira ... to be sacked from his leadership position in the Brazilian Football Confederation"; that was not the case because

> he has dedicated himself to the institution for a long period of 22 years. That is it: five tenures of lots of transparency and hard work leading CBF. And this story will not end before the 2014 World Cup, when this trustworthy man will return the trust of the Brazilian people with the most organised World Cup ever seen in the history of this country. (Fora Ricardo Teixeira 2012)

According to the campaign organisers, they created "a website of public utility for all of us, fans of Mr Teixeira, to get to know everything that this exemplary manager is preparing for the big worldwide sports party". They finished the message making a joke out of the word *fora*, which in Portuguese means "out" or "get out". They dissociated it from the idea of "out" in such a way that the whole text could make sense (and also, make the joke). As they summarised it: "FORA is only an inoffensive acronym for *Feed Otimizado Relacionado a Alguém* [optimised feed related to someone]. And, in this case, that someone is Ricardo Teixeira, lord of the *Tupiniquim* football." Eight months into the campaign, on 12 March 2012, after 23 years leading CBF, Teixeira resigned from his position for medical reasons (official version). In the next section, I analyse the resignation's unfolding conversations on Twitter.

The Resignation and the Unfolding Discussion on Twitter

The resignation provides an interesting moment for analysis because the topic is approached both on social and traditional media, including by Rede Globo. The frame that Globo adopted in this last moment, stressing Teixeira's achievements ahead of CBF,[5] is indeed rather representative of the reasons behind the campaign. My analysis of the conversations is based on a dataset collected from 9 to 18 March 2012—the resignation was on 12 March. The analysis was divided into two parts: first, a more quantitative exploration of the dynamics of the conversations where I use the scripts and techniques proposed by Bruns and Burgess (2011) to identify what kinds of accounts are involved in the conversations and which types of information they are sharing; and second, a more qualitative frame analysis of the topmost retweeted messages where I explore how the resignation resonated on Twitter, with a particular focus on Globo's coverage, one of the main topics of discussion in the aftermath of the announcement.

Twitter Conversations: The General Dynamics

For the collection of the conversations, I used the *yourTwapperkeeper* tool, adopting as keywords the two hashtags most used during the protests (#ForaRicardoTeixeira and #CaiForaRicardoTeixeira) and Teixeira's name. The dataset captured with the hashtags has 832 tweets and the one collected with his name includes 14,926 messages.[6] Even though Facebook was also largely used during the campaign, Twitter was selected because its Application Programming Interface (API) offers more appropriate affordances to collect data from hashtags and keywords. Facebook's API works from pages and groups and does not afford searches for hashtags or keywords, which were important for this study.

About the kinds of accounts involved in the conversations, Figure 1 shows who are the central users in each dataset.[7] The accounts in Figure 1 are among the 10 per cent most active accounts and the graph was organised by the ratio of replies received to sent tweets. This ratio provides an interesting measure to identify those accounts that are important for the conversations. They are not necessarily the most active ones in the dataset, but they are reasonably active and have also a great influence over the content of the interactions (they are generally well replied and/or retweeted). The campaign dataset is dominated by ordinary citizens, including the profile of the creators of the campaign (@foraoficial), and also by non-official accounts of Brazilian clubs. Among the ordinary people, many declared they were football fans or supporters of particular clubs in their profile description, which demonstrates how linked to the football communities the campaign was.

Mainstream media channels, journalists, and satirical Twitter accounts (including fakes) dominated the conversations in the dataset archived with Teixeira's name. The first user, @OLeoBatista, is a satirical fake account of the well-know sports commentator from Globo, Léo Batista. His jokes about Teixeira are highly retweeted, so he has a great resonance over the interactions even if he tweets only a few messages—he had almost 30,000 followers at the time (data from 3 October 2012).

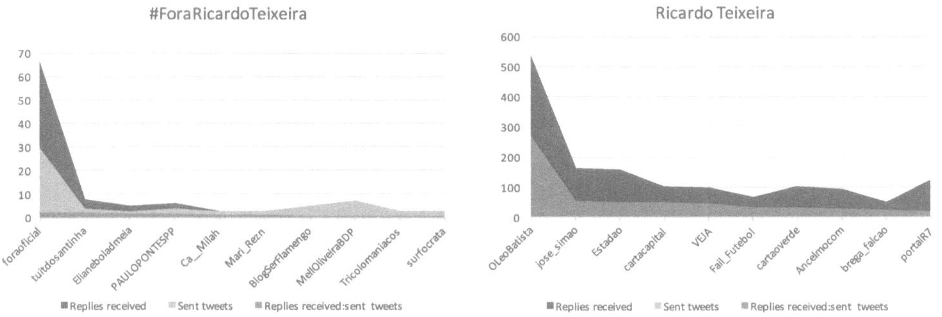

FIGURE 1
Central accounts in both datasets. Only the 10% most active accounts were included and they were ranked by the ratio replies received: sent tweets

Lastly, an important detail about the conversation dynamics is the domains being shared by the users. The two datasets have indeed rather different sources of information included in the messages. Those using his name shared URL's that are from news sites and mainstream media outlets (Table 1). Sports journalists' blogs (such as Blog do Juca and Blog do José Cruz), conventional media and YouTube dominated the top-10 shared domains by the users engaged on the campaign.

Blog do Juca is a famous blog in Brazil and it is maintained by Juca Kfouri, a well-known and respected journalist. Kfouri had a leading role in this case because he has been investigating and reporting Teixeira's controversial activities for years—he was indeed sued for defamation and libel by the leader more than 50 times after he became the president of CBF (Vives 2011). Kfouri won most of the lawsuits and publicly celebrated Teixeira's resignation in his blog.

Besides Kfouri, another important journalist associated with this case is José Cruz, who blogs about the relation between sports and politics. Cruz is also a respected journalist and his blog was a source commonly shared by those using the campaign hashtag. Both can be classified as A-list bloggers in the Brazilian sports environment—A-list blogs are the most popular publicised blogs (Papacharissi 2010).

Finally, the presence of YouTube among the most tweeted domains demonstrates how supporters are sharing user-generated content or appealing to old videos to support their claims. It is worth mentioning that one of the most shared videos shows Teixeira's successor, José Maria Marin, who would later be arrested in Switzerland for corruption (in 2015), taking for him a medal that belonged to a player in an award ceremony of the São Paulo Youth Football Cup.

TABLE 1
Topmost linked internet domains in the posts

Dataset and domain	Type	Occurrences
# Fora Ricardo Teixeira		
http://blogdojuca.uol.com.br	Blog	14
http://www1.folha.uol.com.br	Conventional media outlet website	14
http://www.lancenet.com.br	Conventional media outlet website	12
http://josecruz.blogosfera.uol.com.br	Blog	10
http://diariodonordeste.globo.com	Conventional media outlet website	7
http://veja.abril.com.br	Conventional media outlet website	7
http://www.youtube.com	Social media	6
http://blog.opovo.com.br	Blog	5
http://espn.estadao.com.br	Conventional media outlet website	5
http://globoesporte.globo.com	Conventional media outlet website	5
Ricardo Teixeira		
http://esporte.uol.com.br	Sports news website	366
http://www1.folha.uol.com.br	Conventional media outlet website	316
http://esportes.r7.com	Conventional media outlet website	285
http://globoesporte.globo.com	Conventional media outlet website	229
http://www.lancenet.com.br	Conventional media outlet website	193
http://www.estadao.com.br	Conventional media outlet website	169
http://www.cartacapital.com.br	Conventional media outlet website	141
http://copadomundo.uol.com.br	Sports news website	132
http://veja.abril.com.br	Conventional media outlet website	124
http://g1.globo.com	Conventional media outlet website	113

Twitter Conversations: The Adopted Frames

For the qualitative analysis, the topmost tweeted messages in both datasets were selected.[8] The sample was comprised of 202 posts collected with Teixeira's name (all of them retweeted at least five times) and 100 messages from the campaign. The posts were manually coded, using the frame variables that compose the signature matrix proposed by Gamson and Modigliani (1989).[9] After coding, the data were exported to the R environment, where clustering techniques were adopted to define groups of messages sharing the same frame. This analysis is based on the techniques proposed by Matthes and Kohring (2008) and Vimieiro and Maia (2011), with the addition of the silhouette technique to define the optimal number of groups/frames.

The difference of this analysis in comparison to the studies that it is based on is that here I am working with Twitter content. The particular features of the messages—such as the 140-character limit—give a great importance to more figurative variables in the frame signature matrix, like metaphors and examples, than to more reasoning and argumentative devices, such as causes and solutions. Besides, the topic itself (football) and the intense participation of ordinary people in the conversations also contribute to a more emotional language and to the extensive use of irony and sarcasm. Below, the groups found in each dataset are presented (Table 2). The names of the frames are based on the frequent variables in each group (or the frequent item sets, as they are called in the data-mining area).

In both datasets, we have the dominance of what Iyengar (1991) referred to as the episodic frame. The episodic frame, explains Iyengar (1991, 14), "takes the form of a case study or event-oriented report and depicts public issues in terms of concrete instances". Previous works have identified that there is a dominance of this type of depiction in the news and, especially, on TV, and Iyengar (1991) warns that the effect of the episodic frame is pro-establishment, since it generally attributes responsibility for a matter to an individual or perpetrator rather than to broad societal forces.

In this particular case, the episodic frame is found in tweets that only state that Teixeira resigned from his position. In the case of the messages collected with his name, the episodic frame was identified in 139 tweets, and the defining features of those messages are: their focus on the resignation itself, and the presence of two types of source, journalists/columnists and media company accounts. Regarding those tweets carrying the campaign hashtag and adopting the episodic frame (45 posts), the difference is that these users are clearly celebrating his resignation. These messages can have just the hashtag itself or are articulated with a short phrase mentioning what has happened. Also, they differ from the episodic frame found on the other dataset in terms of the sources: here, ordinary people, mostly football enthusiasts, who feel free to manifest their dislikes, originated the messages.

In the dataset of the campaign, we have two other clusters of messages that also focus on individuals. I called them personalistic frames because they differ slightly from the episodic one (even though they could be referred to as episodic as well) in terms of the main topic of the messages: instead of the resignation itself, they talk about Teixeira and Marin. In the cluster that focus on Teixeira, people are talking about the corruption cases (remembering the ISL and others) and also some messages conjecture about Teixeira's future. Regarding these messages, Twitter users are particularly concerned about the fact that he is probably not going to be punished because he "fled" to the United

TABLE 2
Frames adopted in the topmost tweeted messages in both datasets

Dataset and frame	Defining variables
# Fora Ricardo Teixeira	
Episodic (45 tweets)	• Topic 3: Teixeira's resignation • Source 11: ordinary person, football fan, blogger (not A-list)
Personalistic—Marin (18 tweets)	• Topic 2: Marin (new president) • Solution 3: deposing Marin (#foramarin) • Example 3: medal incident • Consequence 1: no changes • Source 11: ordinary person, football fan, blogger (not A-list)
Systemic (14 tweets)	• Topic 6: Football future • Example 8: World Cup, World Cup Law, etc. • Consequence 1: no changes • Solution 5: reform (e.g. more active clubs, administrative change, CBF elections, etc.)
Personalistic—Teixeira (12 tweets)	• Topic 5: Corruption cases • Topic 7: Teixeira's future • Source 11: ordinary person, football fan, blogger (not A-list) • Slogan/catchphrase 1: "better late than never" (and others, demonstrating how people were relieved he was gone)
Mobilisation (11 tweets)	• Topic 3: Teixeira's resignation • Slogan/catchphrase 4: "Let's go"; "Keep tweeting" (calling for participation) • Source 11: ordinary person, football fan, blogger (not A-list) • Solution 2: civic engagement; popular demonstrations • Source 16: not identified; no longer on Twitter; suspended account
Ricardo Teixeira	
Episodic (139 tweets)	• Topic 3: Teixeira's resignation • Source 8: journalist or columnist • Source 9: media company
Satirical (36 tweets)	1. Source 5: satirical Twitter account 2. Topic 4: Corinthians (traditional Brazilian club) 3. Source 13: account about a Brazilian club (not official; created by fans) 4. Consequence 4: penalty/trouble for Corinthians (joke)
Counter-media (Globo) (27 tweets)	1. Topic 1: Globo's coverage 2. Source 11: ordinary person, football fan, blogger (not A-list) 3. Metaphor 1: Teixeira is a new "saint" (e.g. Dalai Lama, Mother Teresa of Calcutta, the new Pope, or he is a "hero") 4. Metaphor 3: Teixeira is Globo's "godfather"

States immediately after the resignation—so he will not be punished in Brazil. In this cluster, also compounded by mostly ordinary people as sources, they clearly set out that Teixeira is "corrupt", that he stayed for too long in power and that the feeling about having him out is that "it is better late than never"—adverbs such as "finally" and "at long last" are also used to mean the same thing. The focus is clearly on him and on what is going to happen to that "corrupt" person now that he is far from the spotlight.

In the messages that adopt the personalised frame but focus on Marin, the then new president of CBF, users are particularly concerned about the controversial stories that the new leader has in his résumé. A recent episode at that time, where Marin was caught stealing a medal from a junior player during the medal ceremony of a tournament in Brazil, was largely cited, as I mentioned earlier. The embarrassing scene was linked in many messages to justify the concerns and also to suggest that they should get rid of him as well—many messages use the hashtag #foramarin. In this cluster, there are some hopeless users who believe nothing is going to change exactly because Marin is the successor.

In the cluster of what I am calling the engaging frame, people are talking about the resignation as well. They are mostly asking to get Teixeira out (most messages are from the day before the resignation). In this group, there is an appeal that people should continue to tweet about the case, like they were doing previously (to show they care and are watching the follow-ups of the story). They have this belief that they "did something good" for their country and for Brazilian football, particularly.

The last cluster in the campaign dataset is the one that uses a systemic approach. The systemic frame looks at the context, the situation of state football federations in Brazil and points out how difficult it is to change this environment, even with Teixeira out of CBF. Some of them believe that nothing is going to change and others propose that CBF should have an election—hashtags such as #mudacbf (change CBF) and #eleiçãojá (election now) are used, for instance—or that Brazilian clubs should be more active. The World Cup was also often remembered and they questioned whether the organisation of the event was going to be better without Teixeira leading the Local Organising Committee (they believed so).

In the dataset collected with Teixeira's name, two frames that embrace a more critical perspective and, particularly, through a satirical approach were found: one questions Globo's coverage of the resignation and another uses the case to make a joke about the relation between Teixeira and Corinthians. In the first case, what we have got is a cluster of messages, predominantly using ordinary people as sources, which specifically criticise, in a satirical way, the report that *Jornal Nacional* made on the evening of the resignation day. Instead of using arguments or a more rational perspective, the users adopted metaphors to say that Globo's approach made Teixeira a "saint", or the "new Pope" or that Mother Teresa of Calcutta "is under his kindness". Another metaphor, slightly less used, appears in the association to the "godfather" figure or in messages, for instance, that mention that Globo's reporters "almost cried on TV". Other posts state that Globo "made a speech in Ricardo Teixeira's public funeral" and that Globo and Teixeira "should die together, hugging", the latter being a very common expression in Portuguese to mean that two entities are allies.

Lastly, in the case of jokes about Corinthians, the most frequent one referred to Teixeira as part of the squad of the team. In this particular case, the messages stated that once Teixeira had fallen, then, it was supposed to be a penalty for Corinthians (because a player of the team had been taken down).

Analysis: Hyper-commodification, Conflicts and Personalisation of Sports Scandals

The domestic football industry in Brazil has undergone profound changes in the last decade. Neoliberal values and a business orientation started to take shape in this sector in the late 1980s (Helal and Gordon 2002; Ouriques 1999; Proni 2007, 1998; Rodrigues 2007), but it is only in the first decade of the twenty-first century that football showcases clear signs of what it is called hyper-commodification in Brazil (Giulianotti 2002). Since the first presidential term of the leftist Lula, there has been a significant increase in the amount of money circulating in the sector (Bdo 2014; Grafietti et al. 2014; Somoggi 2014) and an expansion of the consumer culture in the country (Yaccoub 2011). Particularly, the recent escalation in the top clubs' media revenues due to the 2011 renegotiation of broadcasting rights (discussed above), and the increase in the revenues coming from ticket sales advanced by the high-priced seating stadiums built or renovated for the 2014 FIFA World Cup, were turning points to a transition in the political-economic organisation of the industry that closely resembles that witnessed in England with the creation of the Premier League in the early 1990s (Vimieiro 2015).

The deepening of football commodification processes has resulted in many controversies and conflicts recently in Brazil. Fans have criticised this consumption-driven approach for many reasons, including for squeezing football's traditional low-class supporter base out of the game—which also happened in Europe after the cultural reorganisation of the industry in the 1990s (Nash 2000, 2001). The campaign *O Maraca é Nosso* (Maracanã is Ours), for instance, had 11 claims, including points against the gentrification, the Europeanisation, and the "shrinkage" of the most famous Brazilian stadium, Maracanã ("A escalação dos 11 pontos" 2012). Conflicts have also emerged involving strong regional traditions, such as the recent attempts to replace regional food with processed products inside some of the new arenas (Maia 2013).

Football's governing bodies have also been criticised for their market orthodoxy, especially because such orthodoxy in an environment that lacks regulatory and control practices has often led to cases of corruption and embezzlement. The government has been targeted for privatising the previous state-owned stadiums, which are now generating high profits for newcoming corporations. Yet, these corporations themselves are also under attack for abusive practices and for not having any expertise whatsoever in managing sports arenas, leading to a model in which football fans are charged high prices for tickets, without finding the expected quality inside the stadiums. Not to mention that all these football-related issues played a significant role in triggering the protests that gripped Brazil during the 2013 FIFA Confederations Cup—which were, by the way, the largest political demonstrations in the country in the last 20 years or so. The campaign #ForaRicardoTeixeira, it is important to stress, emerged within this context.

The great merits of the campaign reside in: the skilled use that citizens made of decentralised media production tools to share with the larger public information that was not publicised, in particular, by Rede Globo; and in the use of social media to mobilise people for online and offline actions that, ultimately, contributed for Teixeira's resignation. About the first, the blog that the campaign organisers kept during the protests became a space where supporters worked together to gather information, material proofs and critical analyses about Teixeira and the vast range of corruption cases involving his name. They collaborated, in particular, with journalists that did more investigative and/or critical work about the scandal, such as Juca Kfouri and José Cruz, bringing to their blog content produced by them and keeping in dialogue with them, who, on the other hand, publicised the campaign actions. About the second, the way they used social media, and, particularly, Twitter, it was so efficient to mobilise supporters and the general public for the cause that led Brazilian cartoonists to illustrate the situation with drawings of Teixeira running away or hiding from Twitter birds (Caracciolo 2011; Coala 2011).

On the other hand, despite the merits of the action in pressing Teixeira out of office, it is important to stress that its personal focus on the leader and, later, also on Marin, ended up preventing the broader issues about the organisation of the sport and its governing bodies being more properly thematised. This tendency to personalisation, other researchers have demonstrated, characterises the news media, being indeed a key criterion of newsworthiness (Galtung and Ruge 1965). Rowe (2016) used the concept of personalisation to analyse the coverage of sports scandals, specifically, the focus that was given to Sepp Blatter in the 2015 FIFA scandal. In that case, particularly, says Rowe (2016, 6), it was rather "tempting for press and public alike to fixate on the strangely compelling visage of Sepp Blatter or to treat a sprawling organization like FIFA as if it was a person afflicted by an all-encompassing pathology". However, the great problem of a personalised frame, such as the one that occurred in the coverage of the 2015 scandal and which was also the case with Teixeira, is to imply in an idea that the simple removal of that person would implicitly resolve the issue. In this sense, even though some of the campaign users concentrated on the big picture, with the systemic frame, it is important to note that this angle was identified only in 14 of the tweets. The distance from the campaign to the time of writing also allows us to assert that there has been no significant change in the broader organisation of CBF and that, today, football insiders have commented, the current president of the institution, Marco Polo Del Nero, does not leave the country because he is scared of being arrested by the Federal Bureau of Investigation for involvement in the same corruption scheme whereby Marin was arrested in 2015 (Moniz 2015). In this sense, the campaign turned out to be pro-establishment, as Iyengar (1991) describes the effect that the dominance of the episodic and/or personalistic frame may have in the social imaginary.

Conclusion

This article combined distinct theoretical and methodological approaches to provide a better understanding of the reasons underlying the failure of sports journalism to produce investigative and critical reports, particularly with regards to sports governing bodies and leaders. The article also explored the responses of contemporary audiences to such failure, using social media and decentralised media production tools to challenge the usual complicity between football organising bodies and broadcast rights holders.

The political economy analysis was important to reveal the historical alliance between Globo and CBF. Such structural dependency is related to the low-quality sports journalism produced by the network and its failure in critically engaging in any investigative work regarding CBF and Teixeira over the years. This symbiotic connection is also behind Teixeira's disdain toward the ISL case allegations expressed in the interview to *Piauí* and the responses of the audience to Globo's coverage of his resignation on *Jornal Nacional*. Fundamentally, the political economy analysis shed light on to the analysis of the protests because it is this history of privileges, omissions and complicity that the supporters sought to challenge with the campaign.

The analysis of the campaign, on the other hand, explored the strategies that football supporters have resorted to in this journalistic environment where the public interest has been left aside for a long time: the use of decentralised media production tools along with social media platforms for activist mobilisation. It is interesting to perceive that, first, there is a critical type of sports journalism being produced in this very same environment (through Blog do Juca, for instance) even though it does not occupy the centre of the media system and, second, that the public is capable of recognising it and, in the #ForaRicardoTeixeira case, productively collaborate with these journalists.

Lastly, it is important to stress that this text did not investigate how such influence in the sports coverage of the business relations of media institutions happens in everyday journalistic routines, which is certainly a task for future research. Recently, however, in the context of the current Brazilian political crisis and of the low-quality political journalism produced about it (by the way, in Brazil, as determined by financial and ideological interests as sports journalism), a former *Jornal Nacional* political editor, Marco Aurélio Mello, gave details about the implicit values in the organisational culture of Globo and of an ongoing scheme of professional rewards in the company that turns up, indirectly, framing the work of the professionals who are there without the need for direct orders about what and how to cover the stories (Mello 2016).

DISCLOSURE STATEMENT

No potential conflict of interest was reported by the author.

NOTES

1. The starting time of Globo's flagship *telenovelas* was also 9 pm, which, therefore, made it the worst timeslot (financially and in terms of programming) for any change.
2. The allegations were covered by the free-to-air TV Record (Globo's main rival), RedeTV and by the pay-for-view channel ESPN Brasil. Other media channels including Web portals, online news, newspapers and magazines such as *Universo Online* (*Uol*), *Terra*, *Folha de São Paulo*, *Estadão*, *Lance*, *Piauí*, *Carta Capital* and *Placar* also covered the story at that time.
3. The ISL case was not covered by Globo, which a search in the company's online platform, G1 (http://g1.globo.com/), is able to confirm. From 1 May 2011 to 31 July 2011, the case was not approached in any of Globo's free-to-air or pay-for-view channels (in the TV newscasts).
4. See http://www.foraricardoteixeira.com.br/ (accessed July 25, 2012).
5. Excerpt available at http://g1.globo.com/jornal-nacional/noticia/2012/03/ricardo-teixeira-foi-o-presidente-que-passou-mais-tempo-frente-da-cbf.html (accessed July 25, 2012).

6. About the representativeness of the data, I used the Streaming Twitter API, particularly with a "spritzer" bandwidth (which means I could collect up to 1 per cent of all Twitter traffic). This does not mean I worked with 1 per cent of the messages about this topic. I probably collected all messages posted about it in the period under analysis. That is because the bandwidth cap of the Streaming API only comes into effect when more than 1 per cent of all tweets posted at the time match the conditions placed on the stream. Gaffney and Puschmann (2014, 57–58) exemplify: "If, for example, a researcher is collecting data for a small conference, spritzer access will be sufficient to capture every tweet posted under the conference hashtag, since in only the most extreme cases will tweets about such an event exceed 1% of all traffic on the platform".
7. This data was generated with the script *metrics.awk* created by Bruns and Burgess (2011).
8. Particularly, I used the script *wordfreq.awk* to process the data and generate the list with the topmost tweeted messages.
9. Variables used here: topics, actors (sources), causes, solutions, consequences, metaphors, examples, slogans/catchphrases and moral judgements.

REFERENCES

Andreff, Wladimir, and Jean-François Bourg. 2006. "Broadcasting Rights and Competition in European Football." In *The Economics of Sport and the Media*, edited by Claude Jeanrenaud and Stefan Késenne, 37–70. Cheltenham, Uk/Northampton, Us: Edward Elgar Publishing Limited.

Bdo. 2014. "7º Valor Das Marcas Dos Clubes Brasileiros: Finanças Dos Clubes [7º Brand Value of Brazilian Clubs: Clubs' Finances]." *Bdo Rcs*. Accessed January 15, 2015. http://Www.Bdobrazil.Com.Br/Pt/Pdfs/Estudos_Zipados/Valor_Das_Marcas_2014.Pdf

Boyle, Raymond. 2006. *Sports Journalism: Context and Issues*. London, England: Sage.

Boyle, Raymond, and Richard Haynes. 2004. *Football in the New Media Age*. London: Routledge.

Brazilian Institute Of Public Opinion And Statistics. 2011. "Esporte Clube Ibope Media." Last Modified October 4. Http://Www.Ibope.Com.Br/Pt-Br/Noticias/Paginas/EsporteClubeIbopeMediaRevelaARela%C3%A7%C3%A3oDoBrasileiroComOsEsportes.Aspx.

Bruns, Axel, and Jean Burgess. 2011. "Gawk Scripts for Twitter Processing" *Mapping Online Publics*, June 22. Http://Www.Mappingonlinepublics.Net/Resources/.

Caracciolo, Leandro. 2011. "Twitter Em Fúria... [Twitter in Rage...] [Image] ." *Terra*. Accessed June 14, 2012. Http://Www.Terra.Com.Br/Esportes/Infograficos/Charges/Galeria/Fotos/10.Jpg

Coala, Fábio. 2011. "Fora Ricardo Teixeira! [Get Out Ricardo Teixeira!] [Image]." Accessed June 14, 2012. Http://Mentirinhas.Com.Br/Wp-Content/Uploads/2011/07/Rteixeira.Jpg

Conn, David. 2012. "Former Fifa President João Havelange 'Received Millions in Bribes' [Globo Counters Record and discards Necessity of Competition for World Cup]." *The Guardian*, July 11. Accessed August 8, 2016. http://Www.Guardian.Co.Uk/Football/2012/Jul/11/Fifa-Joao-Havelange-Bribes-Report

Farina, Allan. 2012. "Globo Rebate Record E Descarta Necessidade De Concorrência Por Copa." *Terra*, February 29. Accessed August 8, 2016. Https://Esportes.Terra.Com.Br/Fute

bol/Copa-2014/Globo-Rebate-Record-E-Descarta-Necessidade-De-Concorrencia-Por-Copa,027b1d81c499a310vgncld200000bbcceb0arcrd.Html

Feltrin, Ricardo. 2011. "Tv Record Abre Fogo Contra Ricardo Teixeira, Cbf E Corinthians [Tv Record Opens Fire Against Ricardo Teixeira, Cbf and Corinthians]." *Folha De São Paulo*, June 13. Accessed August 8, 2016. Http://F5.Folha.Uol.Com.Br/Televisao/948155-Tv-Record-Abre-Fogo-Contra-Ricardo-Teixeira-Cbf-E-Corinthians.Shtml

Feltrin, Ricardo. 2013. "Globo Pagou Multa De R$ 274 Mi À Receita Por Causa Da Copa 2002 [Globo Payed R$ 274 Mi to the Taxation Office because of the 2002 World Cup]." *Uol*, June 29. Accessed August 8, 2016. http://Celebridades.Uol.Com.Br/Ooops/Ultimas-Noticias/2013/06/29/Globo-Pagou-Multa-De-R-274-Mi-A-Receita-Por-Causa-Da-Copa-2002.Htm

Feltrin, Ricardo. 2015. "Pf Investiga Relações Entre Cbf E Globo [Federal Police is Investigating the Relations between CBF and Globo]." *Uol*, July 2. Accessed August 8, 2016. http://Celebridades.Uol.Com.Br/Ooops/Ultimas-Noticias/2015/07/02/Pf-Investiga-Relacoes-Entre-Cbf-E-Globo.Htm

Fora Ricardo Teixeira. 2012. "Os Primeiros 10 Dias [The First 10 Days]." Accessed July 25. http://Foraricardoteixeira.Com.Br/Metricas/

Gaffney, Devin, and Cornelius Puschmann. 2014. "Data Collection on Twitter." In *Twitter and Society*, edited by Katrin Weller, Axel Bruns, Jean Burgess, Merja Mahrt, and Cornelius Puschmann, 55-67. New York: Peter Lang.

Galtung, Johan, and Mari Holmboe Ruge. 1965. "The Structure of Foreign News the Presentation of the Congo, Cuba and Cyprus Crises in Four Norwegian Newspapers." *Journal of Peace Research* 2 (1): 64–90.

Gamson, William A., and Andre Modigliani. 1989. "Media Discourse and Public Opinion on Nuclear Power: A Construcionist Approach." *American Journal of Sociology* 95: 1–37.

Giulianotti, Richard. 2002. "Supporters, Followers, Fans, and Flaneurs: A Taxonomy of Spectator Identities in Football." *Journal of Sport & Social Issues* 26 (1): 25–46.

Grafietti, Cesar, Pasquale Di Caterina, João Dos Santos Cruz Júnior, Alexandre Antonio, Juliana Franceschini, Paulo Ramiro Fernades, Gabriel De Souza Forti, et al. 2014. *Análise Econômico-Financeira Dos Clubes De Futebol Brasileiros De 2014: Dados Financeiros De 2013* [2014 Financial Analysis of Football Brazilian Clubs: 2013 financial statements]. Itaú-Bba.

Hargreaves, John. 1986. *Sport, Power and Culture: A Social and Historical Analysis of Popular Sports in Britain*. Cambridge: Polity Press.

Helal, Ronaldo, and Cesar Gordon. 2002. "A Crise Do Futebol Brasileiro: Perspectivas Para O Século Xxi [Brazilian Football in Crisis: Perspectives for the 21st Century]." *Revista Eco-Pós* 5 (1): 37–53.

Iyengar, Shanto. 1991. *Is Anyone Responsible? How Television Frames Political Issues*. Illinois: University Of Chicago Press.

Kelso, Paul. 2009. "Brazil 2014 World Cup Hopes Hit as Football Chief Ricardo Teixeira Convicted." *The Telegraph*, August 13. Accessed July 14, 2012. http://Www.Telegraph.Co.Uk/Sport/Football/Competitions/World-Cup-2010/6021446/Brazil-2014-World-Cup-Hopes-Hit-As-Football-Chief-Ricardo-Teixeira-Convicted.Html

Leal, Daniel. 2011. "Está Valendo! Tuiteiros Gritam #Foraricardoteixeira [It's on! Tweeters Shout #GetOutRicardoTeixeira]." *Lance!Net*, July 26. Accessed July 23, 2012. http://Www.Lancenet.Com.Br/Copa-Do-Mundo/Internet-Grita-Ricardo-Teixeira_0_524347835.Html

Maia, Chico. 2013. "Movimento De Resistência Do Tropeiro Pode Estar Vencendo a Luta No Mineirão [Tropeiro's Resistance Movement may be Winning the Fight at Mineirão]." *Blog Do Chico Maia*, February 8. http://Blog.Chicomaia.Com.Br/2013/02/08/Movimento-De-Resitencia-Do-Tropeiro-Pode-Estar-Vencendo-A-Luta-No-Mineirao/

Matthes, Jorg, and Matthias Kohring. 2008. "The Content Analysis of Media Frames: Toward Improving Reliability and Validity." *Journal of Communication* 58 (2): 258–279.

Mcchesney, Robert W. 2008. In *The Political Economy Of Media: Enduring Issues, Emerging Dilemmas*, 213–232. New York: Monthly Review Press.

Mello, Marco Aurélio. 2016. "As Engrenagens Do Telejornalismo Da Rede Globo [The Gears of Rede Globo's Broadcast Journalism]." *Ggn: O Jornal De Todos Os Brasis*, March 23. http://Jornalggn.Com.Br/Noticia/As-Engrenagem-Do-Telejornalismo-Da-Rede-Globo

Mello, Fernando, and José Alberto Bombig. 2001. "Globo Enfim Compra a Copa [Globo has Finally bought the World Cup]." *Folha De São Paulo*, October 16. Accessed August 8, 2016. http://Www1.Folha.Uol.Com.Br/Fsp/Esporte/Fk1610200102.Htm

Moniz, Gustavo. 2015. "A Lei Do Silêncio De Del Nero: Confinado No Brasil Por Caso Fifa [The Silence of Del Nero: Confined in Brazil because of the FIFA Scandal]." *El País*, October 23. Accessed August 8, 2016. http://Brasil.Elpais.Com/Brasil/2015/10/22/Deportes/1445540110_680082.Html

Nash, R. 2000. "Contestation in Modern English Professional Football: The Independent Supporters Association Movement." *International Review for the Sociology of Sport* 35 (4): 465–486.

Nash, R. 2001. "English Football Fan Groups in the 1990s: Class, Representation and Fan Power." *Soccer & Society* 2 (1): 39–58.

Ouriques, Nilso. 1999. "O Gol Contra Do Rei: A Lei Pelé E Suas Consequências [The King's Own Goal: the Pelé Law and its Consequences]." *Motrivivencia* 12 (Maio):37-64.

Papacharissi, Zizi. 2010. *A Private Sphere: Democracy in a Digital Age*. Cambridge: Polity Press.

Pinheiro, Daniela. 2011. "The President." *Revista Piauí*, July.

Play The Game. 2015. "Who Took the Bribes? Fifa and the Isl." Last Modified December 7. http://Www.Playthegame.Org/Theme-Pages/Who-Took-The-Bribes-Fifa-Corruption-And-The-Isl/

Proni, Marcelo Weishaupt. 1998. "Esporte-Espetáculo E Futebol-Empresa [Sport/spectacle and Football/Corporation]." Phd Diss., Unicamp.

Proni, Marcelo Weishaupt. 2007. "Marketing E Organização Esportiva: Elementos Para Uma História Recente Do Esporte-Espetáculo [Marketing and Sporting Organization: Elements for a Recent History of the Sport as Spectacle]." *Conexões* 1 (1): 82–94.

Rodrigues, Francisco Xavier Freire. 2007. "O Fim Do Passe E a Modernização Conservadora No Futebol Brasileiro [The End of "Passe" and the Conservative Modernization in Brazilian Football] (2001–2006)." Phd Diss., Ufrgs.

Rosário, Miguel Do. 2013. "Mensalão Da Globo: Se Pagou, Mostra O Darf! [Globo's "Men-Salão": If You've Paid, Show the "Darf"!]" *O Cafezinho*, June 29. http://Www.Ocafezinho.Com/2013/06/29/Mensalao-Da-Globo-Se-Pagou-Mostra-O-Darf/

Rowe, David. 1992. "Modes of Sports Writing." In *Sparks*, edited by Journalism And Popular Culture and Edited By Peter Dahlgren And Colin, 96–112. London: Sage.

Rowe, David. 2005. "Fourth State or Fan Club? Sports Journalism Engages the Popular." In *Journalism: Critical Issues*, edited by Stuart Allan, 125–136. Maidenhead, England And New York, Ny: Open University Press.

Rowe, David. 2007. "Sports Journalism: Still the 'Toy Department' of the News Media?" *Journalism* 8 (4): 385–405.

Rowe, David. 2016. "Sports Journalism and the Fifa Scandal: Personalization, Co-Optation, and Investigation." *Communication & Sport*. doi:10.1177/2167479516642206.

Santos, Anderson David Gomes Dos. 2013a. "A Consolidação De Um Monopólio De Decisões: A Rede Globo E a Transmissão Do Campeonato Brasileiro De Futebol [The Consolidation of a Monopoly of Decisions: Rede Globo and the Broadcasting of the Brazilian Football Championship]." Master's Thesis, Unisinos.

Santos, Anderson David Gomes Dos. 2013b. "A Rede Globo E a Transmissão Do Campeonato Brasileiro [Rede Globo and the Broadcasting of Brazilian Football Championship]." *Revista Eptic Online* 15 (3): 205–215.

Somoggi, Amir. 2014. "Finanças Dos Clubes Brasileiros Em 2013 [Brazilian Clubs' Finances in 2013]." Accessed January 15, 2015. http://Www.Ibdd.Com.Br/Wp-Content/Uploads/2014/05/Financas-Clubes-Brasileiros-2013.Pdf

Vimieiro, Ana Carolina. 2015. "Football Supporter Cultures in Modern-Day Brazil: Hypercommodification, Networked Collectivisms and Digital Productivity." Phd Dissertation, Queensland University Of Technology.

Vimieiro, Ana Carolina, and Rousiley Celi Moreira Maia. 2011. "Análise Indireta De Enquadramentos Da Mídia: Uma Alternativa Metodológica Para a Identificação De Frames Culturais [Indirect Media Frame Analysis: A Methodological Alternative to Identify Cultural Frames]." *Revista Famecos: Mídia, Cultura E Tecnologia* 18 (1): 235–252.

Vives, Fernando. 2011. "O Calo De Ricardo Teixeira [Ricardo Teixeira's Achilles' Heel]." *Carta Capital*, July 18. Accessed October 20, 2012. http://Www.Cartacapital.Com.Br/Sociedade/O-Calo-De-Ricardo-Teixeira/

"Manifestação "#Foraricardoteixeira" Ganha Força No Twitter [#GetOutRicardoTeixeira Gains Momentum on Twitter]." 2011. *Terra*, July 21. Accessed July 20, 2012. http://Esportes.Terra.Com.Br/Futebol/Copa/2014/Noticias/0,,Oi5253044-Ei18776,00-Manifestacao+Foraricardoteixeira+Ganha+Forca+No+Twitter.Html

"O Rio Vai Às Ruas Contra Teixeira [Rio Takes the Streets Against Teixeira]." 2011. *Carta Capital*, July 30.

"A Escalação Dos 11 Pontos Da Campanha [The Campaign's 11 Points Line-up]." 2012. *O Maraca É Nosso*, June 27. http://Maracanosso.Blogspot.Com.Br/2012/06/Escalacao-Dos-11-Pontos-Da-Campanha.Html

"Record Protesta Contra Acordo Entre Globo E Fifa E Ameaça Ir À Justiça [Record Protests against Agreement between Globo and Fifa and Threats go to Court]." 2012. *Uol*, February 29. Accessed August 8, 2016. http://Esporte.Uol.Com.Br/Futebol/Ultimas-Noticias/2012/02/29/Record-Protesta-E-Diz-Que-Contrato-Entre-Globo-E-Fifa-Nao-Foi-Transparente.Htm

Yaccoub, Hilaine. 2011. "A Chamada 'Nova Classe Média': Cultura Material, Inclusão E Distinção Social [The So called "New Middle Class": Material Culture, Inclusion and Social Distinction]." *Horizontes Antropológicos* 17 (36): 197–231.

DATA VISUALISATION IN SPORTS JOURNALISM
Opportunities and challenges of data-driven journalism in German football

Thomas Horky and **Philipp Pelka**

Data visualisation is an area developing strongly in sports journalism. Via the example of football in Germany, this article presents a survey of current potentials of data journalism in sport. We have analysed the challenges of assessing and publishing data in professional online sports journalism. By means of five interviews with experts and an analysis of the content of three special-interest blogs, trends in the use of data in sports reporting, as well as the potentials and dangers, were shown. Here, we can identify, above all, the complexity of football, the incorporation of data without any context, the danger of tailoring data to a topic, as well as mistakes in entering data as problems. For sports journalists, relevant are a lack of (technical) knowledge, the increasing time pressure and growing expectations of recipients. Our analysis reveals that data must not be seen as the equivalent of objectivity. It does not seem possible to capture an entire sporting competition with data-driven journalism. It has become clear that the demands on sports journalists will grow in future, if they want to add value for recipients by applying data.

Introduction

How many calories does my lunch have? How many steps have I taken in the furniture store today? A glance at your smartphone is enough: data are omnipresent and are becoming increasingly important in people's everyday lives. Yet it is not just in everyday life, but also in sport that the presence and effect of data is intensifying. Athletes' performance in training or in competition is monitored by the increased gathering of data, and it is used to guide training and analyse contests. Professional sports journalists exploit this where they make data into a component of their reporting. This article illustrates both the journalists' level and that of recipients. To keep our field of reference within bounds, we are restricting ourselves to football and to online reporting in Germany as our areas of investigation.

There are two reasons for that: recipients can consume the products of online journalism at any time and anywhere. The interaction between journalists and recipients is growing and is placing new demands on journalism. On the other side of matters, football in general—and in Germany especially—has changed markedly. As the way it is played becomes ever-more complex and develops away from a game of individuals to a collective one, journalists face the challenge of finding new approaches for explaining this sport. To this end, they use the almost endless quantity of data gathered during football matches.

> Numbers and data belong to the essence of sport. However, used excessively, statistics also have the opposite effect and compromise comprehensibility ... Can people process this plethora of information at all when reading or listening? We ought to always ask, whether numbers and data really benefit the audience, or whether they do not represent, much rather, useless fan-info, distorting our view of the actual analysis. (Horky and Kamp 2012, 92, translation by Stan Jones)

The possibilities for gathering data develop with technical progress—and, with that, the possibilities for reporting. Thus, data availability increasingly influences sports journalism.

Foundations of Data Journalism

Sports journalism is in the driver's seat for the digital age of mass media. The impact of digitisation is tremendous and leads to fast changes in various fields within sports journalism (Boyle and Haynes 2004; Boyle 2006; Horky and Kamp 2012). One area where this development is visible is data journalism, which demonstrates new opportunities and challenges (Holovaty 2006; Weinacht and Spiller 2014). Data journalism can be defined as data-driven journalism, which adds value by using data-sets or databanks. In that process, the data used become part of the journalistic product and do not just serve research, and so we also talk about "data storytelling" (Matzat 2011).

The changed role and significance of journalism thus becomes clear through the "deluge of data" (Lewis 2015, 322). "The larger turn toward digitization of information in recent times has been connected with a greater role in journalism for the techniques of computer and data sciences", as Lewis and Westlund (2015, 450) explain. They suggest "four conceptual lenses—epistemology, expertise, economics, and ethics" (461) for investigating data journalism.

As Lewis (2015, 321) explains: "Large-scale datasets and their collection, analysis, and interpretation are becoming increasingly salient for making sense of and deriving value from digital information", and describes:

> The overwhelming volume and variety of digital information produced by and about human (and natural) activity, made possible by the growing ubiquity of mobile devices, tracking tools, always-on sensors, and cheap computing storage, among other things ... the particular role of data in journalism—as well as interrelated notions of algorithms, computer code, and programming in the context of news—is only beginning to receive major attention in the scholarly and professional discourse. (Lewis 2015, 322)

The definition of data journalism is not clear from previous concepts of it. Hammond (2015) offers an overview, and several articles investigate the situation and the demands on data journalists in various countries, in Germany (Weinacht and Spiller 2014), in Sweden (Appelgreen and Nygren 2014), in Norway (Karlsen and Stavelin 2014), in Belgium (De Maeyer et al. 2015), in the United Kingdom (Knight 2015) and in the United States (Fink and Anderson 2015). The central findings are similar: data journalists suffer under time pressure, have too few financial resources, and need support with developing and publishing data using particular tools. So far, in the literature we have not discovered any treatment of the special demands in sports journalism.

Depending on the medium, data journalism offers various possibilities for visual display, where the core statements derive from a database. Thus, data journalism profits, above all, from the possibility of illustrating complex and differentiated connections in content simply (Dean 2011).

Data journalism has the potential to uncover scandals, but typically, thematises backgrounds (Beckedahl 2011a; Fink and Anderson 2015). In addition, data-driven journalism detects topics and uncovers or generates relevance in the sense of newsworthiness (Leßmöllmann 2012). A foundation in data, multi-mediality and new narrative forms are hence data journalism's answer to a data-drenched world, which documents and files its social processes in databases (Matzat 2011).

Transparency as a consequence of data journalism's quality demonstrates a new sort of relationship between journalists and recipients. The interaction between data and recipients can be termed a possible corrective for journalism (Matzat 2011).

History of Development

The roots of data journalism lie in the nineteenth century. Florence Nightingale, an English nurse, is considered the pioneer of data visualisation. Because many soldiers in the Crimean War from 1853 to 1856 did not die directly on the battlefield but only later from infections or epidemics, Nightingale proposed the notion that this derived from a lack in hygiene as well as in wound dressing. She demonstrated these faults to the British government by means of the "Polar-Area-Diagram" she developed herself. To this end, Nightingale gathered data herself but also reached back to official data and thus visualised wounded British soldiers' causes of death. Subsequently, British soldiers' mortality rate went down massively after the war; health services in Great Britain were revolutionised. Mendel (2011) described Nightingale as "a pioneer in the visualisation of statistics in this area".

Computer-assisted reporting (subsequently "CAR") can be seen as an early form of today's data journalism. This computer-based research method has been applied in English-speaking environments since the 1960s. In practice, CAR looks for potentially interesting irregularities and peculiarities in databases. CAR, therefore, offers screening and motivates journalists to further researches. Coddington (2015) describes the shift from CAR via data journalism to computational journalism as a "quantitative turn" in journalism. Anderson (2013) deems data journalism generally as a form of computational journalism.

Data journalism specific to sport is, by contrast, a much more recent field. "In Germany, the fans first encountered the fact that you can also count football in 1992. In those days, for the start of the Sat 1. programme, *ran*, a *ran* database was constructed, which provided the audience with information in a new way", as Biermann (2009, 48, translation by Stan Jones) explains. For each Federal League match, two observers monitored the actions on the field and, until 2003, fed these data manually into the databank—since 2007 this has been run by Impire AG (Ebeling 2013). In the

United States since the 1990s, the impact of "Moneyball" in particular in baseball (Lewis 2003) was tremendous and changed the way of dealing with data-driven sports journalism.

In the course of recent years, computer-aided research and the reporting resulting from it has made leaps generally in Germany.

At a time when more transparency and freedom of information underpinning administrative processes are possible, governments are displaying increasing openness. In this sense, political initiatives for the publication of data are discussed and applied, thus offering new potentials for journalistic research. The databases published on Wikileaks (wikileaks.org) in 2006 only became readable for people without background and expert knowledge through analysis and journalistic processing. In addition, we can observe how an increasing number of free and simple tools for displaying and processing data, like Data Wrapper (datawrapper.de), make journalists' work easier—above all, when no finance is available to employ programmers or graphic designers (Krampe 2012).

How Data Journalism Works

The various functions of data journalism are rarely spotlighted. In the United States, Parasie (2015) examined an example of investigative data journalism and verified the process of change through data-processing running in two different directions: a "hypothesis-driven" path and a "data-driven" path. Holovaty (2006) advocated a rethink in the newspaper trade: "Newspapers need to stop the story-centric worldview". Much rather, newspapers should use the data they already collect more or less consciously anyway. In this vein, journalists should, in the first instance, provide information useful to readers.

> Journalists should have less of a concern with what is and isn't "journalism", and more of a concern for important, focused information that is useful to people's lives and helps them understand the world. A newspaper ought to be that: a fair look at current, important information for a readership. (Holovaty 2006)

The preconditions for qualitative data journalism fall into two categories. Alongside exterior circumstances, above all, the immanent characteristics of a data journalistic piece are important. Bradshaw (2010) divides the criteria journalists themselves can influence into four steps: finding data, interrogating data, visualising data and mashing data.

Finding data is the basic requirement for producing a data journalistic product. "Raw data are the basis for data journalism. With them, journalists can stand on their own calculations instead of being dependent on others' interpretations and they are more independent in research and in assessment" (Beckedahl 2011b, translation by Stan Jones). In all this, the willingness of journalists to look for freely accessible data is, above all, paramount—even when this is not always free from legal and/or technical obstacles.

> Data research perhaps also means acquiring data which are not primarily meant for the public at all. (Matzat 2010, translation by Stan Jones)

After obtaining the data, the second step, *interrogating data*, means looking into the available data and presenting it. That does not mean visual presentation but screening and organising data to make them suitable for assessment. This process can be undertaken with the help of special programmes, but does require a large degree of personal input from journalists. Dealing with programmes for extracting the desired data from a databank or a database figures equally among the criteria governing good data journalism (Krampe 2012).

Once the processed data are assessed, then the results have to be visualised and presented. Bradshaw (2010) designates this step as *visualising data*. Usually, visualising data is rather more a task for the graphics department of the respective medium, but more and more journalists are doing it themselves. The reasons given are growing awareness of the possibilities, as well as increasing readiness to experiment.

Mashing data connotes the linking of research results with other databases. Krampe (2012) explains: "That way there often arises a data journalism we can call service-oriented" (translation by Stan Jones). The increased value for the recipients thus generated is an important quality index in data journalism.

> The new way of reporting on these events was certainly only made possible by reporters unafraid of mathematics and familiar with tabular calculations, able to organise data visually and ... asking the right questions. (Rogers 2012, translation by Stan Jones)

Above all, financial resources, as well as the acceptance of data journalism among readers, figure as external criteria for high-quality data journalism. The media business's willingness to invest is an important basis for data journalism, as acquiring, organising, assessing and visualising data demand a lot of time and money. In this context, 50 editors at the German news magazine, *Der Spiegel*, for instance, worked for five months on perusing and assessing the databases published by Wikileaks. The assessment of the "Panama Papers" too, where the *Süddeutsche Zeitung* has taken the lead in Germany, shows the high personnel and financial input. It is false to conclude that higher expenditures simultaneously lead to an increase in quality. In the last analysis, it depends on the readiness of journalists and media companies to assess data intensively (Krampe 2012).

Methods and Scope of Data-gathering in Sport

During a football match, huge quantities of data accrue and are used by sports journalists: players' tracks, ball contacts, shots at goal, but also the temperature of the turf, the number of spectators or the performance data for the referees are recorded (Marr 2015). The data thus collected have meanwhile come to benefit not just the clubs assessing them for training purposes; specialised firms offer the raw data to the media too. Under the heading of "transparent pros", they thus make, among other things, animated 3D analyses possible in the virtual television studio. The raw data made available in the internet likewise offer sports enthusiasts the possibility of envisaging how to bet or reproducing matches in the smallest detail (Krampe 2012).

When data-gathering in sports reporting began, the number of shots at goal, passes or one-on-one contests were still central, but today highly complex computer systems offer a more comprehensive insight into a football match's data. The numbers and statistics gained lead to a large volume of new sorts of information about the match (Wolf 2012). Data-gathering in the Federal League was long performed only out of personal interest. The Deutsche Fußball Liga (German Football League) did not decide until 2011 to officially grant rights to data-gathering (Ebeling 2013).

We distinguish between two methods of compilation of important data for sports journalism. Accordingly, data on paths run, speed and position are gathered to determine the location of an action. Overall, around 2000 trackable actions are subsequently classified using selected characteristics. Whilst people use the so-called tracking system for that, the actions are monitored by colleagues and classified. To this end, trained match observers identify the course of the match and data such as shots at goal, passes, ball contact and thus every significant act in the match.

Tracking, by contrast, is primarily computer-controlled. As a rule, two high-definition cameras, fixed to stadium roofs, are used. These cameras are connected to the data-gatherer's headquarters via mobile servers. An algorithm takes over the actual tracking through automatic image analysis. The data-gatherer only has to provide personnel to adjust the system before the match to the light conditions and the teams' jerseys (Ebeling 2013).

Hypotheses

Assessing the theoretical principles has presented various opportunities for data visualisation in sports journalism, but also problems and demands. We will, therefore, distinguish between advantages and disadvantages as our hypotheses.

Firstly, we can assume that the application of data in sports reporting harbours great potential for journalism when used properly. This is based on data serving as a means to improve journalistic products' credibility and objectivity. In addition, we assume that increased data-gathering facilitates access to data. Because football has meanwhile become notably more complex via tactical and physical developments, demands made by recipients on journalists for explanations and rankings have inevitably expanded. Four hypotheses arise from analysis of the advantages of data visualisation:

H1: Data serve as means to improve journalistic products' credibility and objectivity.

H2: Recipients' demand for analytical journalistic products is large, or respectively, increasing.

H3: Increased data-gathering also facilitates access to data.

H4: Online media are excellently suited to presenting visual data attractively.

Secondly, we assume that use of data in sports reporting is error-prone and thus harbours dangers too. This is based on data being used without an adequate context. An additional danger involves journalists using data selectively and thus producing false conclusions. Furthermore, data are gathered by people, so mistakes cannot be avoided, thus endangering objectivity. We can, moreover, assume that many journalists do not have the necessary expertise to interpret football data properly. This means an analysis of disadvantages of data visualisation in sports journalism in turn produces four hypotheses:

H5: There is a danger of data being used without an adequate context.

H6: Journalists tend to use data selectively. That prejudices objective reporting and thus journalistic quality.

H7: Many journalists do not interpret the data properly, or even do it incorrectly.

H8: Data are gathered by people and can hence never be error-free.

Empirical Method: Expert Interviews and Case Studies

We used two different methods to investigate: initially, we conducted five experts' interviews between October and December 2015; subsequently, we examined the concrete application of data visualisation in sport through three case studies.

In contrast to a conventional interview, expert interviews do not focus on the person but on their expertise on a topic. Critics accuse this method of lacking scholarly comparability (Bogner, Littig, and Menz 2002, 54) due to inconsistent results. To compensate for this weakness, the experts were asked a uniform catalogue of questions, which were individually expanded and adapted according to the interviewee. Our goal was to obtain differing and perceptive viewpoints, from which to gain new insights into a topic. Gläser and Laudel (2009, 117) explain: "The choice of interlocutors decides the nature and quality of the information you receive" (translation by Stan Jones). Hence, the following questions underpinned the selection process:

- Who has relevant information?
- Who is in the best position to provide precise information?
- Who is, most likely, prepared to give information?
- Who is available among the informants?

We chose five experts. Tobias Escher is the co-founder of the football tactics blog, *Spielverlagerung* [*Switching Play*], also presented as a case study. Escher is also a freelance writer for various media. Danial Montazeri is an editor on the sports desk of *Spiegel Online* and is, above all, responsible for analysis of tactics with special emphasis on data. René Martens is a freelance journalist and often deals with the topic of developments in sports journalism. Jörg Seidèl invented *GoalImpact* and runs the eponymous blog. *GoalImpact* is a formula by which we can classify a player using data; we also investigated it as a case study. Christoph Biermann is an editor-in-chief at *11Freunde* [*11Friends*], the "magazine for football culture", and an author of various books on football.

We sent the experts a preliminary questionnaire with the core questions. Some of the interlocutors, therefore, consulted notes during interviews lasting around an hour. The conversations were conducted face-to-face, recorded and held by the authors as audio files. The core questions served as starting points intended for discussion, and the respective emphases in the conversations were correspondingly varied. The following topic areas were discussed:

- Use of data in sports reporting.
- Sourcing and accessing data.
- Recipients' reactions to articles based on data.

- Sources of error in dealing with data.
- Data journalism as a trend on the sports desk.

Statements were excerpted subsequently through qualitative analysis of content; the important arguments were categorised, interpreted and collated in tables (Gläser and Laudel 2009). We examined all statements with regard to the hypotheses and appraised them for their relevance and evaluative worth.

Subsequently, we examined the results of the interviews along with a qualitative analysis of content (Krippendorff 2013) of three special-interest blogs from the area of data journalism in sport. A special-interest blog is devoted mainly to a particular topic area addressing a target group with a high degree of specialist knowledge in that respective area. Independence from editorial or internal publisher's requirements is a big advantage. Opposing that are the financial disadvantages, as such blogs as a rule generate very little profit, or none at all. The number of special-interest blogs in sports is uncountable, some have huge impact for years, other are shooting stars and online just some weeks. Most of them are produced for special audiences like national teams, clubs and their fans, gamblers, fans of special players and provide stats for different groups of users. Our analysis was related to three German- and England-based blogs with a huge impact on the German football scene over a long time, often cited in other media. We chose the blogs *GoalImpact* (goalimpact.com), *WhoScored* (whoscored.com) and *Spielverlagerung* (spielverlagerung.de). We will determine the nature of possible trends through their functioning and especially data-usage.

Overall, our work is explorative, but the results can demonstrate possible trends in sports journalism's data visualisation.

Results

Testing the Hypotheses: Advantages Through Data Visualisation in Sports Journalism

We begin by examining our hypotheses on the advantages and disadvantages of using data in sports reporting. The insights gained from the conversations will subsequently be thematically revisited in the following sections.

Four of the five experts agreed with H1. Biermann did not mention the advantage of the objectivity of data explicitly, yet what he says allows us to conclude that data can be a possible aid to relativisation or correction. Several statements make it clear that the quality of journalistic products can be improved by data. The experts say that data, above all, offer the possibility of explaining more complex circumstances. They note that using data in sports reporting serves as a "recipient-filter". Data-based journalistic products may be able to ensure the circle of recipients is limited to a higher intellectual level—which may be desirable for some media for reasons of image.

This aspect possibly relates to H2. As journalists, both Escher and Montazeri analyse matches by applying data, hence regarding it as a given. Martens, by contrast, mentioned the increased complexity of the game and the recipients' concomitant interest in ranking explicitly. Seidel, the only expert who is not a mainstream journalist, at least notes that dealing with data ought to be linked simultaneously to more profound reporting. Biermann equally confirmed the game's increased complexity, yet warns about more complex reporting needing the necessary space too—in the form of personnel, competence and/or preparedness.

Three of the five experts stressed particularly the great availability of data and thus supported H3. Here it is clear that even the commercial data packets via legal channels, in the form of quotations, for example, have meanwhile become more accessible. Data have obviously become more accessible than some of the classical areas in sports reporting—when, for instance, clubs themselves intervene as media actors.

In addition, not just general accessibility but also filtering of data seems interesting—that way, journalists can access differentiated and individually chosen data-sets. The probability of an exclusive on a topic is extremely high, given the huge quantity of data in an individually filtered search, which, in turn, should prompt tackling this topic.

Three of the five experts address the good opportunities in online media for visualisation and thus support H4. The number of visualisation tools available, often free, is clearly large and would interest small editorial operations or blogs without a graphics department, or respectively, a licence for particular tools. One advantage of visually presenting data in online media is the possible interactivity. Martens points to the potential modernising of familiar forms of text by incorporating data—and their visualisation too.

Testing the Hypotheses: Disadvantages of Data Visualisation in Sports Journalism

Statements by three of the five experts support H5, to the effect that data are used without an adequate context. Here, Seidel notes that the organisation of data in sports generally happens only rarely. Martens remarks that appearances often eclipse organisation and information, whilst Escher laments the lack of analysis of existing data. Biermann, by contrast, says data are used, above all, anecdotally. He thinks data cannot offer any information about the course of a match, let alone about success or failure.

All five experts support H6 on journalists' tendency to customise data, with the quality of reporting suffering accordingly. They note in particular conscious disregard of data. In this way, challenging the respective article's stated proposition is avoided. Furthermore, they mention editors' ingrained expectations about certain players. This induces sports journalists to reduce players to certain attributes. The view of other, possibly more meaningful, data are thus constrained. Montazari's mention of the cost of working with data can be seen as a reason for the danger of customising data. Escher points to people's habit of making things as simple as possible—customising data is thus as normal as it is inevitable.

Four of the five experts supported H7 about many journalists not interpreting data properly, or even wrongly. Montazeri and Escher argue giving examples, and Seidel and Martens only indirectly agree. Escher laments the rejection of tactical measures in analysing statistics. Hence, a bad passing record, for instance, features regularly as a criticism, although this is possibly based on risk-taking as ordered by the coach.

Montazeri sees many sports journalists' lack of expertise behind erroneous interpretation of data. For Martens, the problems of interpreting data are one step further back. That means lacking expertise causes erroneous use of analytical tools, making it completely impossible to interpret the relevant data. Seidel also criticises sports journalists as often incapable of identifying the really relevant data.

H8, that data gathered by people cannot be error-free, is affirmed by three of the five experts. Escher and Montazeri evince the fact that the various data-providers differ. This may arise with monitoring possession via various algorithms and, with actions like one-on-one contests, via differing interpretations. Differences in gathering unambiguous data can, however, only be attributed to mistakes by the processor responsible.

Escher and Montazeri additionally added that not all data relevant to an analysis are gathered. This need not be seen as a mistake, but rather as a technical failing. Biermann mentioned the financial aspect—the risk of mistakes is certainly higher due to possible savings by data-gathering firms.

Case Studies: Special-interest Blogs as Trendsetters in Data Journalism?

GoalImpact

Seidel founded the blog, *GoalImpact*, in November 2012. He developed an algorithm as a filter showing the influence of individual players on their team's performance. The so-called *GoalImpact* shows how strongly on average a team's goal tally depends on an individual player. In developing the formula to calculate a footballer's performance index, Seidel followed car racing. Transferring this on to football, Seidel rejected taking passing records, shots at goal, players' tracks and other parameters into account. Seidel changes the secret formula at irregular intervals. In this way, he successively allows factors like season, teammates or a player's experience to come in. The databank meanwhile contains over 45,000 players and is the basis for the blog's journalistic output.

Seidel chooses different types of articles and displays. Thus, for example, anticipated league tables or a team's "optimal eleven" are presented with the aid of *GoalImpact*. In addition, Seidel writes articles where various clubs' squad composition or transfer policy is examined using *GoalImpact*.

Between 20,000 and 50,000 users visit goalImpact.com every month. *GoalImpact* is used repeatedly by other media to illustrate developments or comparisons of individuals. *GoalImpact* is known and accepted as a statistical index, particularly in the English-speaking world. The majority of calls on goalImpact.com come from the United States, which relates to the greater presence of American data journalism. This fact is why Seidel has been presenting the blog in English since February 2013.

WhoScored

The English blog, *WhoScored*, was founded in 2008 and provides users with match plans, statistical livetickers and a databank containing more than 15,000 teams and more than 25,000 players. *WhoScored* assesses players according to their actions in matches, as collated by the data-provider, Opta. Thus, players can at best attain the top score of 10.0. The assessment is purely statistical in nature, the weighting of individual actions, like goals, assists, passing record, anticipations, tackles or fouls is, however, secret.

In the so-called "Match Centre", filters provide users with data from the match selected according to their own interests. With this, *WhoScored* offers the possibility of combining several player statistics to compare individual actors or teams. Alongside the databank and the tools in the "Match Centre", there are also articles organising the data journalistically and presenting them visually. The regular contributions as a rule focus on individual players. Using visualised data, the authors adduce, for example, the influences of defensive midfield players on the team's possession ratings. The graphic elements play an equivalent role to the text passages, which are often supplemented with further data as evidence.

Implementing such a comprehensive databank, and the contextually appropriate integration of it into a journalistic setting, is *WhoScored*'s greatest quality index.

Spielverlagerung

Spielverlagerung is a blog founded in 2011 and concerned primarily with football tactics. The authors were inspired by the English tactics blog, *ZonalMarking*79 (zonal-marking.net), and analyse matches for notable tactical features. These are presented journalistically using graphics produced by the tool, Inkscape80 (inkscape.org), and freely available data. *Spielverlagerung* has published more than 1800 articles, together with special numbers for major tournaments. The blog registers on average around 700,000 visits a month, with about half generated via Facebook.

Spielverlagerung's most common text form is match analysis. Here, the course of matches is replicated through strategic and tactic interactions and explained to users. Data are employed for this as support and illustration. They are not only integrated into graphic form but also into continuous text. Alongside match analyses, *Spielverlagerung* also offers them for individual players. This form of portrait is as a rule richer in data than a match analysis. To describe playing styles and tasks on the field visually, the authors use data, exhibiting two main methods for that. They often adopt graphics from other special-interest blogs, clarifying them accordingly. However, on their own initiative, the authors also gather data from databanks, like *WhoScored*, for instance, and produce their own graphics from it.

Spielverlagerung differs from *GoalImpact* and *WhoScored* by not focusing on data, but these serve rather to check observations and the conclusions drawn from them. Larger media noticed the blog because of its increasing appeal on social networks, where *Spielverlagerung* can boast more than 25,000 fans on Facebook and more than 17,000 followers on Twitter. That brought co-operation with ZDF (Second German Television), the *RuhrNachrichten*, *RevierSport*, *11Freunde* and Eurosport. There may be a trend visible here, where established media align themselves with successful blogs. Since the success of *Spielverlagerung*, more analyses of tactics and data journalism have appeared in traditional media's sports reporting.

Discussion and Evaluation

Advantages for Journalists

Using data in sports reporting primarily serves objectivity.

> A journalist receives an independent assessment of a player. An evaluation, which doesn't depend on the ups and downs of the everyday job. (Seidel, experts' interview[1])

In addition, data promote consideration of one's own conclusions before writing a text; some phenomena from the course of a match can, however, only be registered in data. That includes, for example, accuracy of passing. Journalists can certainly rely on their observations, but they will never be able, with any certainty, to say anything objective about individual actors' passing games. To convey their impressions to recipients credibly, presenting suitable statistics for special topic areas is, therefore, essential—and also, because the users themselves can access a lot of data.

> Data endow a text with authority. If you can provide certain numbers, then you have that certain air of persuasiveness. (Martens, experts' interview)

However, data do not only play a supporting role, but an investigative one too. Thus, data can prompt sports journalists to go beyond a possibly fixed view of individual players or of the match as such. This way, new topics, as yet not covered by other media, are unearthed.

Alongside the gain in objectivity, data journalism appearing increasingly in sports coverage can also enable editors to effect changes in readership. Data-based journalistic products interest, above all, those users who do not want to approach a topic superficially but more intensively.

> This other approach to the game produces another audience demanding things be explained. (Martens, experts' interview)

Data journalism can lead to increased quality for the media. Thus, the culture of discussing commentaries among respective articles can improve.

> We often observe that users argue in their commentaries using data. (Escher, experts' interview)

The cause might be that data journalism's products tend to be read and commented on by users engaged more intensively with the topic area.

Data journalism is an area where journalists enjoy, relatively, considerable freedom. New approaches, not limited by media partners or institutions, are available through data. That means journalists can find new approaches for articles, where they do not depend on individuals being available (Martens, experts' interview).

Using data does not offer just variety in topics but also in styles. For example, you can use data in portraits to show future developments as well. In addition, data can fulfil anecdotal purposes and so serve to entertain alongside informing. (Biermann, experts' interview)

Data can enrich familiar presentation forms visually too. In particular, financially embarrassed media, without access to photo agencies, can quickly produce attractive graphics to topic-related data with free tools and thus divide texts into topic sections.

Advantages for Recipients

Many of the given advantages for journalists are relevant for their recipients, too. Recipients enjoy advantages through the increasing influence of data on sports reporting. Data journalism "can offer readers research environments facilitating immersion in large databases" (Matzat 2011, translation by Stan Jones). Journalistic products, like *WhoScored*, or the official homepage of the Federal League (bundesliga.de) facilitate the targeted filtering of data desired by users.

In addition, the credibility aspect is not just an important factor on the part of journalists, but also with recipients. Just as a journalist wants to lend his text authority, so users want to be able to rely on the respective utterances. Furthermore, more complex connotations become comprehensible. Optimally, recipients' interest is awakened and increased by dint of data, making media consumption not only easier for users but also more worthwhile. The same goes for objectivity. If journalists use data properly, objective information is presented to recipients (Escher, experts' interview).

Dangers and Problems of Data Journalism for Football

Data journalism in sports also displays disadvantages. Among other things, these relate to online media's need for topicality.

> Online journalism has the problems of the fixture list being so tightly packed and of simply so many games happening on a Saturday and of the pressure for clean copy. Of course, Mondays you could still happily follow up with a data-based piece on the weekend's top match. But how would that suit the mind-set of online chief editors? (Martens, experts' interview)

Football's Complexity

Football is commonly known as a simple game. This assumption clearly rests, however, on the simplicity of the rules. Match phases, by contrast, are highly complex and thus demand highly differentiating observation from journalists. On a descriptive level, football seems utterly easy to grasp; a qualitative statement about actions on the field is, however, difficult even for experts.

> You can define many indices containing a value in themselves and expressing what happens on the field. You cannot, however, define generally what value holds good. There are very many descriptive statistics, but they haven't any predictive quality about whether a player's action is actually productive for the team or not. (Seidel, experts' interview)

Thus, data can indeed give a quick insight into the number of a player's passes, but not their effects. For a journalist to process data usefully, well-founded expertise is necessary: in this sense, the number of passes has to include several important factors, like their distance, their success rate and their direction. The strategic stance of the team also plays a role, as a team looking to counter-attack has less possession than their opponents, leading necessarily to a relatively lesser number of passes.

> In contrast to sports like baseball, for instance, where performance can be relatively clearly measured via data, football is difficult to monitor. (Montazeri, experts' interview)

Including Data Without Contextualisation

Given football's complexity, its simultaneous popularity and the resulting tailoring of journalistic products for mass appeal, it does not seem surprising that data are often presented without any proper context. "People often ... try to reduce football's complexity to individual values" (Biermann, experts' interview).

Journalists using data without providing any proper context for recipients points to an "inflation in data usage" (Biermann, experts' interview). This is, above all, a threat because more and more media can afford expensive access to databanks like Opta. If such a tool is available, then, of course, given its costs, it should also be used often.

> If you are, however, pressured by your boss to use data, you can run into difficulties—particularly when you've no prior knowledge. (Escher, experts' interview)

This lack of prior knowledge can be, on one hand, technical, so that a journalist, for example, is overtaxed by the tool's filtering function. On the other, the prior knowledge can be professional, if journalists do not know which data could be somehow important in judging a fullback's performance.

> It's certainly very tempting to such people to adopt statistics and deduce mundane things from them. (Montazeri, experts' interview)

Here, the combination of several problems in data handling appears in sports reporting. The data are presented without a proper context and also show that actions in football can only rarely be classified as clearly good or bad. In addition, data not suiting the message are not found or are even deliberately ignored.

> Statistics actually ought to widen your viewpoint and be additional aids—they can, however, also narrow your view. (Montazeri, experts' interview)

This brings the objectivity and authority of data into question, and it becomes equally clear that sports journalists have difficulty dealing with data.

> In data journalism, it's a matter of making connections and not of processing data. (Patzwald 2011, 7, translation by Stan Jones)

Mistakes in Gathering Data: The Human Factor

In sports journalism, why are data so often used without any context? Possibly it is

> the danger that, based on the data you have, you succumb to a certain fascination—and so possibly tell stories, which are, in part, not necessarily relevant. (Martens, experts' interview)

The endless possibilities available through data-gathering perhaps do lead sports journalists to use "data for data's sake". The above-mentioned pressure from editors to use costly access to data can be very significant. In addition, the danger exists of placing appearances ahead of contents and hence not adding value for recipients.

> For the World Cup, the *New York Times* had produced an article with a goalkeeper's movements ... but the context was missing. That means there was no explanation of why the goalkeeper did this or that movement—for example, based on differing strategies in

> defensive posture. Here, an explanation of that sort would have been more than meaningful. The whole thing did indeed look nice, but that was all. (Martens, experts' interview)

A further error-source in handling data is people themselves. In part, data-gathering, in fact, functions via computers, yet there are tasks carried out by people and hence prone to mistakes. These mistakes can result from confusing situations in a match, but commercial reasons can also play a role.

> Data providers are, in the last analysis, no more than businesses too, and possible savings can also be sometimes linked with negligence in collection. (Biermann, experts' interview)

A further problem is that data differ from provider to provider. Thus, differing values arise and hinder sport journalists' work. Whoever is bound to a certain provider by their editor will pick the corresponding values—although doubts over the objectivity and authority of these statistics arise from another provider's diverging results (Montazeri, experts' interview). By contrast, whoever does not work with any particular provider can choose between two differing results. Here, it is probable that a journalist will use the value that best suits the points made in their article.

The Danger of Customising

In looking for reasons why teams succeed or fail, sports journalists repeatedly exploit data. Increased use of data is particularly noticeable when a team has lost several matches in a row, is in a "crisis", so that this is, for example, explained through the number of one-on-one contests lost.

> Football is not nuclear physics—but notably more complex than most journalists assume. Here, it's not enough to say: the player played well because he won eight contests. (Montazeri, experts' interview)

Together with the absolute number of contests and the success rate, you also have to note contests' locations. Thus, winning a contest deep in the opposition's half almost inevitably triggers a direct chance of a goal. Winning a contest deep in your own half, by contrast, is only any use when the ball can subsequently be cleared out of the danger zone. It, therefore, seems plausible "that sports journalists often take the easy way". (Biermann, experts' interview)

> The most blatant error-source is journalists not understanding the numbers. I find tactics play a huge role right there. Certain pressing moves, for example, immediately affect the passing statistics. Not understanding such mechanisms probably leads to you customising your report of the game somehow or other. (Montazeri, experts' interview)

Whoever cannot follow the tactical moves necessarily has problems with organising the data properly. Sports journalists customising data seems understandable against the background of the pressure for actuality and possible editorial pressure obliging the inclusion of data. The difficulty remains, however, and forms the basis for new demands on sports journalism.

Looking Ahead: Conclusion and Future Demands

In this analysis of data-driven sports journalism, we demonstrated the complexity of football, the incorporation of data without any context, the danger of tailoring data to a topic, as well as mistakes in entering data as problems. It seems clear that relevant for professional sports journalists are a lack of (technical) knowledge, the increasing time pressure and growing expectations of recipients.

The large quantity of data gathered and the easier access result in interesting potentials for data journalism within sports journalism, or respectively, in football reporting. Certainly the greatest potential lies in the variety of topics, "because you can explain things that weren't explicable previously" (Escher, experts' interview). Data and tactics are topics well suited to combination in a journalistic context. Furthermore, journalists' observations on tactical moves can be checked using data.

Alongside the supporting and objective aspect, data can also be used to display developments and derive new conclusions from them. These, in turn, prompt further research by journalists and recipients, who are familiar with data use and have themselves access to them. Data, moreover, enable development of topic areas apart from sports.

> For example, with the World Cup in Brazil, you could certainly have written yet more incisive pieces on venues, on the infrastructure or the costs—sufficient data material existed. (Martens, experts' interview)

The obligation to publish the accounts of the clubs, which appear as limited companies, gave sports journalists access, for example, to important commercial data. Instead of a mention in reports, these data could have been more precisely analysed and linked to the sports results. That would have generated a considerable added value for recipients.

The visual aspect of data journalism also contains huge potential, above all in online media. Thus, there is a large variety of software for visualising processed data and for establishing various thematic aspects. A player portrait can, for example, be livened up stylistically and its content improved by a sports journalist organising the respective player's performance data into a visualised player profile. Such graphics can display players' strengths and weaknesses on a factual level. Data from individual scenes can also serve as evidence when describing a mode of play.

The advantages, potentials and dangers of integrating data into sports journalism's products have shown how the demands made on sports journalists are changing.

> One of the most important (and least technical) skills in understanding data is asking good questions. An appropriate question shares an interest you have in the data, tries to convey it to others, and is curiosity-oriented rather than math-orientated. Visualizing data is just like any other type of communication: success is defined by your audience's ability to pick up on, and be excited about, your insight. (Fry 2008, 4)

Matzat explains:

> Data journalism assumes that journalists are ready to share their research sources with recipients. The sources become examinable but also re-usable. (Matzat 2010), translation by Stan Jones)

As the users can access much data, sports journalists have to think a step further and process and interpret data more rigorously to generate added value for recipients. To accomplish this, editors and journalists have to be ready to do that bit more—above all, when using new technical aids for research and/or for processing data. Even if a lot of data are freely accessible, the increased editorial component in data journalism in sports is not only labour-intensive but also costly.

In the end, data journalism requires *computer-literacy*, meaning journalists' capacity to use computers and even exhibit knowledge of programming. A journalist must act as a link in the editorial department, functioning, on one hand, as a channel between editors and programmers and, on the other, assuming the role of producer of data-based articles. This person must not necessarily be able to program, but must know what is technically possible with what effort. Future data journalists in sports will, not least, have to be able to make that clear to the publishing side too (Matzat 2011). The investigation by Fink and Anderson (2015) confirmed these conclusions as they looked at the skills, organisational roles as well as personal values (privacy) of general data journalists in the United States and established four relevant constraints on data journalists: lack of time, lack of tools, lack of manpower and lack of legal resources.

With the frequent on-the-spot assignments in sports journalism as well, some rethinking is possibly needed. As a rule, a representative of an online editorial desk sits in the press box at matches and begins producing articles. Depending on the personnel assigned or on the organisation of the editorial desk, the journalist in the stadium writes the match report and/or a follow-up review. The latter is often strongly linked to individual players and is intended to attach an interesting story to them.

> This thinking in stories and personalities can hugely distort your view on the match as a whole. (Martens, experts' interview)

To sum up: data journalism in sports figures as a journalistic form of expression characterised by numerical data. Whilst presenting informative data is distinguished rather more by its nature as a service for recipients, journalistic added value can, above all, be generated where the content combines several sets of differing and relevant data.

A basis exists for a fundamental interest in data by dint of the increasing presence of them in people's everyday lives and by the general advance in applications of technology. The recipients' role is changing concomitant with data-sets being published by governments, associations and clubs, and with the degree of accessibility to what data providers gather. Using data makes the way journalists work more transparent and can act as a corrective, as, particularly in online media, direct user-feedback often ensues, where recipients themselves argue in part through data. Ultimately, using data in sports reporting can, in this way, improve what journalists produce. However, the ongoing development of football demands a high degree of analytical organisation from journalists. Special-interest blogs, above all, make clear the possibility for new sorts of display modes and approaches to visualisation. The blogs presented above have shown how data can be integrated into suitable contexts.

Overall, we can deduce a change in demands on sports journalists. Hence, the point actually is not to see data in isolation but in relation to other data and in the context of elements of matchplay tactics. In addition, sports journalists must accompany a readiness to work harder on researching and processing data with also improving their technical skills. However, the most important precondition for working more intensively with data in sports is understanding how to ask the right questions before starting research.

DISCLOSURE STATEMENT

No potential conflict of interest was reported by the authors.

NOTE

1. All experts' interviews translated by Stan Jones.

REFERENCES

Anderson, Chris W. 2013. "Towards a Sociology of Computational and Algorithmic Journalism." *New Media & Society* 15 (7): 1005–1021.

Appelgreen, Ester, and Gunnar Nygren. 2014. "Data Journalism in Sweden. Introducing New Methods and Genres of Journalism into "Old" Organizations." *Digital Journalism* 2 (3): 394–405.

Beckedahl, Markus. 2011a. "Datenjournalismus und die Zukunft der Berichterstattung [Data Journalism and the Future of Reporting]." Netzpolitik Blog. Accessed January 5. https://netzpolitik.org/2011/gastbeitrag-datenjournalismus-und-die-zukunft-der-berichterstattung/

Beckedahl, Markus. 2011b. "Neue Recherchewege—Datenjournalismus [New Ways of Investigation—Data Journalism]." *Netzpolitik Blog*. Accessed November 17. https://netzpolitik.org/2011/zapp-neue-recherchewege-datenjournalismus/

Biermann, Christoph. 2009. *Die Fußball-Matrix—Auf der Suche nach dem perfekten Spiel* [Football Matrix—Searching for the Perfect Game]. Köln: Kiepenheuer & Witsch.

Bogner, Alexander, Beate Littig, and Wolfgang Menz, eds. 2002. *Das Experteninterview* [The Expert Interview]. Wiesbaden: VS.

Boyle, Raymond. 2006. *Sports Journalism. Context and Issues*. London: Sage.

Boyle, Raymond, and Richard Haynes. 2004. *Football in the New Media Age*. London: Routledge.

Bradshaw, Paul. 2010. "How to be a Good Data Journalist." *The Guardian*, October 1. http://www.theguardian.com/news/datablog/2010/oct/01/data-journalism-how-to-guide.

Coddington, Mark. 2015. "Clarifying Journalism's Quantitative Turn." *Digital Journalism* 3 (3): 331–348.

Dean, Talisa. 2011. "Online-Journalismus zwischen Daten und Multimedia [Online Journalism between Data and Multimedia]." *Datenjournal Blog*. Accessed December 7. http://www.datenjournal.de/dossier/einstieg.html

Ebeling, Felix. 2013. "Datenjournalismus in der Sportberichterstattung: Der Einfluss von Daten auf die Berichterstattung am Beispiel der Impire AG [Data Journalism in Sport Reporting: The Impact of Dta on Reporting with the Example of Impire AG]." Unpublished BA-Thesis, Macromedia University, Hamburg.

Fink, Katherine, and C. W. Anderson. 2015. "Data Journalism in the United States. Beyond the "Usual Suspects"." *Journalism Studies* 16 (4): 467–481.

Fry, Ben. 2008. *Visualizing Data: Exploring and Explaining Data with the Processing Environment*. Sebastopol, CA: O'Reilly.

Gläser, Jochen, and Grit Laudel. 2009. *Experteninterviews und qualitative Inhaltsanalysen* [Expert Interviews and Qualitative Content Analysis]. Wiesbaden: VS.

Hammond, Philip. 2015. "From Computer-Assisted to Data-Driven: Journalism and Big Data." *Journalism*, December 15. doi: 10.1177/1464884915620205.

Holovaty, Adrian. 2006. "A Fundamental Way Newspaper Sites Need to Change." *Holovaty Blog*. Accessed September 6. http://www.holovaty.com/writing/fundamental-change/

Horky, Thomas, and Christian Kamp. 2012. *Sport: Basiswissen für die Medienpraxis* [Sports: Basic Knowledge for Media Practice]. Köln: Herbert von Halem.

Karlsen, Joakim, and Eirik Stavelin. 2014. "Computational Journalism in Norwegian Newsrooms." *Journalism Practice* 8 (1): 34–48.

Knight, Megan. 2015. "Data Journalism in the UK: A Preliminary Analysis of Form and Content." *Journal of Media Practice* 16 (1): 55–72.

Krampe, Anna-Lena. 2012. "Voraussetzungen für guten Datenjournalismus—äußere Kriterien [Requirements for Good Data Journalism—Exterior Criteria]." *Datenschätze Blog,* Online-Ressource. Accessed September 25. https://datenschaetze.wordpress.com

Krippendorff, Klaus. 2013. *Content Analysis: An Introduction to its Methodology*. Los Angeles, CA: SAGE.

Leßmöllmann, Anette. 2012. "Datenjournalismus: Chancen für den Journalismus von morgen [Data Journalism: Chances for Tomorrow's Journalism]." *Journalistik Journal*. Accessed March 29. http://journalistik-journal.lookingintomedia.com/?p=843

Lewis, Michael. 2003. *Moneyball: The Art of Winning an Unfair Game*. New York: W.W. Norton.

Lewis, Seth C. 2015. "Journalism in an Era of Big Data." *Digital Journalism* 3 (3): 321–330.

Lewis, Seth C., and Oscar Westlund. 2015. "Big Data and Journalism." *Digital Journalism* 3 (3): 447–466.

De Maeyer, Juliette, Manon Libert, David Domingo, François Heinderyckx, and Florence Le Cam. 2015. "Waiting for Data Journalism. A Qualitative Assessment of the Anecdotal Take-Up of Data Journalism in French-Speaking Belgium." *Digital Journalism* 3 (3): 432–446.

Marr, Bernhard. 2015. "How Big Data and Analytics are Changing Football." *Smartdatacollective.com*. Accessed July 28. http://www.smartdatacollective.com/bernardmarr/332906/how-big-data-and-analytics-are-changing-football

Matzat, Lorenz. 2010. "Data Driven Journalism: Versuch einer Definition [Data-Driven Journalism: Attempt of a Definition]." *Open Data Network*. Accessed April 16. http://opendata-network.org/2010/04/data-driven-journalism-versuch-einer-definition/

Matzat, Lorenz. 2011. "Datenjournalismus [Data Journalism]." *Bundeszentrale für politische Bildung*. Accessed October 26. http://www.bpb.de/gesellschaft/medien/opendata/64069/daten-journalismus

Mendel, Anja. 2011. "Florence Nightingale: Eine Vorreiterin des Datenjournalismus [Florence Nightingale: A Pioneer of Data Journalism]." *Datenjournal Blog*. Accessed December 7. http://www.datenjournal.de/dossier/einstieg.html

Parasie, Sylvain. 2015. "Data-Driven Revelation? Epistemological Tensions in Investigative Journalism in the Age of "Big Data"." *Digital Journalism* 3 (3): 364–380.

Patzwald, Marc. 2011. "Erzählen nach Zahlen. Datenjournalismus zwischen neuen Formen und alten Ideen [Talking with Numbers. Data Journalism between New Forms and Old Ideas]." *EPD Medien* 32: 7–9.

Rogers, Simon. 2012. "Change—Wie Daten den Journalismus verändern [Change—How Data Changes Journalism]." *Deutschlandfunk Diskurs*. Accessed February 22. http://diskurs.dradio.de/2012/02/22/change-wie-daten-den-journalismus-verandern/

Weinacht, Stefan, and Ralf Spiller. 2014. "Datenjournalismus in Deutschland. Eine explorative Untersuchung zu Rollenbildern von Datenjournalisten [Data Journalism in Germany. An Explorative Survey of Role Models of Data Journalists]." *Publizistik* 59 (4): 411–433.

Wolf, Tanja. 2012. "Statistik 2.0: Die Tracking-Technik im modernen Fußball [Statistics 2.0: Technic of Tracking in Modern Football]." *Conrad Blog*. Accessed June 20. http://blog.conrad.de/statistik-2-0-die-tracking-technik-im-modernen-fussball/52247/

PRESSURE ON PRINTED PRESS

How soccer clubs determine journalism in the German Bundesliga

Christoph G. Grimmer

Digital media have influenced everyday life to a large extent. They have particular influence on jobs in the communication realm such as journalism. Clubs and federations communicate directly with their reference groups without being reliant on intermediate traditional media. Consequently, they have acquired communicative superiority in the highly competitive field of professional sports information. This research addresses how collaboration and relationships between sports and media work through expert interviews with the head spokespersons of 18 German Bundesliga clubs and an online survey among print sports journalists who report on these clubs (adjusted sample N = 174). An integrative analysis contrasts results from spokespersons and journalists. Both sides see journalists as more dependent on the spokespersons than vice versa. None of the spokespersons interprets their role as a service provider for the media but journalists do. Additionally, 87 percent of the journalists expect clubs to increase pressure on their reporting in the future. Assessing honesty, more than 90 percent state that spokespersons withhold certain information or do not tell the truth constantly. Also, 73 percent criticize authorization of interviews as modern censorship. The digital revolution, however, has changed journalistic roles and initiated a journalistic advancement as illustrated by new sports channels, programs, and formats.

Introduction

Soccer has become a global industry and target of wide-ranging interests. This holds true not just for major events such as the FIFA World Cup, UEFA European Football Championship, or UEFA Champions League, but also for league competitions. The German Bundesliga has had a prosperous development. At the beginning of 2016, the Deutsche Fußball Liga GmbH (German Football League, also known as the DFL) announced their 11th consecutive sales record with 2.62 billion in 2014–2015 (DFL 2016a, 2).

Beside its economic importance, one can differentiate four other aspects that must be considered for assessing soccer's significance in Germany. First, the Bundesliga is ranked second in UEFA rankings for club competitions. Six years ago, it was in the fourth position behind England, Spain, and Italy. Second, the Bundesliga attracts strong media attention. More than 800 print reporters are permanently accredited per season

(Grimmer 2014). The sale of broadcasting rights generates proceeds of more than 730 million per year (DFL 2016a, 26). From 2017 on, the Bundesliga will receive more than 1 billion each season (DFL 2016b).

Third, the preceding numbers are strongly related to soccer's social demand. More than 13 million spectators attended games within the latest seasons—42,685 per match on average, more than 90 percent of stadiums' capacities (DFL 2016a, 23, 48). Millions more watch live television broadcasts or highlights of games. Many of the highest-rated television broadcasts in Germany are soccer matches (Agf 2016).

Fourth, sports in general is growing in political relevance. Beyond major issues such as corruption, doping, and referendums on hosting events such as the Olympics, the question of whether soccer clubs should pay for police and security on match days or public funds should be used to build stadiums (e.g., Munich 2001 and Freiburg 2015) are major issues in Germany.

In sum, soccer is becoming more relevant in economic, sporting, media, social, and political spheres. However, its controversies are also becoming more significant. Athletes opt for doping to become global elites. Tactical fouls replace fair play. Processes of awarding major sporting events are controversial and lack transparency. Attention is focused on a small numbers of sports, in particular soccer.

As such, tensions appear to be growing between the soccer establishment and the media that reports it. Sports journalists always have been faced with the apparently contradictory task of promoting and criticizing the teams they cover. They assess and judge on-pitch performances and off-pitch decisions. While the exchange between players and journalists formerly took place behind the scenes, nowadays television cameras are permanent companions. As a consequence, protagonists may, on the one hand, behave in a friendlier manner but, on the other hand, any conflict becomes more visible. Several disputes between sports figures—amongst others Stefan Effenberg in 1999, Rudi Völler in 2003, Klaus Augenthaler in 2007, Thomas Doll in 2008, Bastian Schweinsteiger in 2011, and Bruno Labbadia in 2012—and the media illustrate strained relations between their respective representatives.

Club spokespersons, installed numerously during the Bundesliga's rapid professionalization which has been substantially driven by the UEFA European Championship 1996, face those issues as moderators of these tense relations. They simultaneously must address internal demands and external expectations (Stoldt, Dittmore, and Branvold 2012). Journalists are not just faced with a counterpart directing the clubs' communication; their work is affected by technical developments. Sports federations, clubs, and athletes now can communicate directly with their public (Williams and Chinn 2010). Journalists are threatened with loss of their importance as an intermediary of information between organizations and the general public. Under these conditions, one must ask how journalists perceive their current role in the information process and how they assess cooperation and collaboration with spokespersons as public relations (PR) ambassadors of sports clubs, managers, and athletes.

Following is a review of the literature about the relation between sports and journalism in the digital age. Next is a presentation of the results from surveys of sports journalists and spokespersons in the German Bundesliga related to crucial issues such as authorization of interviews and then a discussion of major findings. The final section puts the results in a wider context of patterns and trends, and concludes with the limitations of the current study.

Literature Review

The advent of online, social, and digital media has disrupted traditional forms of communication and journalism practice (Gibbs and Haynes 2013; Wilson and Supa 2013). Whereas in former times print, television, and radio have been clearly distinct, in the online environment all three types are applied and can be combined in online storytelling via podcasts, streams, etc. This merging of media outlets often causes in-house competition between traditional outlets and online channels. The online-first principle has strengthened internet media and weakened traditional distribution channels (Whiteside 2014). Competing for advertising partners, information most commonly is offered free of charge today.

Driven by digital technologies, global information flow is easy, cheap, and rapid as never before. According to Boyle (2013, 95), "sports journalism has in many ways been one of the areas of journalism most profoundly affected by this change." The media sports market in particular is characterized by instant gathering, reporting, and dissemination of information, tense competition and myriad challenges for communication professionals, and a heavy decline of the print media sector as more people turn to online outlets for news and journalistic content.

24/7 and the Media Lifecycle

Technological infrastructure and reasonable charges for Web usage make possible ubiquitous online use for almost everyone, anywhere and anytime. This development is driven to a huge extent by television with its 24-hour news and, in particular, live coverage (Sugden and Tomlinson 2010). In Germany, Sky Sport News HD—the country's first 24-hour sports information provider—has broadcast news, interviews, news conferences, statistics, and much, much more in a continuous loop since December 2011. "The opportunities for a sports journalist to step back from a story and dig deeper have become less frequent" (Boyle 2006, 135). Circulation of information has picked up the pace, and the half-life period of information has decreased.

In addition to the impact of the 24/7 news culture on traditional media, social media have fueled a faster pace of information flow more than traditional inter-media competitors in the former communication market (Kian and Murray 2014). They accelerate the process of rolling news and raise the pressure to break information instantly (Hutchins and Rowe 2010; Li et al. 2015). Thus, the digital infrastructure of modern media makes scoops immediately a common good (Boyle and Haynes 2014; Haynes 2013).

Traditionally, an evolution of new media forces existing media to adjust their orientation of content, verbalization, visualization, dramaturgy, or related issues, and to develop new forms of topic identification, storytelling, and content distribution. Interaction and struggle between old and new media is addressed by the so-called media lifecycle model (Lehman-Wilzig and Cohen-Avigdor 2004). To offer additional value for readers, listeners, and viewers, existing media have to change their nature and journalistic practice (Boyle 2012).

Thus, newspapers were not replaced by radio, and television did not replace newspapers, radio, and cinema. Technologies co-exist and share inter-media power relations (Curran and Jean Seaton 2009). Similarly, online and social media have had an impact on the character of existing communication. They have not eradicated traditional media outlets but rather disrupt former patterns of journalism, consumption, and practice. This is in line with Haynes' (2013, 57) position "suggesting a co-existence between media forms rather than some sort of dominance by any one platform." In line with this, social media may affect the creation of news stories, but importance and traction still is conveyed via traditional media.

Quality of and in "New" Sports Journalism

Based upon the idea of 24/7 coverage and media interdependencies, it must be questioned how the internet has changed news coverage and how the quality *of* and *in* the new sports journalism can be judged. The rise of the internet enables people, in general, and communication professionals, in particular, to access more information at a lower investment of time and money (Butler, Zimmerman, and Hutton 2013). Li et al. (2015) surveyed 133 Chinese sports journalists who reported gathering news as a primary motivation for using social media.

A recent international study, however, revealed a lack of sources named in print sports journalism (Horky and Nieland 2013). Broadcasting in the context of major sporting events is dominated by a huge extension of live coverage and within this an increase of discursive formats such as expert talks (Grimmer, Horky, and Winkler 2016). Connected with this, the rise in the cost of broadcasting rights and production has added to the predicament between objective reporting and promoting one's own broadcasting product.

The media focus on elite sports and major sporting events, while investigative reporting and topics such as doping and/or corruption receive little attention. Social media has relevance as inspiration for news stories, yet journalists still privilege elite sources (Jordaan 2013; Paulussen and Harder 2014). Thus, journalists "hesitate to use information retrieved from social media as direct and quoted sources in news reporting" (Lecheler and Kruikemeier 2016, 156). Because online sources so far have not substituted offline sources, they rather serve as a supplemental gimmick in the daily news-sourcing process.

English (2016) compared the acceptance of Twitter by sports desks in Australia, India, and the United Kingdom. He combined a content analysis of more than 4100 print and online articles with 36 in-depth interviews. Only 183 print media stories contained some type of Twitter content. Interestingly, the highest Twitter adoption was found in the United Kingdom, where 8.0 percent of all articles included Twitter material, followed by Australia (3.9 percent) and India (2.0 percent). Thus, it seems "evident, that cultural and commercial aspects of the respective nations' media systems impact on rates of adoption" (English 2016, 497). India's relatively low adoption is closely linked to the existing power of its print industry as well as an in general lower online and Twitter usage.

In China, Li et al. (2015) surveyed journalists on their social media perceptions and adoption. The results showed that the reporters' views were ambivalent. Although some felt a closer relation with athletes due to personal and/or private information on social media platforms, others acknowledged a more distant one because top athletes no longer are dependent on coverage by traditional media.

In the end, one can argue about the quality of sports journalism in the digital age that is shaped by the increasing pace of information circulation and storytelling. An increasing number of sports organizations have released regulations and/or guidelines for social media activities for teams and athletes participating in major competitions (Boyle and Haynes 2014). Because many newspaper stories are not original, Davies (2009) coined the expression *churnalism* to describe PR information that is re-warmed by journalists and then conveyed via traditional media as unbiased and fact-checked journalism.

Challenges for Journalists in the Digital Age

Technological innovations and new platforms are changing the nature of traditional journalism and information-gathering practices (Gibbs and Haynes 2013; Sheffer and Schultz 2010; Wilson and Supa 2013). In the battle for news, competition is not just between journalists and between media, but nowadays includes athletes, clubs, and federations that promote information on their respective (personal or corporate) websites and other media channels such as social network sites (Coombs and Osborne 2012). Burk, Grimmer, and Pawlowski (2016) examined the use of corporate club PR channels and found a high usage in particular for club websites, magazines, and email information, as well as email newsletters to get information about club issues.

> The increasing economic and political importance of the public relations practice that is growing up around the sports industry presents a challenge to journalists working in this field. But the challenges they face are similar to journalists in other areas ... Sport, with its mixture of entertainment, drama and news values, offers a particular challenge for journalists in their need to both inform and entertain in an increasingly fast-paced news environment while addressing, in many cases, an increasingly knowledgeable audience. (Boyle 2006, 181)

The internet and social media, in particular, offer enriched possibilities to break news worldwide, drive traffic on platforms with targeted content, and develop new revenue streams (Coombs and Osborne 2012). Concurrently, players have aimed marketing goals at an international audience as well (Bowman and Cranmer 2014). Driven by these trends, journalists have less access today than they had decades ago (Suggs 2015, 2016). Four out of five Chinese sports journalists questioned by Li et al. (2015) noted that social media threatened traditional print media. In particular, social media have accelerated the pace in information gathering and news reporting. For instance, monitoring information on social network sites has increased professional pressure. Only a small percentage of respondents noted a professional simplification based on more news sources and more available information than before the digital era (Li et al. 2015).

In Germany, sports journalists assess social media mostly as either relevant or extremely relevant for their work. The majority agrees that athletes' social media use has made it more difficult to provide news exclusively, yet 87.5 percent of these journalists gather information by following actors from the field of sports (Nölleke, Grimmer, and Horky 2016). The fans themselves have become an additional important player in today's sport media complex. Boyle (2012) expects more conversation between journalists, readers, and supporters. At the same time, in stadiums and at training grounds, fans can distribute breaking news immediately via online media before journalists can get the story to any editor (Butler, Zimmerman, and Hutton 2013).

Moreover, the audience itself can choose from a variety of news platforms, such as Twitter accounts from elite sports figures and 24/7 televised media conferences. Boyle (2013, 96) illustrates that sport journalists have to offer "something more than the supposed ringside seat." Against the backdrop of *citizen journalism* and the increase in sources and channels, Li et al. (2015) found three main reasons that contribute to journalists' pessimism toward journalism in the digital age: (1) competition between an increased number of media outlets, (2) lower estimation for professional journalists because of the rising amount of citizen journalists, and (3) higher requirements in terms of skills (social media, research, information gathering and monitoring, and verification strategies).

Situation in the Print Media Market

It has become obvious that sports journalism has altered in the course of recent decades due to the shift from analog to digital. Journalists tend to lose (or already have lost) their classical gatekeeping function (Butler, Zimmerman, and Hutton 2013; Li et al. 2015). They compete with citizen journalists in producing and distributing information on the news market (McEnnis 2013). Probably more than ever, their predicament is how to offer non-complicit, rigorous, and well-founded journalism at a time of economic difficulties in the media industry (Boyle 2013).

These circumstances are applicable especially for print journalism. Fewer reporters than before face an increasing number of expectations in terms of monitoring information channels, identifying accurate news, getting original content, and writing specifically for different outlets (Butler, Zimmerman, and Hutton 2013; Pedersen 2014). According to Boyle (2006, 2012), print journalists are more concerned with comment and analysis than traditional reporting. At the same time, sports journalists provide entertainment and amusement.

> The sports reporter who once faced a single deadline for copy in print is now beholden to multiple deadlines and tasked with producing multiple versions of the same story, as the sports department is forced to meet the increasing demands of consumers in a world of blogging, streaming, and live chats. (Butler, Zimmerman, and Hutton 2013, 220)

Digital media open up the possibility of promoting coverage of mainstream media (Wilson and Supa 2013; Schultz and Sheffer 2010). Although television remains fundamental for the live sports media experience (Boyle 2012), the internet has driven an audience to print coverage (Boyle 2006). However, digital technology has usurped important selling propositions of twentieth-century print journalism, notably exclusivity (Meikle and Young 2011). Ironically, "selling" proposition is an outdated term in the age of free online content. According to Anderson (2009), a decline in newspaper circulation was ascertainable in the United States before the internet (r)evolution; responsible for this were things such as the suburbanization of America, the drop of advertising revenues, and changes in tax rules.

Nevertheless, there are detrimental characteristics of print media in the digital era. As Butler, Zimmerman, and Hutton (2013, 220) note, "breaking stories do not wait 24 hours." The frequency of publication is probably the most important structural disadvantage compared to television or radio (live broadcasting) and online media (24/7 rolling news). Secondly, users (and sports fans) can select from among a variety of media outlets in the news marketplace. A third crucial issue is the availability of information free of charge at the click of a mouse. Consequently, newspapers lost financial resources in the past decades, tried to save money by cutting personnel costs, and now face a growing PR market (Davies 2009; Hobsbawn 2010). Media organizations are called upon to find solutions for the economic predicament to sustain their work (Boyle and Haynes 2014). Some journalists benefited individually from the rise of online journalism and newspapers' decline by recognizing opportunities in the transition from print to online (Kian and Zimmerman 2012).

Coombs and Osborne (2012) point out that clubs' PR departments, often composed of former journalists, frequently treat reporters as second-class citizens instead of supporting them in doing their jobs. Moreover, the dependency of sports (events, federations, clubs, leagues, athletes) on mainstream media coverage dropped as sports organizations have become financially underwritten by an inflated broadcasting rights market and fueled by technically driven opportunities of self-promotion. In the past 20–25 years, the distance between journalists and sports has widened. This is presumably due to the professionalization and commercialization of sports as well as the money flowing to elite sports stars, the common value, and public interest.

Research Gap and Research Questions

The literature review up to here has highlighted radical shifts in the sports communication profession during the past two decades, in particular since the new millennium. The impact of the internet, with its myriad utilization possibilities such as research or distribution of information in the 24/7 always-on environment, has affected and changed journalism in the digital age (Gibbs and Haynes 2013). Following the initial "online first" mentality, media companies' battle for users provoked free content on websites, particularly having an impact on the traditional print media. Moreover, in a time of economic crises in journalism, PR are a viable competitor in the race for clicks, market share, and television ratings. In sports, organizations and athletes now can communicate directly with their audiences without intermediaries such as journalists. This drives the question of how sports representatives and journalists manage their professional collaboration and cooperation.

Isaacson (2010) provides an overview on PR research. The studies mentioned concentrate on sports information directors and their professional duties, but "little is known about media–practitioner relationships in sport public relations" (Isaacson 2010, 603). Apart from sports communication, more than 150 studies have examined some aspect of relations between PR practitioners as news sources and journalists as media gatekeepers since the 1960s (Sallot and Johnson 2006). Whereas PR practitioners used to actively promote a club or federation, they now manage an increased number of media requests and decide who may get an interview with which athlete, coach, manager, and/or official. "The consumer demand that exists for sport information has the potential to influence the power balance of the relationships" (Isaacson 2010, 603).

In addition, social media may "speed up" (Boyle 2012, 58) the struggle for prerogative interpretation between PR interests (subjectivity) and journalistic ethos and critique (neutrality). The literature makes it obvious that few have investigated the media–practitioner relationship in sports (Isaacson 2010, 604). So far, little, if anything, is known about the quality of media relations in the digital age (Gibbs and Haynes 2013; Neijens and Smit 2006; Shaw and White 2004; Wilson and Supa 2013). In particular, studies on journalists' experiences with and the perception of club spokespersons in sports are missing (with some limitations; Coombs and Osborne 2012; Pincus et al. 1993; Suggs 2016).

In the German-speaking area, few studies have been conducted in this broader field. Studies on club PR either have focused on working issues in an international context (Jungels 2007) or compared PR working conditions in different sports (Ziegler 2008). Moreover, primarily quantitative approaches were applied (i.e. Schaffrath 2012), except for a survey among the Austrian Swimming Federation (Fenz 2009; see Macnamara [2014] for qualitative interviews apart from sports communication). Just one study examined both journalists and PR practitioners but in the context of events taking place only once a year such as golf, tennis, and equestrian sports events (Ellert 2006).

Based upon these considerations and the concomitant research gap, the following research questions were derived:

RQ1: How do sports journalists assess club PR practitioners' relevance and vice versa?

RQ2: How do club PR practitioners manage the (journalistic) demand for sports information?

RQ3: How does the collaboration between journalists and club PR practitioners run?

RQ4: How do journalists and club PR practitioners justify and assess authorization of interviews?

RQ5: How do sports journalists and club PR practitioners evaluate their mutual relationship?

Methodology

Sample

The sample for the current study was journalists in the realm of the German Bundesliga and the clubs' head PR practitioners. Because of the small number of Bundesliga soccer clubs, a full census was intended. On the other side, two motives were essential in concentrating on print journalists only: proximity and competition.

Print sports journalists usually have the most regular and intensive collaboration with clubs or federations. Whereas radio or television reporters in Germany normally rotate in covering events, print journalists observe training sessions and news conferences on a daily basis. Thus, they have a daily dependence on information and should be able to assess the PR work most reliably and accurately.

Whereas audiovisual media, and in particular online media, have diverse opportunities to produce and distribute interesting coverage, print journalism is in crisis and increasingly less demanded. The affected journalists must cope with these circumstances. Accordingly, it seems particularly worthwhile to assess how print journalists evaluate their working conditions.

Research Method and Instrument

A combination of qualitative and quantitative methods was chosen for this study. Several reasons have been crucial for this approach. First and foremost, qualitative methods facilitate new insights and perspectives which were previously unknown. Secondly, it seemed inevitable to survey Bundesliga club PR practitioners personally since it marks a certain effort on the side of academia and in addition the spokespersons get in touch with the scholar they share their knowledge with. The advantages of the quantitative method are the comparability of results and the chance to survey a higher sample.

An interview guide was created as an instrument for the personal interviews with the clubs' PR practitioners. Each of five thematic horizons had a quite general question which summed up each horizon's interview questions.

Horizon 1: Professional daily life—which challenges does your job as PR practitioner in the German Bundesliga have (professionally, personally, physically)?
Horizon 2: The club's PR concept—which goals do you pursue for the club and how do you try to achieve them (organizational, conceptual, operational)?
Horizon 3: Self-concept—what is your main challenge in this job and how do you define your area of responsibility (conditions, competencies, job interpretation)?
Horizon 4: Auto and hetero stereotypes—what do you think of how you are perceived by others in your role as PR practitioners and how do you wish to be seen?
Horizon 5: Collaboration of PR and media—how do you proceed to meet the journalists' requirements without negotiating the club's expectations (expectations, strategies, instruments)?

The written survey among PR practitioners had a similar structure (three main horizons: person, club, work). With just 6 out of 35 questions concerning demographic parameters, 29 questions remained targeting the PR work and collaboration with journalists. Journalists answered 58 questions, of which 46 were concerning the research questions. These targeted in particular the public image of Bundesliga clubs, their PR goals, PR methods, and PR communication tools, as well as in particular the PR practitioner's role for his/her club, on the one hand, and the media, on the other hand.

Data Collection

At the beginning of 2011, a pre-test was conducted for both surveys and based on those results minor adjustments were made to the research instruments. To validate results, journalists were surveyed online. I derived questions from a review of the literature and theoretical considerations. The questionnaire was executed online from April 19 to May 31, 2011 (end of the league competition in Germany), with 254 journalists opening the online interface. The net sample reduced to 174 because some journalists finished the questionnaire at early stages or did not cover Bundesliga soccer.

Based on the number of journalists who are permanently accredited by the clubs, one can assume that 803 reporters cover the clubs regularly. This is tantamount to a usable response rate of 21.7 percent.

Personal interview was the chosen method to obtain information and insights on the comparatively unexplored field of collaboration between journalists and sports PR workers. Therefore, I conducted face-to-face expert interviews with 18 heads of club communications from March 1 to May 24, 2011. The interviews lasted 27–111 minutes, with an average of 64 minutes. Subsequent to the interviews, the PR practitioners filled out a nine-page questionnaire to obtain data comparable to the journalists' survey.

Data Analysis

One club PR practitioner did not want to be mentioned in the study after the completed interview. Thus, calculations include 17 of 18 Bundesliga clubs (94.4 percent). Because of the mixed methods of qualitative expert interviews with PR practitioners and quantitative questionnaires with both groups, results initially had to be analyzed separately and then later related to each other from the perspective of the research questions.

In terms of confidentiality of sources, the club's PR practitioners had the chance to give their interviews or at least crucial quotes anonymously. For publication, all quotes were authorized. This was not a burden probably because they are communication experts and conducted the interviews this way; only linguistic expressions were changed, but no content-related adjustments were executed.

Results

Relevance of Journalists and Spokespersons

Club PR practitioners rated the status of journalists as high or very high. Interestingly, there were big differences comparing print, television, radio, and online reporters. For print journalists, 88.2 percent of PR workers said they had a very high importance while 11.8 percent assessed a high relevance. In second place, 76.5 percent gave television journalists a very high status and 23.5 percent affirmed a high relevance. For radio journalists, the evaluation was nearly balanced with 52.9 percent rating them very high and 47.1 percent rating them high. Surprisingly, the status of online journalists appears to be comparatively low. Just 29.4 percent assessed a very high rating, with 64.7 percent rating them high and 5.9 percent low. Despite a crisis in the German print media market, print journalists still have the highest relevance in the Bundesliga journalism realm.

These results are confirmed by the importance rating for specific media types in the Bundesliga context. Just 15 of the 17 questioned PR practitioners were willing to award points for a selection of media types. Each PR expert had to adjudge six points: three for the most important media type, two for the second place, and one for the third most relevant media. Twenty-eight out of 90 points in total were awarded to daily tabloid press such as *Bild*, one of the newspapers with the most sales and highest circulation in Germany, followed by daily quality press such as local, regional, and national newspapers (24 points). News agencies were placed third (13), closely followed by public television (11) and private television (10). This appears surprising because the pay television channel Sky is the biggest sponsor of the German Bundesliga, paying roughly 700 million per season and having the privilege of conducting the first interviews after Bundesliga games. Ranked sixth were sports magazines (4). This was unexpected as well because renowned magazines *kicker* and *SportBild* are well-respected print products and receive great attention from sports and in particular soccer fans. Weekly newspapers, public and private radio stations, and online media did not get any points.

> Media business in the Bundesliga has got a manageable size some time. You know the colleagues after some years—not everybody personally, but the names and where to put, which media. And that's quite important. Reliability is something that we can and should offer independently of sportive success or critical moments. (Tobias Sparwasser, 1. FSV Mainz 05)[1]

Club PR practitioners also were asked with which media's journalists they maintain the best relationship. Again print journalism was in the top position (41.2 percent), followed by television (29.4 percent), radio (11.8 percent), and agencies (5.9 percent). Two PR practitioners (11.8 percent) were not poised to judge this question.

In the face-to-face interviews, the PR workers were questioned about the objectives in their collaboration with journalists. As evidenced by Sparwasser's quote, reliability is one of the main goals, independent of failure or any other crisis. Bayern Munich's media director Markus Hörwick appreciated a similar relationship: "I wish that journalists see me as correct and reliable that one can say: Ok, we don't get everything from him, but we know that he does the best possible for us—what we really do." Other practitioners pointed out that working together in the German Bundesliga depends on individual relationships, independent from any media type. Thus, one cannot say that collaboration with quality press works better than with tabloid newspapers.

> I know which people I can trust, who I can give some background information for explanation, where I can trust that I am not cited immediately. You have to know who just abuses you and with whom you can have a professional, trustful and partner-like collaboration. That all happens with the knowledge that you are not rowing in the same boat! Interests are often completely different between the club and journalists. (Gerd Voss, VfL Wolfsburg)

Both groups were questioned about role interpretations (Table 1). The majority classified club PR practitioners as mediators between the club and the media. Interestingly, nearly 30 percent of the journalists said PR workers were service providers for media professionals, but none of the spokespersons did, seeing themselves instead as the clubs' advisors in media issues.

Surveying the relevance of PR practitioners in the Bundesliga soccer context, 50 percent of journalists assessed PR practitioners as unimportant for their media work. Just 8.2 percent rated the clubs' PR workers as very important and another 35.2 percent as important. Surprisingly, 6.6 percent evaluated the spokesperson's job as very unimportant for the journalists' work.

TABLE 1
Role interpretation (%)

Statement	Spokespersons (N = 17)	Journalists (N = 174)
Mediator between club and media	76.5	56.9
Service provider for media and journalists	0	28.7
Club's advisor	17.6	5.7
Open statements	5.9	8.6

PR Management of Journalistic Demand

Clubs' PR practitioners must cope with a myriad of public inquiries, in particular media requests. Interviews with the Bundesliga spokespersons revealed three ways of dealing with public and media interest. First and foremost, they select the most sensible information and interview requests. "After Louis van Gaal is away now, the journalists expect that they can talk to Franck Ribéry," Bayern Munich's media director Markus Hörwick said one day after the manager's dismissal. "Everybody knows that Ribéry would 'explode,'" because it was an open secret that they did not have a good relationship. "So it's my job to withdraw him from the business, so that he doesn't make any nonsense," Hörwick explained. In this situation, the club would have found it inappropriate to let someone talk who is most likely happy about the separation with van Gaal.

> It is absolutely clear that *kicker* as a soccer magazine has got a better chance to get an interview than *Super Illu* [German *Playboy*]. But that could be meaningful as well. Our player Marcel Schmelzer comes from Magdeburg [former East Germany] ... I have informed myself before I spoke to him. Indeed, the former sex magazine *Super Illu* has changed its content and is one of the top-sold magazines in the former DDR, so that he has recently given a bigger interview. (Josef Schneck, Borussia Dortmund)

Schneck illustrates deliberations in terms of media inquiries. Newspapers, magazines, and radio and television stations that report regularly about the club and that have a close thematic sports focus normally are preferred. But there can be arguments such as newspaper circulation, viewing rates, and market shares for whether to favor print products that do not report regularly on soccer or the club in particular.

The second way to deal with media interest is to influence the journalists' work. This can be a kind of support, as Markus Sieger (1899 Hoffenheim) said: "You can steal the journalists' thunder if you sometimes just say: 'Yes, that's the case. This will happen;'" or the PR practitioners can try to use their network and long-established relationships with specific reporters. In urgent matters, there is a chance to "prevent stories because of good arguments or good relations" (Oliver Schraft, VfB Stuttgart). Katharina Wildermuth (1. FC Nürnberg) explained that she launched a report by a main regional newspaper to level expectations toward a young player after another newspaper had reported very critically about the club's talent.

A third—and the smoothest—way is to guide media attention. "Every Monday we release an interview called 'Standpunkt' [Standpoint] on our Web page with an important person in our club," said Markus Aretz (Borussia Mönchengladbach). "Therewith we want to stake a claim and to give newspapers the chance to cite out of it. This works relatively well." Other PR practitioners confirmed the impression that journalists are thankful to get any kind of information from the club, and that this information is not seldom published one-to-one the next day.

Related to these strategies, club PR practitioners were asked several criteria for successful PR work. Figure 1 illustrates the importance of positive coverage, gaining journalists' trust, and prohibiting critical issues. It shows that positive reporting and prohibiting negative coverage are of main relevance, with 41.2 percent assessing both criteria as very important and 52.9 percent as important.

Independent of these three criteria solely for PR practitioners, both groups were questioned about the relevance of PR "soft skills." Two aspects were revealed as particularly interesting due to a contrary response from the two groups. Spokespersons unanimously rated secrecy as very important, whereas journalists' responses were more inconsistent: very important (38.5 percent), important (46.0 percent), unimportant (12.6 percent), and very unimportant (2.3 percent).[2] Responses also were inconsistent for persuasion. Spokespeople rated this mostly as very important (70.6 percent) or important (23.5 percent), whereas journalists mostly expressed that this is unimportant (48.3 percent) or important (36.2 percent). Just 10.9 percent agreed with the PR practitioners, rating it as having very important relevance.[3]

Finally, the journalists were asked if they approve or deny statements regarding PR purposes (Figure 2). They nearly unanimously said that clubs' efforts to shape a positive image are legitimate and that it is their own journalistic duty to work as independently and unaffected as possible. The statement that the clubs' efforts to influence coverage are too strong was confirmed by 43.7 percent. Only 19.5 percent were convinced that clubs' PR work helps them in their news coverage. The open statements (6.9 percent) did not bring forth any new insights but mostly were descriptions in their own words that were similar to the three already mentioned.

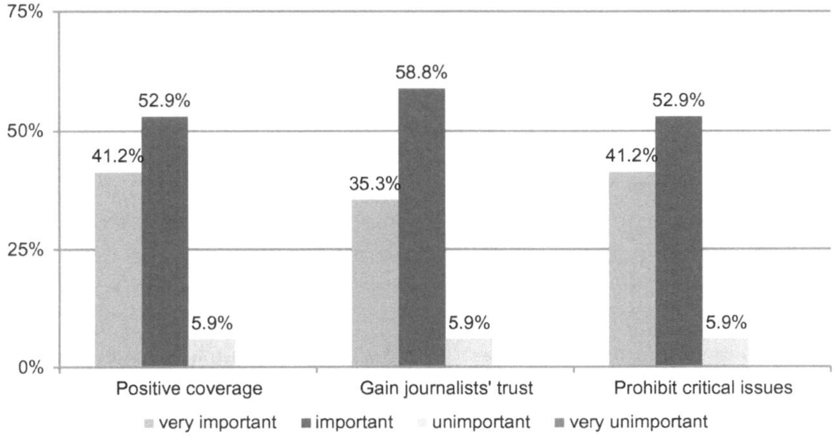

FIGURE 1
Criteria for successful PR (N = 17 spokespersons)

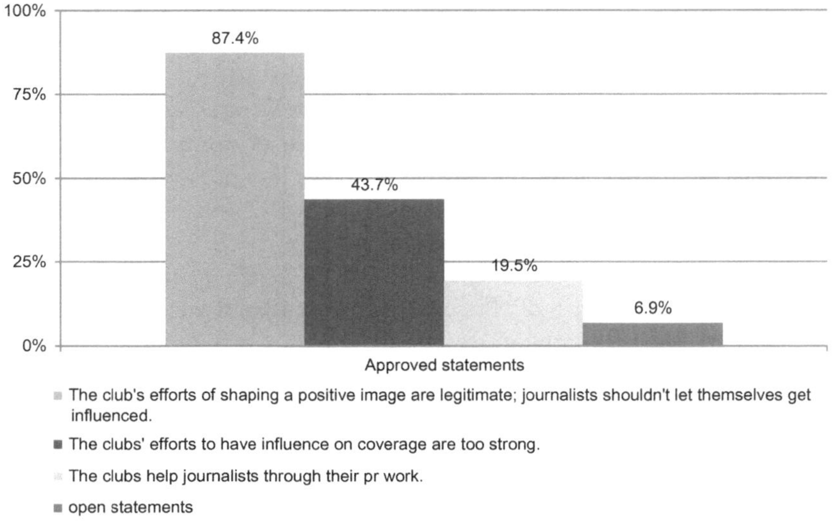

FIGURE 2

Purpose of PR; multiple responses allowed ($N = 174$ journalists)

Information Seeking and News Coverage

Journalists and PR practitioners were called upon to assess collaboration such as handling media inquiries, the influence on journalists' coverage, and dealing with (supposed unfair) coverage and critiques. Figure 3 illustrates how journalists meet spokespersons and how they assess the PR workers' honesty. Less than 6 percent of journalists are sure that their counterparts do not lie. This is an alarming result, challenging the collaboration between both sides and in a broader sense all of Bundesliga soccer journalism. About 46 percent of the journalists believed they are confronted with dishonest PR workers—approximately the same percentage of journalists who assume that PR professionals at least withhold certain information.

Meinolf Sprink (Bayer 04 Leverkusen) illustrates the PR perspective: "By definition we stand on opposite sides of the river. Maybe journalists or PR workers can sometimes swim a bit in this river, but they should never forget from which riverside they come." This may explain the divergent judgments offered in Table 2.

Whereas journalists believe they get short answers only, PR practitioners mostly say they provide detailed answers and additional background information. This indicates an obvious disagreement in openness and transparency. Just 25.3 percent of journalists had the impression of receiving more information than they asked for. None of the PR workers declared just giving brief answers. Of course, response behavior might have been influenced by social desirability, but it reveals PR professionals striving to be cooperative.

In the long run, journalistic coverage is the most problematic issue. It is the product and result of behind-the-scenes cooperation between both groups, and it is what sometimes millions of fans and people track and therewith the basis for shaping public opinion.

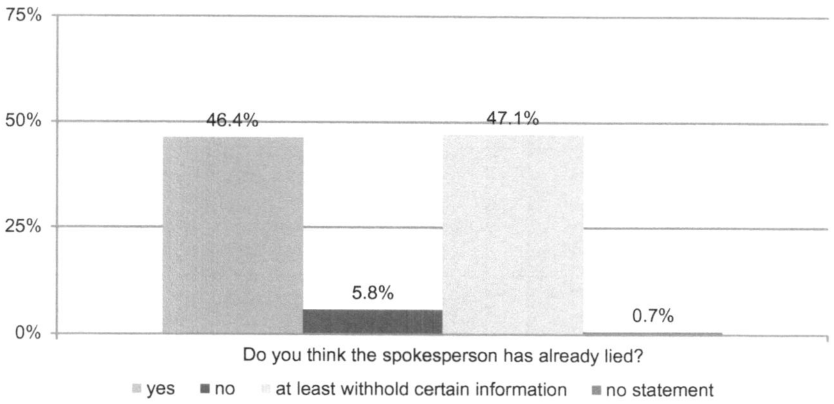

FIGURE 3
Honesty of spokespersons (N = 138 journalists)

TABLE 2
Dealing with media inquiries (%)

Statement	Spokespersons (N = 17)	Journalists (N = 146)
Detailed answer and additional background information	88.2	25.3
Detailed answers	11.8	30.8
Short answers	0	42.5
No statement	0	1.4

> If a newspaper writes throughout the week: "The player isn't able to kick a ball, he's useless," and he plays a bad pass at the beginning, everybody starts to whistle. If they write: "He is a pretty good player," despite three bad passes, everybody says: "Come on, it will work the next time." (Christopher Lymberopoulos, 1. FC Köln)

This statement illustrates the strong influence of media coverage (Table 3). Asked for a justifiable criticism limit, the PR workers almost unanimously explained that they appreciate critique that is not personal. "Roman Weidenfeller, our goalkeeper, once had a season in which he made some mistakes. One newspaper called him 'Weidenfehler' [*fehler* = mistake]," said Josef Schneck (Borussia Dortmund). "I think it's one part of my job to not just say: 'Thank you very much and see you next week.' If critique becomes personal I speak to the journalist and ask: 'Has it been necessary'?"

Following up on this, PR practitioners stated how they deal with supposed (unfair) coverage. As multiple responses were allowed, 100 percent agreed with the statement that they talk to the journalist and clear up the incident; another 23.5 percent said the incident influences the relationship if no clarification follows, and 11.8 percent declared that they do not insist on a clarification due to possible repercussions.

Asked about this issue, journalists confirmed the PR attitude. "The spokesman is worried about thematization of scandals and negative issues" was given as a statement, and 27.5 percent of the journalists assessed it as very accurate, 57.0 percent as accurate, and 14.1 percent as inaccurate; 1.3 percent did not make any assessment.

TABLE 3
Influence on coverage (%)

Statement: Spokespersons influence on media coverage	Spokespersons (N = 17)	Journalists (N = 146)
Very large influence	23.5	2.7
Large influence	58.8	12.3
Some influence	17.6	44.5
No influence	0	40.4

In the past, there have been several occasions on which clubs wanted to guide information seeking and journalistic coverage. In 2009, Bayern Munich fined defender Philipp Lahm who previously had criticized the club, manager Louis van Gaal, and teammates in an interview with a respected newspaper. The interview was organized and conducted without the club's knowledge and published on match day. In a media release, Bayern Munich declared that Lahm had "offended internal rules in a striking and inexcusable manner" (own translation). The club further stated a contractual agreement required that interviews be requested and confirmed by the club.

Questioned about athletes' contractual obligation not to criticize the club, any officials or teammates, journalists assessed such restrictions mostly as harmful for journalism (Figure 4). More than half of the respondents rated such obligations as incapacitating for players. A bit surprising is the result that less than half the journalists indicated that no other sport handles this issue as strictly as soccer. Thus, there must be sports other than soccer in which contractual obligations are at least as harsh. Thirty-eight percent of the journalists stated that they would organize contractual obligations in a similar way if they were working for a club.

An example from the recent past that reveals a strong gatekeeper function and illustrates the PR practitioners' distinct role for journalists' information gathering is the severance of Bayern Munich's medical department in April 2015. After 38 years working for the German championship record-holders, team physician Hans-Wilhelm Müller-Wohlfahrt declared his immediate withdrawal. It was officially known by media reporting that Müller-Wohlfahrt and head coach Pep Guardiola had a strained relationship. As Guardiola was asked for background information on the issue during the first news conference after this incident, media director Markus Hörwick intervened:

> The club has got three, four extremely important days ahead [Champions League quarterfinal second leg against FC Porto after a 1–3 defeat in the first match]. We should not reopen the subject and explain issues which are as they are. It is not ok to interpret anything. (Winter 2015)

To receive a comprehensive evaluation, journalists were asked to give a general grade for the spokespersons' work. The scale was oriented to grading in German schools (1 = very good, 6 = very bad). Due to sometimes low respondent numbers, the grades must be interpreted carefully. In total, 125 journalists rated the practitioners' work with a 2.32. Above average were the clubs 1. FSV Mainz 05 (1.67; $N = 3$), VfL Wolfsburg (1.75; $N = 4$), Borussia Dortmund (1.83; $N = 6$), Bayern Munich (1.96; $N = 27$), SC Freiburg (2.00; $N = 2$), and Borussia Mönchengladbach (2.25; $N = 4$). Eight clubs represented the "midfield:" FC Schalke 04 (2.33; $N = 5$), VfB Stuttgart (2.38; $N = 13$),

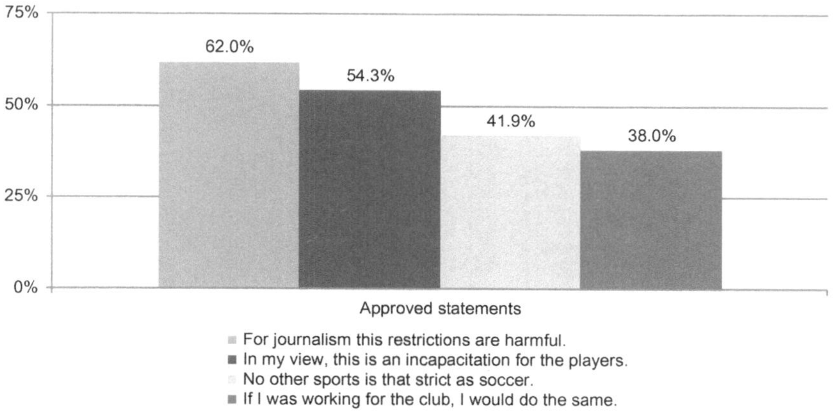

FIGURE 4
Contractual obligation not to criticize; multiple responses allowed (N = 129 journalists)

Hamburger SV (2.67; $N = 12$), Eintracht Frankfurt (2.67; $N = 7$), 1. FC Köln (2.67; $N = 7$), Bayer 04 Leverkusen (2.75; $N = 4$), Hannover 96 (2.75; $N = 4$), and 1. FC Nürnberg (2.86; $N = 7$). At the bottom of the rankings were 1899 Hoffenheim (3.00; $N = 4$), 1. FC Kaiserslautern (3.00; $N = 5$), FC St. Pauli (3.00; $N = 4$), and Werder Bremen (3.57; $N = 7$).

Authorization of Interviews

As mentioned previously, soccer players must participate in interviews with their club's agreement. With the exception of news conferences and mixed-zone interviews, journalists must get permission to print or publish quotes or full interviews. The authorization process often is unpopular with journalists. In this matter, representatives of both sides have been confronted with several issues regarding authorization and its handling (Figure 5).

Whereas journalists mostly state that spokespeople are responsible for authorizing interviews, the PR practitioners preponderantly indicated that they conduct proofreading and approval jointly with the respective player. Just 11.9 percent of journalists did not apply for authorization, and a few journalists sought permission from the player and/or agent directly.

Looking at the handling of authorization requests, results show a "friendly burden." Journalists were given three statements to evaluate. The majority (60.5 percent) agreed with the statement "I mostly get the permission to publish the interview." At least 39.5 percent confirmed the statement "The spokesperson or one of his/her staff members frequently calls me to discuss phrases/expressions." These impressions show the common practice that clubs want to manage communication as best as possible and try to exert their influence. Just 3.1 percent stated, however, that the release of their conducted interview had been forbidden.

But why are changes in interviews necessary? Both sides were asked about this. The proportional distribution reveals interesting differences in terms of the perceptions of PR practitioners and journalists (Figure 6). Whereas 70.6 percent of spokespersons

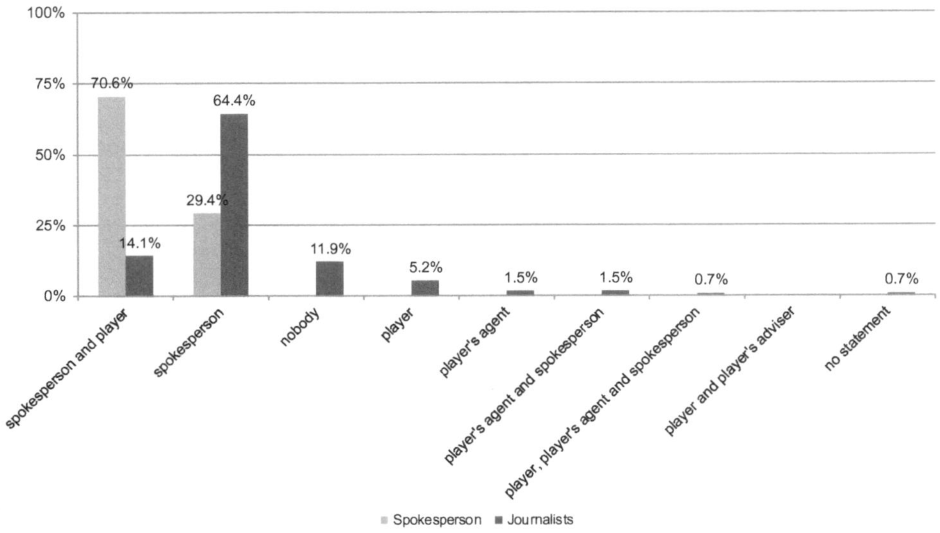

FIGURE 5
Authorization of interviews ($N = 17$ spokespersons; $N = 135$ journalists)

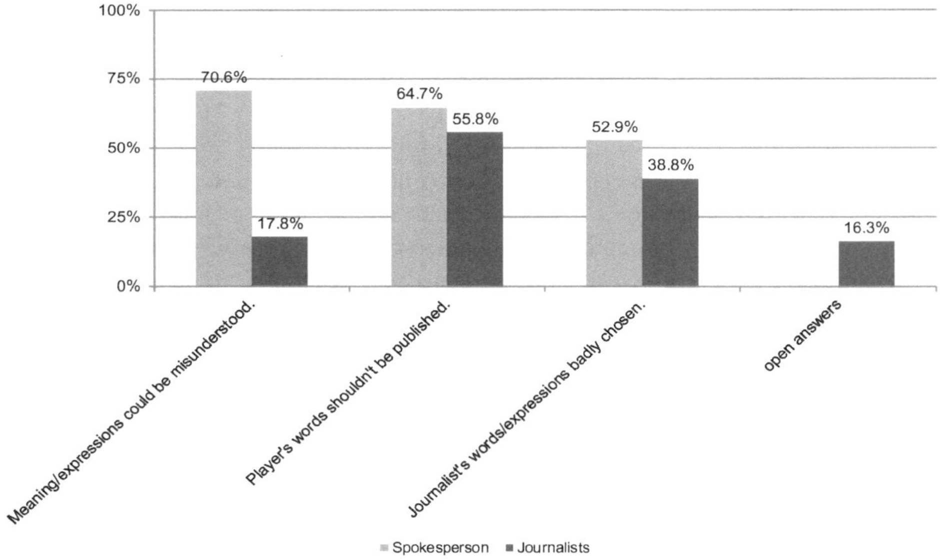

FIGURE 6
Causes for changes in interviews before release; multiple responses allowed ($N = 17$ spokespersons; $N = 135$ journalists)

stated that chosen expressions could be misunderstood, 55.8 percent of journalists declared that "player's words shouldn't be published" as most important reason. Based on this information, one can suspect that spokespeople explain desired changes at the expense of the players.

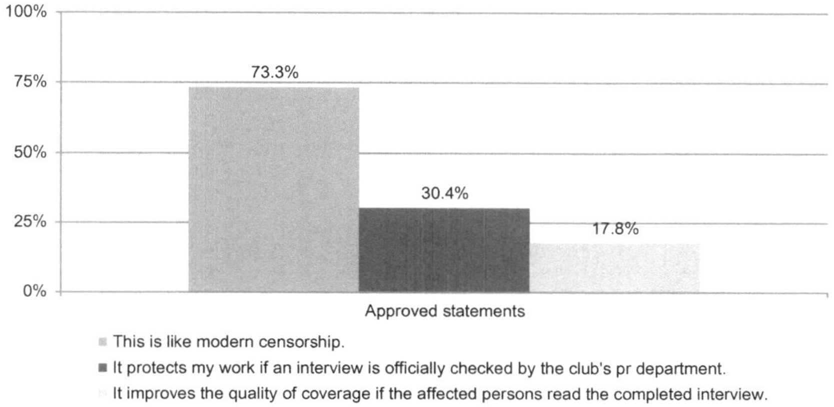

FIGURE 7
Journalists' view on authorization; multiple responses allowed (N = 135 journalists)

Journalists assess authorization of interviews predominantly as modern censorship (Figure 7). Just 30.4 percent of journalists consider an authorization as protection for the work because it prevents subsequent trouble. Only a few journalists were willing to assess authorization as an improvement of journalistic work; sometimes spelling and grammatical mistakes can be eradicated or the club/athlete edits additional information, thereby making the interview more profound and substantial.

The range of authorization practices appears homogeneous and at the same time quite broad. "I try to make as small revisions as possible since I know that it is unpopular with journalists," said Katharina Wildermuth (1. FC Nürnberg). Markus Aretz, working for Borussia Mönchengladbach, is aware of his responsibility: "I think the way you handle authorization of interviews decides whether it is accepted by journalists or not." His colleague Christian Gruber, who formerly worked for 1. FC Kaiserslautern, pointed toward honesty in the clubs: "In particular, it is dreadful when people—mostly not players, but club officials—do not stand by what they said." Other spokespersons did not care about the journalists' authorization perception. "Everybody has to follow some rules. I don't care whether it is unpopular or not," said Christian Bönig (formerly FC St. Pauli, now Hannover 96).

Evaluation of Mutual Relationships

Finally, journalists and PR practitioners were questioned about different aspects in terms of their mutual relationship. They assessed some statements to characterize their interdependent relationship (Table 4). Multiple responses were allowed.

The statement that received most consent focused on the professional collaboration between the groups. "Knowing the other's needs/requirement" was the second most important assessment. Looking at the two remaining statements, however, responses turned out slightly different. Whereas spokespersons rated collaboration as "give and take" rather than as "friendly interaction without any problems," journalists preferred "friendly interaction" to "give and take." The following quote illustrates a give-and-take mentality on the club's side.

TABLE 4
Assessment of relation (%)

Statement: The relation between spokespersons and journalists is characterized by ...	Spokespersons (N = 17)	Journalists (N = 153)
A professional collaboration	100	62.1
Knowing the other's needs/requirements	64.7	43.1
A "give and take"	29.4	20.9
A friendly interaction without any problems	11.8	28.1

> There are journalists with which I have this ideal relation. Trust is grown over the years. I can tell them everything and at the end of our conversation I can ask: "What will you write for tomorrow now?" Or I can call him and say: "What is your story for tomorrow?" You can talk about it openly. There are several journalists with which you can have such a good relationship. But you cannot tie it up to specific media. Thus, you cannot say you can work this way solely with serious quality newspapers and not with tabloid press. Moreover, it depends on the person and the relation that is grown over time. (Markus Aretz, Borussia Mönchengladbach)

Jörn Wolf (Hamburger SV) stressed development in the media business and focused on his mission: "Journalists want more and more, and we [in the clubs] try to go further and further away. Nevertheless you have to try to bring it together." To better classify collaboration in the German Bundesliga, journalists were asked to compare soccer with media relations in other sports (Figure 8).

In terms of collaboration (easier versus more difficult), access (more open versus more reserved), interaction (more personal versus more impersonal), and sentiment (more relaxed versus more formal), journalists voted almost entirely in favor of other sports. Only professionality of PR work was an advantage for soccer as opposed to other sports. Some spokespersons' statements supported the journalists' assessments, indicating a sometimes strained relationship. "I am annoyed because three or four years ago we have played in the third division. They are privileged to report about a Bundesliga soccer club. The most important sports issue is content of their newspaper," explained Markus Sieger (1899 Hoffenheim), tracing back to journalists' individual dissatisfaction and high expectations.

Christopher Lymberopoulos (1. FC Köln) emphasized the competitive media realm in the German Bundesliga: "There is big competition. If I give one journalist some information, the other one is pissed off. When I decide to make a daily press conference, they say: 'No, we don't want this either, because we will then have similar reporting.' I always live in this field of tension." His colleague Meinolf Sprink (Bayer 04 Leverkusen) supported the perception of a tense relationship: "Per definition journalists are opponents. I have got a mandate, he has got a mandate—this is escalation level."

Based upon this mandate definition, a question addressed the mutual dependency of both stakeholders (Table 5). Roughly the same percentage acknowledged an equal dependency. The remaining portion agreed that journalists are more dependent on spokespeople than vice versa. Just 11.1 percent of journalists and 5.9 percent of PR practitioners said that spokespersons are more dependent.

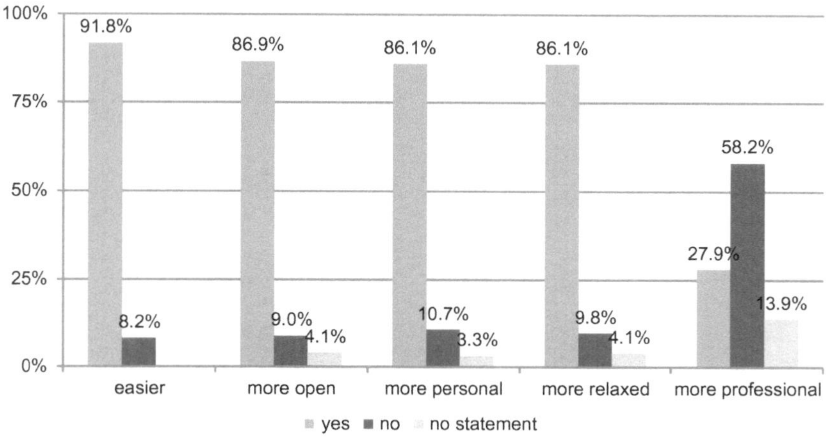

FIGURE 8
Comparison of PR work for other sports with Bundesliga (N = 122 journalists)

TABLE 5
Mutual dependency (%)

Statement	Spokespersons (N = 17)	Journalists (N = 153)
Equal dependency	47.1	47.7
Journalists are more dependent	47.1	41.2
Spokespersons are more dependent	5.9	11.1

> I tell everyone: "Come in!" I'd like to have a collegiate relation with journalists ... Once I was a young journalist, too. I know that everyone enjoys their job when they come to our club grounds and say: "Ok, today Bayern Munich. That's cool" ... A personal relation to journalists is important because you can clarify many things on a personal basis. That is not possible when you have got just a distanced and official contact. (Markus Hörwick, Bayern Munich)

Thomas Spiegel (FC Schalke 04) pointed out another important attitude toward each other:

> Mutual respect and mutual understanding should be the basis for a fruitful culture which is not necessarily dominated by bright sunshine. If this is recognized, one can solve conflicts. We should acknowledge and accept that one has to get along with each other—not to forget that we do not sit in the same boat.

Directing the attention to journalists' expectations for the future, one has to be worried (Figure 9). The majority expects increasing pressure on their upcoming reporting.

Discussion

The purpose of the study was to examine the media–practitioner relationship in sports' PR, which has been influenced by the professionalization of PR and an economic

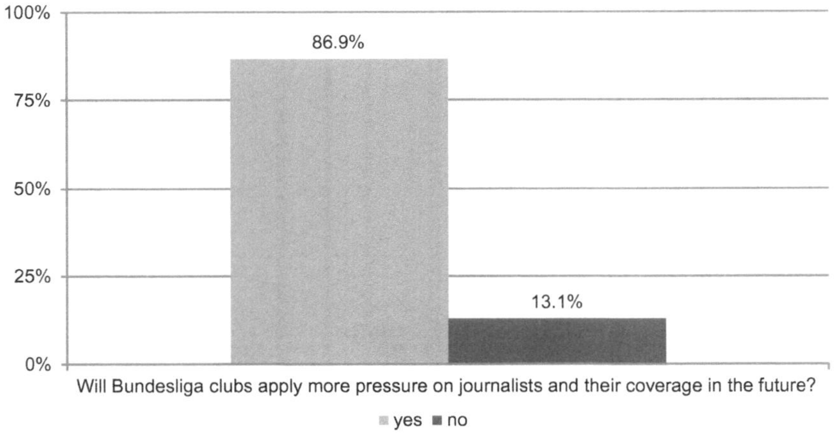

FIGURE 9
Outlook for increasing pressure (*N* = 122 journalists)

struggle in journalism, particularly in print media. The study focused on the collaboration of PR practitioners and journalists in the context of professional soccer in Germany. Swirled by digital progression, clubs have built their own communication channels and interact with interest groups without intermediaries such as journalists.

The results confirm an imbalance of power and dependency. Journalists are more reliant on PR professionals than vice versa in the German Bundesliga context. Interestingly, both parties agreed with this appraisal. A strained collaboration does not necessarily mean a bad relationship because tension between two fields of practice can be "a sign of health in a media ecosystem" (Macnamara 2014, 747).

The majority of journalists and all of the surveyed spokespersons, however, see an all-in-all professional collaboration with members of the other side. A critical issue is the authorization of interviews; 75 percent of journalists regarded this as a form of modern censorship, just 30 percent considered it a kind of journalistic protection, and less than 18 percent appreciated an improvement in coverage when sources read an interview ahead of its release. The most important issue for changes in interviews during authorization was PR practitioners' worry about misunderstandings of what has been said, something journalists regarded as a muzzle for players. The majority of journalists regarded as harmful to their reporting players' contractual obligations against criticizing teammates, the manager, and club. More than half the journalists see this is as incapacitating for players.

Regarding spokespersons' influence on media coverage, journalists and PR practitioners provided contradicting results. The answers might be influenced by social desirability. The spokespersons' job is to manage the news agenda and the club's reputation. In contrast, journalists are expected to report critically and unaffectedly. Therefore, spokespersons attested to a (very) large influence whereas journalists preponderantly assessed none or just some impact. According to Sallot and Johnson (2006), journalists admitting a higher influence for PR practitioners on the news reported having a better relationship with the practitioners. If this holds true for the German Bundesliga, relations ought to be relatively bad.

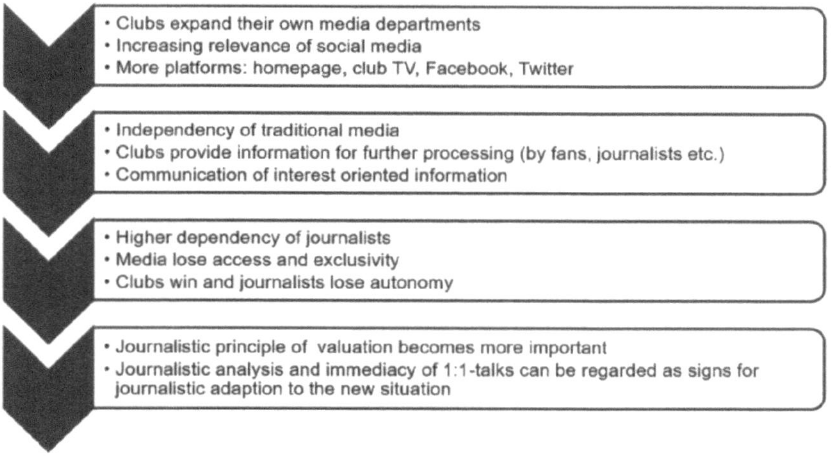

FIGURE 10
Process of PR impact on journalists' profession

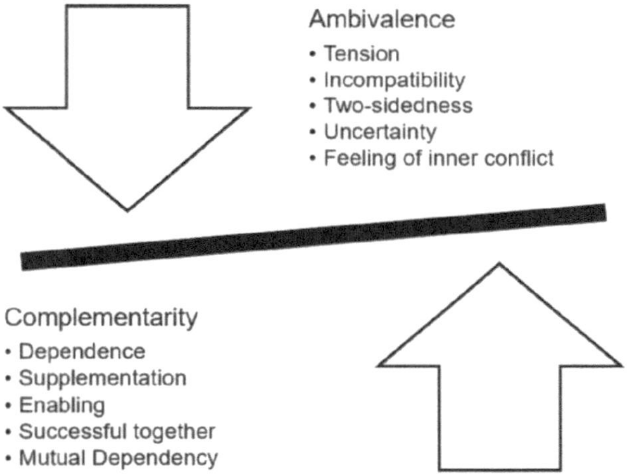

FIGURE 11
Ambivalence and complementarity of clubs' spokespersons and journalists

Dealing with media inquiries is a crucial aspect of the professional collaboration between journalists and PR practitioners. As above with spokespersons' influence on media coverage, the results were contradictory. PR professionals said they provide detailed answers and additional background information, whereas journalists stated they mostly receive just brief answers. Additionally, journalists questioned spokespersons' honesty; less than 6 percent were convinced that the spokesperson they regularly cooperate with has not yet lied.

Handling demand for sports information, PR practitioners try to shape a positive club image and reputation and to avoid coverage of adverse issues. To establish a fruitful collaboration with journalists, spokespersons first and foremost try to gain journalists' trust. Journalists assess these efforts as legitimate and consider it their duty not to be influenced but to provide unbiased reports. Only 20 percent of media professionals interpreted the clubs' PR work as helpful, but both parties assessed the representatives of the other side as relevant. Print journalists remain very important for the spokespersons' work, even above television, radio, and online journalists. Thus, print journalists in the Bundesliga context still resist the print media market crisis in Germany. On the other hand, journalists assess spokespersons as mediators between the clubs and media. More than 25 percent of the print reporters surveyed said PR practitioners were service provider for journalists.

Conclusion

This study addressed the media–practitioner relationship in sports, which had been comparatively uninvestigated before (Isaacson 2010, 604). A mixed method of expert interviews followed by a questionnaire with PR practitioners in the German Bundesliga accompanied by an online survey of print journalists reporting on these clubs addressed the quality of media relations as well as experiences and the perception of club spokespersons and vice versa. Because most studies available chose quantitative instruments (Jungels 2007; Schaffrath 2012; Ziegler 2008), the main part of this study was a personal expert survey with the PR heads of all the German Bundesliga clubs.

Within the past decade, the clubs steadily expanded their media staff. Driven by the internet, social media, and new communication outlets, they established platforms such as homepages, club television, and profiles on social network sites. Digital technology gave the teams the opportunity to communicate directly with target groups without intermediaries such as journalists. Thus, the clubs provide interest-oriented information for further processing (Figure 10).

The clubs' new opportunities create challenges for journalists. Because most of the clubs face high media demands, they offer regular news conferences for all journalists. The chance to receive exclusive information has dropped drastically. Instead, clubs publish news on their own media outlets first, particularly via digital media. Traditional media have lost access to officials, managers, and players, and with this they lost exclusivity of information.

Consequently, as the Bundesliga clubs won autonomy, journalists lost it because they now are reliant on the (interest-oriented) information provided by the clubs. Journalists nowadays often receive common information; therefore, the journalistic function must be questioned in the Bundesliga context. Several adaptations indicate realignment of professional sports journalism. The principle of valuation seems to be more important. This is in line with an increase in interviews in general sports reporting and expert interviews during live sports broadcasting (Grimmer, Horky, and Winkler 2016).

Tying to the media lifecycle (Lehman-Wilzig and Cohen-Avigdor 2004), distinct adaptations have become obvious in recent years in professional soccer coverage. Journalists have been forced to implement innovative programs and formats to be able to provide fans and users with additional value. Thus, it can be concluded that the digital revolution has initiated a journalistic advancement and changed journalistic roles (Gibbs and Haynes 2013). In the German media market, new channels (24-hour live sports broadcasting), new programs (90-minute discussions on soccer by former players using specific television tools for illustration), and new formats (3D tactical analysis) have emerged.

Media relations in the German Bundesliga hint at an imbalance of power in highly demanded sports. Focusing on professional sports, the German media market seems comparable to other European media markets. Taking into account that television rights holders usually have the easiest access to the clubs, print media must find their way. Additionally, due to online media, the print media must differentiate itself from other media outlets and handle the periodical publication handicap.

The most important aspect that makes this study internationally transferable is the power of soccer in Germany. One can assume that print journalists are confronted with similar challenges covering other famous, financially powerful, and socially demanded leagues such as the English Premier League, Primera División in Spain, or the professional sports leagues in the United States, and sports series events like Formula 1. Thus, it can be hypothesized that findings existent in terms of first division soccer in Germany can be transferred to other popular sport leagues worldwide.

Professional collaboration of spokespersons and media representatives is characterized by ambivalence and complementarity (Figure 11). Distrust, incompatibility of interests, and skepticism toward the other's side honesty can lead to a feeling of inner conflict. On one hand, journalists need PR practitioners for information and access to players, managers, and officials; on the other hand, journalists' work was easier without spokespersons as intermediaries. The same applies for PR professionals; they know the importance of traditional media, but they also know about journalists seeking negative aspects, conflicts, and scandals. Yet, both parties maintain a complementary relationship and are reliant on the other side to do a good job every day. Journalists and spokespersons are mutually dependent because they enable each other's work. There were no spokespersons without any journalists, and journalists are conditional on information provided by PR practitioners.

Limitations

Although some kind of generalizability was sought, the study solely analyzed media relations in the German Bundesliga soccer realm, and on the media side only print journalists were surveyed. Thus, it is hard (not to say inadmissible) to speak about media relations in general. As always, the applied methods have not just strengths but also weaknesses. Expert interviews are reliant on the interviewer and personal sympathy between the academic and the interviewee. A replication of this study is impossible because the conversational situation would change.

Future studies first should take into account not just print reporters, but also television, radio, and online journalists. Secondly, researchers could undertake a comparative study including leagues and/or sports from different countries to provide evidence of generalizability of the findings.

DISCLOSURE STATEMENT

No potential conflict of interest was reported by the author.

FUNDING

This work was supported by a PhD bursary at the University of Hamburg.

NOTES

1. All PR practitioners' statements were translated by the author.
2. No statement was made by 0.6 percent of the journalists.
3. Journalists' residual response behavior: very unimportant (4.0 percent), no statement (0.6 percent); spokespersons residual response behavior: unimportant (5.9 percent).

REFERENCES

Agf. 2016. "Jahreshitlisten." Arbeitsgemeinschaft Fernsehforschung ["Annual Ranking." Television Research Partnership], February 29. https://www.agf.de/daten/tvdaten/hitliste/?name=hitliste_20jahre

Anderson, Doug. 2009. "Is the great American newspaper dead?" The Nielsen Company, April 13. http://www.nielsen.com/us/en/insights/news/2009/is-the-great-american-newspaper-dead.html

Bowman, Nicholas D., and Gregory A. Cranmer. 2014. "SocialMediaSport: The Fan as a (Mediated) Participant in Spectator Sports." In *Routledge Handbook of Sport and New Media*, edited by Andrew C. Billings and Marie Hardin, 213–224. New York: Routledge.

Boyle, Raymond. 2006. *Sports Journalism: Context and Issues*. London: Sage.

Boyle, Raymond. 2012. "Social Media Sport? Journalism, Public Relations and Sport." In *We Love to Hate Each Other: Mediated Football Fan Culture*, edited by Roy Krøvel and Thore Roksvold, 45–62. Gothenburg: Nordicom.

Boyle, Raymond. 2013. "Reflections on Communication and Sport: On Journalism and Digital Culture." *Communication & Sport* 1 (1–2): 88–99.

Boyle, Raymond, and Richard Haynes. 2014. "Sport, Public Relations and Social Media." In *Routledge Handbook of Sport and New Media*, edited by Andrew C. Billings and Marie Hardin, 133–142. New York: Routledge.

Burk, Verena, Christoph G. Grimmer, and Tim Pawlowski. 2016. "'Same, Same—but Different!' On Consumers' Use of Corporate PR Media in Sports." *Journal of Sport Management* 30 (4): 353–368. doi:10.1123/JSM.2015-0180.

Butler, Bryan, Matthew H. Zimmerman, and Sharon Hutton. 2013. "Turning the Page with Newspapers: Influence of the Internet on Sports Coverage." In *Routledge Handbook of Sport Communication*, edited by Paul M. Pedersen, 219–227. London: Routledge.

Coombs, Danielle S., and Anne Osborne. 2012. "Sports Journalists and England's Barclays Premier League: A Case Study Examining Reporters' Takes on Modern Football." *International Journal of Sport Communication* 5 (3): 413–425.

Curran, James, and J. Jean Seaton. 2009. *Power Without Responsibility: The Press, Broadcasting and Internet in Britain*. London: Routledge.

Davies, Nick. 2009. *Flat Earth News: An Award-Winning Reporter Exposes Falsehood, Distortion and Propaganda in the Global Media*. London: Vintage.

DFL. 2016a. "Bundesliga Report 2016. Die wirtschaftliche Situation im Lizenzfußball [Bundesliga Report 2016. The economic situation in German licensed soccer]." Deutsche Fußball Liga, January 22. http://s.bundesliga.de/assets/doc/1070000/1066709_original.pdf.

DFL. 2016b. "DFL überspringt erstmals Milliarden-Marke bei nationalen Medien-Rechten: Pro Saison durchschnittlich 1,16 Milliarden Euro *ab* 2017/18 [DFL exceeds billion mark in national media rights for the first time: on average 1.16 billion Euro per season from 2017/18 on]." Deutsche Fußball Liga, June 9. http://s.bundesliga.de/assets/doc/1090000/1087912_original.pdf.

Ellert, Guido. 2006. *Konzilianz von PR und Medien im Sport. Theoretische Annäherung und empirische Erkenntnisse* [Conciliation of public relations and media in sports. Theoretical approach and empirical insights]. Dissertation, Technische Universität München.

English, Peter. 2016. "Twitter's Diffusion in Sports Journalism: Role Models, Laggards and Followers of the Social Media Innovation." *New Media & Society* 18 (3): 484–501. doi:10.1177/1461444814544886.

Fenz, Karin. 2009. *Beruf: Pressesprecher. Das Berufsbild des Öffentlichkeitsarbeiters einer Sportorganisation anhand des Österreichischen Schwimmverbandes (OSV)* [Profession: spokesman. The job profile of public relations practitioners in sport organizations in the context of the Austrian Swimming Federation (OSV)]. Hamburg: Diplomica.

Gibbs, Chris, and Richard Haynes. 2013. "A Phenomenological Investigation into How Twitter has Changed the Nature of Sport Media Relations." *International Journal of Sport Communication* 6 (4): 394–408.

Grimmer, Christoph G. 2014. *Kooperation oder Kontrolle? Eine empirische Untersuchung zum Spannungsverhältnis von Pressesprechern in der Fußball-Bundesliga und Journalisten* [Cooperation or Control? An empirical study on the collaboration of public relations practitioners in the German Bundesliga and journalists]. Köln: Herbert von Halem Verlag.

Grimmer, Christoph G., Thomas Horky, and Sabine Winkler. 2016. "Fußball satt! Aber was läuft da eigentlich? Eine Analyse zu Fußballübertragungen im Fernsehen [Soccer in abundance! But what is actually reported? An analysis on soccer broadcastings in German television]." *Fachjournalist Online*, February 11. http://www.fachjournalist.de/fussball-satt-aber-was-laeuft-da-eigentlich-eine-analyse-zu-fussball-uebertragungen-im-fernsehen/.

Haynes, Richard. 2013. "Sports Journalists, Social Networks, and Strategic Communications Management in the UK." In *Crossmediale Kommunikation und Verwertung von Sportveranstaltungen: Tagungsband zum Internationalen Hamburger Symposium, Sport, Ökonomie und Medien' 2012*, edited by Andreas Hebbel-Seeger, and Thomas Horky, 46–58. Aachen: Meyer & Meyer.

Hobsbawn, Julia, ed. 2010. *Where the Truth Lies: Trust and Morality in the Business of PR Journalism and Communications*. London: Atlantic Books.

Horky, Thomas, and Jörg-Uwe Nieland. 2013. *International Sports Press Survey*. Norderstedt: BoD.

Hutchins, Brett, and David Rowe. 2010. "Reconfiguring Media Sport for the Online World: An Inquiry Into 'Sports News and Digital Media'." *International Journal of Communication* 4: 696–718.

Isaacson, Tom. 2010. "Sports Public Relations." In *Handbook of Public Relations*, edited by Robert L. Heath, 599–609. Los Angeles, CA: Sage.

Jordaan, Marenet. 2013. "Poke me, I'm a Journalist: The Impact of Facebook and Twitter on Newsroom Routines and Cultures at two South African Weeklies." *Ecquid Novi: African Journalism Studies* 34 (1): 21–35. doi:10.1080/02560054.2013.767421.

Jungels, Dirk. 2007. *Professionelle Kommunikatoren in professionellen Clubs. Eine theoretische und empirische Studie bei europäischen Fußballvereinen* [Professional communicators in professional clubs. A theoretical and empirical study on European soccer clubs]. Köln-Pulheim: MedienSportVerlag.

Kian, Edward M., and Ray Murray. 2014. "Curmudgeons but Yet Adapters: Impact of Web 2.0 and Twitter on Newspaper Sports Journalists' Jobs, Responsibilities, and Routines." *#ISOJ Journal* 4 (1): 61–77.

Kian, Edward M., and Matthew M. Zimmerman. 2012. "The Medium of the Future: Top Sports Writers Discuss Transitioning from Newspapers to Online Journalism." *International Journal of Sport Communication* 5 (3): 285–304.

Lecheler, Sophie, and Sanne Kruikemeier. 2016. "Re-evaluating Journalistic Routines in a Digital Age: A Review of Research on the Use of Online sources." *New Media & Society* 18 (1): 156–171. doi:10.1177/1461444815600412.

Lehman-Wilzig, Sam, and Nava Cohen-Avigdor. 2004. "The Natural Life Cycle of New Media Evolution: Inter-Media Struggle for Survival in the Internet age." *New Media & Society* 6 (6): 707–730. doi:10.1177/146144804042524.

Li, Bo, Sarah Stokowski, Steven W. Dittmore, and Olan K. M. Scott. 2015. "For Better or For Worse: The Impact of Social Media on Chinese Sports Journalists." *Communication & Sport*. doi:10.1177/2167479515617279. http://com.sagepub.com/content/early/2015/11/27/2167479515617279.abstract

Macnamara, Jim. 2014. "Journalism–PR Relations Revisited: The Good News, the Bad News, and Insights into Tomorrow's News." *Public Relations Review* 40 (5): 739–750. doi:10.1016/j.pubrev.2014.07.002.

McEnnis, Simon. 2013. "Raising Our Game: Effects of Citizen Journalism on Twitter for Professional Identity and Working Practices of British Sport Journalists." *International Journal of Sport Communication* 6 (4): 423–433.

Meikle, Graham, and Sherman Young, eds. 2011. *Media Convergence: Networked Digital Media in Everyday Life*. London: Palgrave.

Neijens, Peter, and Edith Smit. 2006. "Dutch Public Relations Practitioners and Journalists: Antagonists no More." *Public Relations Review* 32 (3): 232–240. doi:10.1016/j.pubrev.2006.05.015.

Nölleke, Daniel, Christoph G. Grimmer, and Thomas Horky. 2016. "News Sources and Follow-Up Communication—Facets of Complementarity between Sports Journalism and Social Media." *Journalism Practice*. doi:10.1080/17512786.2015.1125761. http://www.tandfonline.com/doi/full/10.1080/17512786.2015.1125761

Paulussen, Steve, and Raymond A. Harder. 2014. "Social Media References in Newspapers: Facebook, Twitter and YouTube as Sources in Newspaper Journalism." *Journalism Practice* 8 (5): 542–551. doi:10.1080/17512786.2014.894327.

Pedersen, Paul M. 2014. "The Changing Role of Sports Media Producers." In *Routledge Handbook of Sport and New Media*, edited by Andrew C. Billings and Marie Hardin, 101–109. New York: Routledge.

Pincus, J. David, Tony Rimmer, Robert E. Rayfield, and Fritz Cropp. 1993. "Newspaper Editors' Perceptions of Public Relations: How Business, News, and Sports Editors Differ." *Journal of Public Relations Research* 5 (1): 27–45. doi:10.1207/s1532754xjprr0501_02.

Sallot, Lynne M., and Elizabeth A. Johnson. 2006. "Investigating Relationships Between Journalists and Public Relations Practitioners: Working Together to Set, Frame and Build the Public Agenda, 1991–2004." *Public Relations Review* 32: 151–159. doi:10.1016/j.pubrev.2006.02.008.

Schaffrath, Michael. 2012. *Sport-PR als Beruf. Empirische Studie zum Aufgaben- und Anforderungsprofil von Pressesprechern im Sport* [Sport Public Relations as a profession. Empirical study on duties and requirements of public relations practitioners]. Berlin: LIT.

Schultz, Brad, and Mary L. Sheffer. 2010. "An Exploratory Study of How Twitter Is Affecting Sports Journalism." *International Journal of Sport Communication* 3 (2): 226–239.

Shaw, Thomasena, and Candace White. 2004. "Public Relations and Journalism Educators' Perceptions of Media Relations." *Public Relations Review* 30: 493–502. doi:10.1016/j.pubrev.2004.08.004.

Sheffer, Mary L., and Brad Schultz. 2010. "Paradigm Shift or Passing Fad? Twitter and Sports Journalism." *International Journal of Sport Communication* 3 (4): 472–484.

Stoldt, G. Clayton, Stephen W. Dittmore, and Scott E. Branvold. 2012. *Sport Public Relations: Managing Stakeholder Communication*. Champaign, IL: Human Kinetics.

Sugden, John, and Alan Tomlinson. 2010. "What Beckham Had for Breakfast: The Rolling Menu of 24/7 Sports News." In *The Rise of 24-Hour News Television. Global Perspectives*, edited by Stephen Cushion, and Justin Lewis, 151–166. New York: Lang.

Suggs, David Welch. 2015. "Valuing the Media: Access and Autonomy as Functions of Legitimacy for Journalists." *International Journal of Sport Communication* 8 (1): 46–67.

Suggs, Welch 2016. "Tensions in the Press Box: Understanding Relationships Among Sports Media and Source Organizations." *Communication & Sport* 4 (3): 261–281. doi:10.1177/2167479515577191.

Whiteside, Erin A. 2014. "New Media and the Changing Role of Sports Information." In *Routledge Handbook of Sport and New Media*, edited by Andrew C. Billings, and Marie Hardin, 143–152. New York: Routledge.

Williams, Jo, and Susan J. Chinn. 2010. "Meeting Relationship-Marketing Goals through Social Media: A Conceptual Model for Sport Marketers." *International Journal of Sport Communication* 3 (4): 422–437.

Wilson, Drew, and Dustin W. Supa. 2013. "Examining Modern Media Relations: An Exploratory Study of the Effect of Twitter on the Public Relations-Journalist Relationship." *Public Relations Journal* 7 (3): 1–20.

Winter, Sebastian. 2015. "Pressekonferenz als Farce: Maulkorb für Guardiola [Press conference as a farce: muzzle for Guardiola]." Spiegel Online, April 17. http://www.spiegel.de/sport/fussball/mueller-wohlfahrt-pressekonferenz-mit-guardiola-wird-zur-farce-a-1029219.html.

Ziegler, Hannah. 2008. *PR in der Bundesliga—zwischen Ehrenamt und Professionalität. Eine Online-Befragung von Pressesprechern aus Basketball, Handball und Volleyball.* (unpublished diploma thesis).

THE STATE OF SPORT PHOTOJOURNALISM
Concepts, practice and challenges

Richard Haynes, Adrian Hadland and **Paul Lambert**

Based on a global survey of photojournalism and case studies of recent transformations in the use of photography in sport, this paper critically analyses current professional practices of sport photojournalists focusing on the contemporary challenges faced by this industry. Rhetoric proclaiming the death of the photographer in the age of video technology and self-mass communication of digital photographs has presented a major challenge to the survival of photographers and photography as a professional practice in news media. In the specific field of sport photojournalism, photographers have faced added challenges of accreditation to sport with the selective access to sporting venues or events through commercial licensing of "preferred media partners" and increasing management of "image rights" and anti-piracy measures. This has occurred at a time when sport images and the digital distribution of sporting images are greater than ever. The data for this article are taken from a World Press Photo Foundation–University of Stirling longitudinal project on photojournalism and represents the views and experiences of over 700 photographers who are engaged in sports photojournalism.

Introduction

> To save money, instead of hiring real sports photographers, sports/news publications are telling their sportswriters to shoot games with their cellphones and use these still pictures to illustrate their sports columns. This puts freelance sports photographers out of work, and results in lousy pictures. (Sports photojournalist, World Press Photo survey, 2016)

London. Thursday 9 August 2012. Jamaican sprinter Usain Bolt wins the 200 metres Olympic final, making him the first man to successfully defend both Olympic sprint titles. "Half man, half superhero", gushed the admiring *Daily Telegraph* of London. Within minutes of his success, Bolt borrows a camera from one of the photographers crowding around him and mimics their moves, down on one knee, turning the camera on the cameras. Then, with a Jamaican flag wrapped around his shoulders, Bolt assumes the frozen archer position that has become his signature. In mid pose, he turns to his right and smiles. The photograph is used across the entire front page not just of the *Telegraph* the next morning, which accompanies the image with the words

"The Greatest", but all around the world. The use of powerfully evocative images in print, online and on television has not just tracked Bolt's stellar career, a partnership he acknowledged with his little camera show in the Olympic Stadium in London, it has been a fundamental component of the transformation of sport in the contemporary era.

But, just as sports and sports journalism have evolved and changed, so too has the process by which sport images are captured, transmitted and published. Sports photojournalists[1] must grapple with a range of challenges that collectively threaten the very sustainability and future of their art, ironically at a moment when the image has never been as ubiquitous or as important as an expression of human creativity or as a medium for demonstrating athletic prowess. With billions of images uploaded on to the internet every day, the field has become crowded. The massification of image production has also coincided with media company cutbacks as legacy businesses struggle to adjust to the disruption of the digital era. If any sector has suffered from the commonly described "crisis" of journalism (Reinardy 2011), photojournalists have been among them. In newspapers, photographers and photographic departments are frequently the first to go, at times suffering disproportionate cutbacks, especially in America (Anderson 2013; Mortensen 2014). The findings of this research reflect the impact of this crisis on the work patterns and prospects of those making a living illustrating news storytelling with images. There have been shifts, too, within the photographic industry marked notably by the concentration of photographic agencies, many of which have been bought up by big corporate players such as Getty Images.[2]

In the specific field of sport photojournalism, photographers have faced added challenges of accreditation to sport with the selective access to sporting venues or events through commercial licensing of "preferred media partners" (Edwards 2015; Greenslade 2010, 2013) and increasing management of "image rights" and anti-piracy measures (Haynes 2007). This has occurred at a time when sport images and the digital distribution of sporting images proliferate.

This confluence of developments provokes a series of questions concerning the current state and future of sports photography: How are sports photographers coping in the digital era? What are the key challenges they face? Is there a future for professional sports photography?

Surprisingly, very little research has been conducted on photographers generally and there is almost nothing on sports photographers in particular. This article aims to begin the process of addressing this absence. It does so by considering recent data from more than 700 professional photographers involved in sport to varying degrees. This study focuses on the changing practices of sport photojournalism based on an international survey of photographers. It is therefore based on the experiences, perceptions, professional values and practices of sport photojournalists, which have been relatively ignored in the field of sport and communications more broadly. The results provide fascinating insights into the world of sports photography and into the challenges, opportunities and threats faced by sports photographers on a daily basis.

Sport Photojournalism: Literature Review

Beyond work commissioned by World Press Photo (see, especially, Campbell 2013) only a handful of research studies have been published on photojournalists as a group (Caple 2013; Mortensen 2014; Pantti and Bakker 2009; Papadopolous and Pantti 2011; Taylor 2000). Often this research included other groups, such as amateur or citizen photographers (see Allan 2015). Mäenpää's (2014) is one of the few papers dedicated specifically to photojournalists. Mäenpää's work is based on Finnish data obtained from 20 interviews and an online survey of 200 people and while the focus is on photojournalists' values, the respondents include a wide range of people associated with the photography industry, such as graphic designers and art directors. Vauclare and Debeauvais (2015) have also published a French-language study of French photographers commissioned by the Ministry of Culture and Communication (for an overview, see Sutton 2015).

Sport photojournalism is an established part of the sport–media complex, which has been identified as the dominant mode of elite sport and increasingly is characterised as being heavily commodified, mediatised and global in a digitally networked communications environment (Hutchins and Rowe 2012). In spite of the broadening of the media–sport complex, both in terms of networked media sport and globalisation, the cultures of sport continue to reflect some deep-seated prejudices in terms of sexism, racism and homophobia (Messner and Cooky 2010). As well as the very important issue of media representation of women, ethnic minorities and the LGBT community in sport, the issue of equality in media sport and communications is of genuine concern in the context of this study. For example, the paucity of women in sport media professions and the "gendered" roles which they tend to occupy continues to present a major challenge to the industry in terms of equality and diversity (Franks and O'Neill 2015).

Recent studies on the changing nature of photojournalism, both in terms of the professional role of photographers in news outlets and transformations in visual storytelling, have also emphasised the impact of processes of digitisation and networked communications on the profession (Campbell 2013; Yaschur 2011; Zavoina and Reichert 2000).

As has been recognised more broadly in the media and communications industries, digitisation has transformed "media work" (Deuze 2007) and convergent, networked communications have transformed the power relations between producers, distributors and consumers of media (Castells 2013). Most notable in the case of photojournalists has been a shift from the standard production of the printed still image to more diversified roles of digital visual storytelling; producing videos and slideshows for online news content, which sit alongside the more established editorial shots of events, people and places.

One of the central questions such developments pose is what are the continuities and discontinuities from print photojournalism, long established in the twentieth century, and the user-created, software-enabled, networked photography, which has blossomed in the early twenty-first century? A common observation would suggest there are significant discontinuities in terms of the scale of popular photography and image distribution, but it is less clear whether the actual form of photography has been transformed quite as radically. As Manovich (2016) has identified, this raises a further question concerning variability, that is, has the recent explosion of digital photography led to more diversity in image capture and distribution? Or, conversely, has it led to more repetition of themes, uniformity and social mimicry? For example, while "the selfie" may be a new visual form, it is also a uniformly mimicked and creatively constrained visual culture.

Newsrooms and photographers, of course, have changed their routines to accommodate such changes, and many news outlets now join the online conversation on Twitter or Instagram to provide instantaneous visual feeds from breaking news stories. Photojournalism has always adapted to technological advances, whether it be the move to colour printing in the 1970s and 1980s, or the shift to digital in the 1990s. For example, research in the late 1990s by Russial and Wanta (1998) revealed sport photojournalism, especially during the coverage of major events like the Olympic Games or the Super Bowl, was at the forefront of adaptations to digital photography, even where cost and variable quality issues constrained the use of such technologies in everyday news-gathering routines. They also noted how recruitment patterns changed in terms of skillsets, where the ability to process photographs in a dark room were usurped by computer literacy and an ability to edit images in specialist software packages such as Photoshop.

In the context of sports media, the expansion of digital content across news services (print, broadcast, online, mobile) and, in particular, through the rise of networked social media, means that sport photography has mushroomed in both volume and contributors, most of which is supplied by amateurs sharing their images online through applications such as Instagram, Pinterest, Facebook, Twitter and Snapchat, among many others. For professional photojournalists, the broadening of visual culture around sport may be viewed as a direct challenge to their previously privileged position to provide visual storytelling around sport. The multi-variegated access to images from sport, where a sport star's "selfie" can become a more socially valued mode of engagement than a professional photograph, can potentially undermine the economic value of professional sport photography as the main visual record of an event or sport star.

A challenge also comes from the user-generated images of fans, whose access to networked mobile photography brings new perspectives on the sporting event which can be instantaneously produced, distributed and shared during live action to various online communities. The speed of distribution is key to the cultural capital of fan-made digital photography from sport, and in terms of accessibility to a visual record of an event, usurps the professional distribution of images that have to be processed via editorial controls and syndication. In short, fan-made media, in this case sporting images distributed in networked social media, do not face the same professionalised, routinised and conventionalised practices of sport photojournalists. However, they may quite rapidly become distributed and shared as the visual image telling the story of a sport event or happening that render industrially produced media images as either redundant or lacking relevance to the fan experience.

In addition to the competition brought by fan-made media, the expansion of digital images from sport online has brought with it new constraints and forms of sport industry regulation. As the volume of sporting images increased, so too have attempts to increase regulation of accredited access to sporting venues, as well as mechanisms to increase the control of licensing rights of sporting images in the online environment. This is mainly due to an increased awareness on the part of governing bodies of sport, individual venues and professional sports clubs of the value of visual culture in sport

(Hutchins and Rowe 2012). The ownership and control of intellectual property rights to sport, in particular the regulation of the rights of access to either broadcast or distribute commercial images from sport, have become incredibly lucrative aspects of contemporary sport economics (Haynes 2007). For example, there has been a marked increase in preferred media partnerships between sports organisations and media outlets that are prepared to collaborate on exclusivity contracts regarding access and syndication of images to competing new organisations.

In the Premier League (football) in England, this has included exclusive media partnerships between Newcastle United F.C. and media outlets Sky Sports and the national *Daily Mirror* newspaper (Edwards 2015), as well as internally run photography syndication by Southampton F.C. (Greenslade 2010), which effectively monopolises the commercialisation of images from these stadia. In other cases, such as Nottingham Forest F.C., football clubs in England have taken access rights away from particular news outlets because sports journalists have upset the owners of such clubs with critical news stories (Greenslade 2013). For news agencies and the fans, such developments present a closure on access to what may be privately owned sports organisations but are more broadly viewed as essential parts of the local community and cultural traditions of the area.

In particular, from within our general survey of international photojournalists from the World Press Photo competition, we were interested in gathering some basic data on the range and specialisation of photographers on the sports they covered. We wanted to know about the demographic breakdown of sport photojournalism in relation to the wider survey, including gender balance and regional distribution, as well as how these factors related to the coverage of particular sports.

Through a survey of photographers around the world, we were keen to analyse the extent to which the processes identified above are actually having an influence on the practices of those working in a sporting context. To what extent have sport photographers adopted the broader visual culture of digital media and introduced video capture into their work? How many photographers have identified the issue of access to sporting venues and events as a problem or a challenge to their daily work in sport? Are developments in networked social media felt by photographers to be affecting the value of their work in sport? Our analysis of sport photojournalists around the world is, therefore, a first attempt to map some of the key patterns of work in the contemporary networked digital media environment, and the extent to which issues related to access and social media are viewed as having an impact on the practices of sport photojournalists.

Methods

Our focus on sport photojournalists draws on data from a broader questionnaire survey of photography practice and routines in wider news contexts. The broader study investigates the attitudes and values of photographers on a range of issues relevant to contemporary developments in their profession, covering, for instance, employment arrangements, professional practices and opinions about future developments in the field (see Hadland, Campbell, and Lambert 2015). Many of these issues are relevant to the study of sports photojournalism and will be factors in the contemporary responsibilities and work roles of professionals in the industry, many of whom are struggling to survive the impacts of declining circulations in newspapers and the proliferation of images online (Anderson 2013; Mortensen 2014).

We gained access to a sample of more than 700 sports photographers through collaboration with the World Press Photo Foundation (WPP), host of a leading international photography competition. In early 2016, 5775 photographers from more than 100 countries and territories sent in their work to be judged across a variety of categories, including best sports photograph (single image and story). After submitting their work, the entrants were contacted by email and encouraged to link to a voluntary online survey. More than a third of the entrants, 1991 photographers, responded and worked their way through almost 70 questions about subjects ranging from equipment and pay to ethics.[3] A similar survey was undertaken in early 2015 (see Hadland, Campbell, and Lambert 2015), but the 2016 study (which is due to be published by the end of 2016) has a special focus on photographers working in sport.

Photographers responding to the survey were commonly engaged in multiple forms of photography at the same time. In the 2016 survey, 713 of the 1991 respondents (36 per cent) indicated that sports photography was one of the forms of photography that they undertook (usually in combination with other forms). Of these respondents, 362 (or 18 per cent of the full sample) reported that sports photography was the major focus of their news work. The survey also collected information on the income (if any) generated by respondents through their photography, as well as data on other features of their employment status. By comparing responses across several related questions, we could also identify 284 respondents whose answers indicated that they generated an important element of their income through sports photography.[4] Most of our results below are presented for each of these three groups: the wider category of 713 who engage in some level of sports photography; the 362 respondents who report that sports photography is one of their main activities; and the smaller group of 284 for whom sports photography is an important element of their income.

Results are presented below in the form of summary statistics that give a profile applicable to the respective groups of sports photographers. This is contrasted, when relevant, with a corresponding figure for all survey respondents, and with indicators of the statistical significance of the difference between the relevant group of sports photographers and others. In broad terms, a significant difference between the group and others suggests that the pattern of difference in the profiles, as revealed in our sample of data, is strong enough that it is very plausible that the difference holds genuinely in the underlying population of all photographers and photojournalists.

Results and Analysis

Table 1 presents a number of summary statistics about sports photography among the survey respondents. Based on our data, the average sports photojournalist is male, well-educated (usually to degree level) and in his late 30s or early 40s. He is more likely to be employed by a media company or agency than self-employed, though the proportion is roughly 60:40. This is higher than for the photojournalists in this study as a whole, most of whom are self-employed.

TABLE 1
Aspects of sports photojournalism from the 2016 WPP survey

	All responses (*N* = 1991)	Any sports photography (*N* = 713)	Mostly sports photography (*N* = 362)	Sports photography important part of income (*N* = 284)
Panel 1: Background characteristics				
Percentage female	15.5	8.7*	6.6*	4.9*
Percentage aged 30–50	67.5	69.3	67.1	66.2
Percentage employed (cf. self-employed)	43.4	59.6*	58.6*	61.6*
Panel 2: Percentage saying access to sports venues is... (*N* = 921)				
"Difficult" or "very difficult"	20.6	18.5*	19.7	18.7
"Difficult" or "very difficult" (women)	28.2	16.7*	18.2	7.7
"Difficult" or "very difficult" (self-employed)	23.5	20.0*	18.8	20.4
"Difficult" or "very difficult" (photographers covering football)	19.0	18.4	19.3	18.5
Becoming a little/much harder to access grounds in last few years		34.8	39.0	40.5
Panel 3: Range of sports covered (%)				
Those who "cover a wide range of sports"		42.9	56.9	59.9
Those who cover "a small number"		29.7	28.5	30.3
Those who only shoot one or two sports		19.4	12.7	9.9
Those employed rather than self-employed (of those covering football)		34.0	36.8	34.4
Panel 4: Risks related to livelihood from sports photography (% mentioning...)				
Access/rights restrictions		47.4	50.8	50.7
Amateur/citizen photography		35.5	39.0	41.6
Social media		15.4	18.5	17.3
Copyright issues		28.3	30.9	30.6
Cost of equipment		37.0	40.9	39.8

Note: Analysis of 1991 respondents to the 2016 WPP questionnaire.
*In first two panels, an asterisk indicates that the category proportion is significantly different from the value for all other respondents at the 95 per cent statistical significance level.

In our sample, there are proportionally fewer sports photographers in Africa and Europe compared to the Americas. For example, of the 220 respondents from either North America or Australasia in this year's study, 53 (24 per cent) said they mainly worked in sports photography. This compares to 18 per cent across the sample as a whole, and reminds us that those patterns revealed in the sample for those respondents who are engaged in sports photography are for respondents from a somewhat different national distribution to those of photographers as a whole.

The gender gap, already so evident in photojournalism as a whole, is even more pronounced in sports photojournalism, the data suggest. Across our whole sample, over two years, the gender spread is roughly 85 per cent male and 15 per cent female. Among the sports photojournalists, only 6.6 per cent are female and 93.4 per cent are male, and the gender disparity increases when we isolate those photographers for whom sports photography is an important part of their livelihood.

Many of the sports photographers covered a wide range of sports, particularly those who gained relatively more of their income from sport. For all those undertaking sports photography, 43 per cent report covering a wide range of sports, 30 per cent a few sports, and 19 per cent report that they shoot only one or two sports.

Respondents were also asked to indicate which from a list of popular sports they were engaged in covering. Figure 1 summarises the responses received.

We can see that football/soccer is by far the most covered sport with around 70–80 per cent of the sports photojournalists surveyed saying that it is one of the sports they most often work on. There is a considerable gap before other sports feature as among those that respondents most often cover—e.g. basketball, athletics and tennis are mentioned by around a third of relevant respondents.

In terms of the link between country and football, sports photographers in Asia, Africa, and Central and South America were more likely to cover football than any other sport. By contrast, North American sports photographers were more likely to be covering golf, basketball or ice hockey than photographers from other regions. Sports photographers focusing on football were relatively less likely to be self-employed than other sports photographers.

As a group, just under 20 per cent of the respondents said they found it difficult (or very difficult) to gain entrance to stadiums or clubs. A third of all the sports respondents said they believed this had become more difficult in recent years. It is possible that difficulties of access are more pronounced for women photographers than men. From all respondents who answered a question on access to sports venues, a higher proportion (28 per cent) of women described access as "difficult" or "very difficult", compared to 20 per cent of their male counterparts. However, this pattern does not hold for those respondents for whom sports photography is a relatively more important part of their professional lives—in these groups, more men than women report difficulties of access. However, self-employment status, and also data on what specific sports were covered, was not strongly linked to reported difficulties of access. Additionally, many respondents (in all categories) reported that in their view it had become harder to access sports venues over the last few years (34 per cent of all responses among people engaged in sports photography). Though access may not be an especially prominent issue in the mindset of respondents, it is clearly influencing a number of photographers, and many believe it has been increasingly problematic in the recent past.

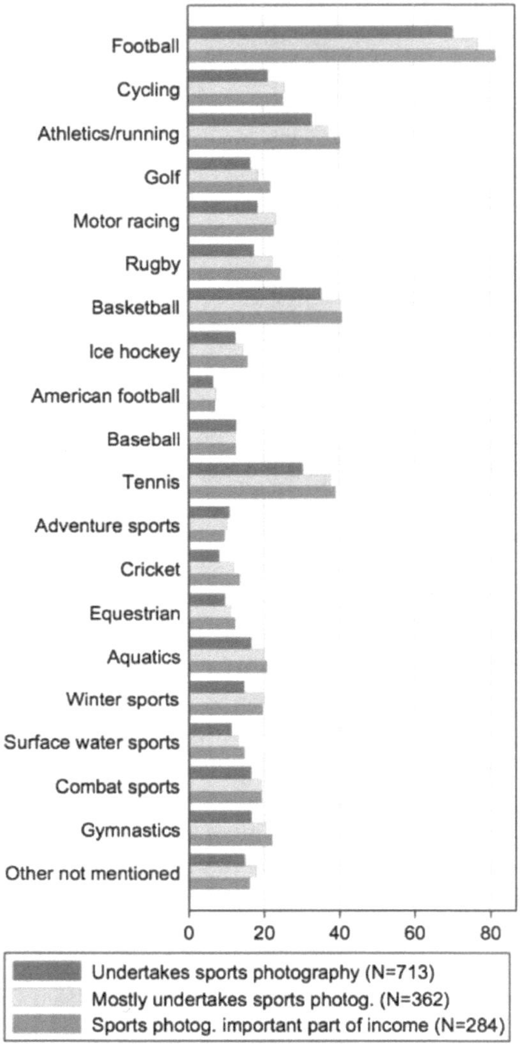

FIGURE 1
Percentage of respondents shooting images in the listed sports

Respondents were also asked to identify if they considered a number of factors that are thought to be relevant to the practice of sports photography as potential threats to their livelihoods (Table 1, panel 4). Around 50 per cent of relevant respondents listed access to venues as an issue that was a risk to their livelihood as sports photographers. The cost of equipment and the threat of amateur photographers was cited by around 40 per cent while copyright infringements concerned around 30 per cent and social media around 15 per cent. Concerns were generally higher in those groups where photography was a more important part of their income, and it was noticeable that North American and Australasian sports photographers (the regions with higher levels of sports photography amongst the sample) were considerably more concerned about the threat of amateurism (with 55 per cent expressing that this was a serious danger).

In an open section of the questionnaire where respondents were invited to give more detail on their livelihoods as sports photojournalists, some respondents expressed their concerns with the use of "hobbyist" photographers working on low or no commissions often producing poor-quality images. A similar sentiment is expressed in the comments in the quote at the beginning of the introduction of this article, which were also taken from the open section of the questionnaire.

The rising cost of equipment was cited by many of the respondents as a real threat to the sustainability of their work as sports photographers. Ordinarily, the sports photographer needs much larger, more expensive lenses than other types of photographer in order to capture the high-speed, close-up action shot that are the hallmark of their business. Male photographers (20 per cent) appeared to be slightly more worried than female photographers (13 per cent) about the cost of equipment and African and Central/South American photographers considerably more concerned about this than their counterparts in Europe, Asia and North America.

Table 2 summarises some other ways in which sports photographers were similar to or different from the other photographers who participated in the WPP survey in 2016. On many issues the pattern is one of similarity, for instance with few significant differences between sports and other photographers in levels of social media use and in experiences of the use of images without permission (panel 1); in attitudes to financial circumstances (panel 2); and in general satisfaction with the profession (panel 3).

There are, however, a few exceptions: sports photographers, particularly those for whom sports photography is a relatively more important part of their livelihood, are relatively less likely to use a film camera than other photographers (panel 1), but when using digital images they are also relatively less likely to report that they often enhance images such as by adjusting contrast or colour (panel 1). In terms of their financial situation, sports photographers are somewhat more positive about their circumstances than other photographers, and it is certainly the case that among survey respondents, those who were engaged in sports photography reported on average higher annual incomes from photography than those who were not (panel 2). Lastly, panel 3 suggests that sports photographers generally felt they had more control over their daily work than did other photographers, although in contrast they were slightly more likely to report that their work could be edited without their permission. This latter pattern may suggest that sports journalists work in an environment in which they feel relatively autonomous and are generally satisfied by their circumstances, but are nevertheless aware that the products of their work may be controlled by others such as editors.

Regression models allow us to assess the relative influence of nominated explanatory factors upon an outcome of interest, in a manner that controls for other relevant differences between cases. In Table 3, results from four regression models are shown. Models 1a and 1b summarise relative influences upon the probability of a respondent stating that amateur/citizen photography is an important risk to their livelihood in sports photography, and Models 2a and 2b summarise similarly selected influences upon the probability of stating that access restrictions are an important risk.

Overall, the models show that the highlighted factors are in combination only a small influence upon the chances of mentioning these risks (evident in the small pseudo-R^2 values, which indicate the percentage variation in the outcome that can be attributed to the various explanatory variables). The table also shows in summary form whether or not the highlighted measures had a distinctive and significant impact upon

TABLE 2
Aspects of photography as experienced by sports photojournalists in the 2016 WPP survey

	All responses (*N* = 1991)	Any sports photography (*N* = 713)	Mostly sports photography (*N* = 362)	Sports photography important part of income (*N* = 284)
Panel 1: Digital practices and social media (%)				
Using film camera	17.7	9.1*	8.0*	6.3*
Often/always enhance digital images (e.g. contrast, hue)	43.5	34.6*	30.4*	32.0*
Images used without permission	75.3	77.6	76.0	76.0
Often/always uses social media	51.0	48.3	47.2	46.1
Panel 2: Financial situation at present				
Difficult/very difficult (%)	35.6	28.1*	32.3	28.5*
Worse than last year (%)	31.0	31.8	34.5	32.4
Income less or a lot less now compared to 5 years ago (%)	38.4	35.8	40.2	37.9
Imputed mean annual income from photography (US$)	25,600	30,500*	30,500*	35,800*
Panel 3: Indicators of satisfaction with photography (% happy with, or % stating that they have control over...)				
Current mix of assignments	62.1	63.5	63.0	63.0
Control over what work I do	30.2	40.3*	39.8*	43.3*
Work rarely edited without permit	79.1	75.3*	74.3*	75.0
Not too overwhelmed by technology change	73.5	72.9	74.0	76.1
Feel photography is valued	50.5	51.6	51.4	51.4
Positive on future of photography	51.6	50.4	48.3	48.2

Note: Analysis of 1991 respondents to the 2016 WPP questionnaire.
*The category proportion is significantly different from the value for all other respondents at the 95 per cent statistical significance level.

TABLE 3
Logistic regression model results for influences on mentioning "amateur/citizen photographers" and "access restrictions" as "an important risk to your livelihood as a sports photojournalist"

	Amateur/citizen photography a threat to livelihood		Access restrictions a threat to livelihood	
	Model 1a	**Model 1b**	**Model 2a**	**Model 2b**
Gender				
Male (reference)	0	0	0	0
Female	ns	ns	ns	ns
Age				
29 years old or younger	–	–	ns	ns
30–49 years (reference)	0	0	0	0
50 years old or older	ns	ns	ns	ns
Continent				
North America or Australasia	+++	+++	ns	+
All other continents (reference)	0	0	0	0
Sports covered				
Mentions football		+++		+++
Any other mentions (reference)		0		0
Positive financial situation (Likert score, 1 = very difficult, 5 = very good)		–		ns
Pseudo-R^2	0.024	0.040	0.003	0.012
N	713	713	713	713

Note: Analysis restricted to 713 cases who reported some level of sports photographic activity. Reference category coefficients are zero by design.
ns: no significant effect. +, +++ indicate significant effects in a positive direction at the 90 and 99 per cent significance thresholds. – indicates significant effect in a negative direction at the 90 per cent significance threshold.

the outcome. Only a few variables are seen to have a discernible influence across the models (net of the effects of other variables).

From Models 1a and 1b, we see that photographers based in the North America or Australasia were more likely to mention amateur photography as a threat, but gender was not influential net of other measures, and age was associated only with a slight pattern (whereby younger respondents were more likely to consider amateur photography a threat). In Model 1b, we see that those photographers who mentioned shooting images of football were relatively more likely to see amateur photography as a threat, but having a more positive attitude to their current financial situation was associated with a lower chance of seeing amateur photography as a threat (net of other factors). From Models 2a and 2b, we see that gender, age and continent have no important influences (net of each other) upon the chances of regarding access restrictions as an important threat (Model 2a), however, when we also take account of field of photography and financial attitudes, we see a slight pattern whereby those who shoot football are relatively more likely to mention the threat of access restrictions, and, in the context of the other variables included in the model, a slight influence of continent in which those based in North America and Australasia are slightly more likely to mention access as an issue (net of other factors included in the models).

Conclusion

At the outset of this paper, we identified three key questions concerning the current practices and outlook for photojournalists specialising in sport: How are sports photographers coping in the digital era? What are the challenges they face? Is there a future for professional sports photography? Certainly, the results and analysis give us an initial impression of the answers.

In terms of how sports photojournalists are coping in the digital era, in spite of the restructuring of the industry and the "crisis" so frequently alluded to, the loss of formal employed positions and the technical challenges, photojournalists who mainly cover sport are doing relatively well. Their income is generally higher than photographers as a whole and they are somewhat more positive about their circumstances than are other photojournalists. Sports photographers are more likely to be formally employed by media companies and only a relatively modest proportion are finding access to stadia and sport clubs difficult. Most photographers tend to cover a wide range of sports, particularly those who gain relatively more of their income from sport. The sports photographers who participated in this study generally felt they had more control over their daily work than did other photographers, while the general feeling was that sports photographers tended to work in an environment in which they felt relatively autonomous and were generally satisfied with their circumstances.

There were some national and regional variations in terms of general conditions of work with, for instance, sports photographers in Asia, Africa, and Central and South America more likely to cover football than any other sport.

The key challenges were identified in the study as the persistent gender gap in sports photojournalism, pervasive copyright infringements, the anticipation of increasingly difficult access to sports stadia and athletes, the rising cost of equipment, and the threat of both social media and amateur photographers. There were gender-based and regional variations in how keenly these challenges were felt.

The question of the future sustainability of sports photojournalism is less clear from the data. Certainly there are challenges and the manner in which these are resolved or allowed to develop will have an impact on the profession going forward as well as on the representation of sport. The gradual disappearance of women sports photographers will not help correct the sexism, racism, homophobia and lack of diversity already evident in the cultures of sport. The capturing of iconic sports moments and their inspirational impact may be undermined by a lack of quality images and inadequate equipment. A new narcissistic aesthetic of subject-generated content may be looming. These diverse factors may encourage or discourage young people from entering the profession or force sports photojournalists in their prime to leave.

In highlighting the threat of amateur photographers, free images, copyright theft and dwindling levels of full employment, the data support the notion that sports photojournalists have been in the frontline of the crisis spawned by the advent of online news and images. They have, however, been slightly less affected than news photojournalists as a whole. Certainly, it is important to track the work patterns, trends and vulnerabilities of those who make a living populating the world online and offline with quality images. This study is a reminder of the importance of gathering data from the people who have made such a profound contribution to the commercialisation and sustainability of sport itself. Given the scarcity of studies on photojournalists, and on sports photojournalism in particular, there is evidently a need for more in-depth research in this area.

DISCLOSURE STATEMENT

No potential conflict of interest was reported by the authors.

FUNDING

This work was supported by the World Press Photo Foundation [grant number 2016].

NOTES

1. Photojournalists describe themselves in many different ways from visual story-tellers to sports photojournalists. In this paper, photographers covering mainly sport and sports photojournalists are interchangeable concepts. Variations in proportion of time spent taking pictures of sport or the extent to which income is determined by sports work are outlined as relevant.
2. Getty Images has a history of aggressive purchasing in the sector, including sports photography agency Allsport in 1998, the Image Bank in 1999, Mediavast in 2007 and Jupiterimages in 2009.
3. A full copy of the survey questionnaire is available at http://rms.stir.ac.uk/converis-stirling/person/18027.
4. This number was calculated by identifying those who mainly worked in photography and who also stated either (1) that they mostly undertake sports photography and that photography generated the bulk of their income (266 respondents), or (2) in response to a separate independent question, that sports was the type of photography that generated most of their income (148 respondents).

REFERENCES

Allan, Stuart. 2015. "Introduction." *Journalism Practice* 9 (4): 455–464. doi:10.1080/17512786.2015.1030131.

Anderson, Monica. 2013. "At Newspapers, Photographers Feel the Brunt of Job Cuts." http://www.pewresearch.org/fact-tank/2013/11/11/at-newspapers-photographers-feel-the-brunt-of-job-cuts/

Campbell, David. 2013. *Visual Storytelling in the Age of Post-Industrialist Journalism*. Research Project published under the auspices of the World Press Photo Academy. https://www.david-campbell.org/multimedia/world-press-photo-multimedia-research/

Caple, Helen. 2013. *Photojournalism: A Social Semiotic Approach*. Basingstoke: Palgrave MacMillan.

Castells, Manuel. 2013. *Communication Power*. 2nd ed. Oxford: Oxford University Press.

Deuze, Mark. 2007. *Media Work*. Cambridge, MA: Polity.

Edwards, Luke. 2015. "Newcastle Owner Mike Ashley's 'Preferred Media Partners' Strategy Threatens Objective and Independent Press." *The Telegraph*. Accessed July 31 2015. http://www.telegraph.co.uk/sport/football/teams/newcastle-united/11777127/Mike-Ashleys-preferred-media-partners-strategy-at-Newcastle-threatens-an-objective-and-independent-press.html

Franks, Suzanne, and Deirdre O'Neill. 2015. "Women Reporting Sport: Still a Man's Game?" *Journalism* 17 (4): 474–492.

Greenslade, Roy. 2010. "Proclaiming Press Freedom as Football Clubs Ban Journalists May Be Own Goal." *The Guardian*. Accessed August 9 2010. https://www.theguardian.com/media/greenslade/2010/aug/09/southampton-fc-press-freedom

Greenslade, Roy. 2013. "MPs Condemn Football Clubs for Banning Journalists." *The Guardian*. Accessed December 10 2013. https://www.theguardian.com/media/greenslade/2013/dec/10/nationalunionofjournalists-newcastleunited

Hadland, Adrian, David Campbell, and Paul Lambert. 2015. *The State of News Photography: The Lives and Livelihoods of Photojournalists in the Digital Age*. Research Report. Oxford: Reuters Institute for the Study of Journalism, University of Oxford.

Haynes, Richard. 2007. "Footballers' Image Rights in the New Media Age." *European Sport Management Quarterly* 7 (4): 361–374.

Hutchins, Brett, and David Rowe. 2012. *Sport beyond Television: The Internet, Digital Media and the Rise of Networked Media Sport*. London: Routledge.

Mäenpää, Jenni. 2014. "Rethinking Photojournalism: The Changing Work Practices and Professionalism of Photojournalists in the Digital Age." *Nordicom Review* 35 (2): 91–104.

Manovich, Lev. 2016. *Instagram and Contemporary Image*. http://manovich.net/index.php/projects/instagram-and-contemporary-image

Messner, Michael A., and Cheryl Cooky. 2010. *Gender in Televised Sports: News and Highlights Shows, 1989–2009*. University of Southern California Center for Feminist Research. http://dornsife.usc.edu/cfr/gender-in-televised-sports/

Mortensen, Tara Marie. 2014. "Blurry and Centred or Clear and Balanced?" *Journalism Practice* 8 (6): 704–725. doi:10.1080/17512786.2014.892703.

Pantti, Mervi, and Piet Bakker. 2009. "Misfortunes, Memories and Sunsets: Non-Professional Images in Dutch News Media." *International Journal of Cultural Studies* 12: 471–489. doi:10.1177/1367877909337860.

Papadopolous, Kari Anden, and Mervi Pantti. 2011. *Amateur Images and Global News*. Bristol: Intellect.

Reinardy, Scott. 2011. "Newspaper Journalism in Crisis: Burnout on the Rise Eroding Young Journalists' Career Commitment." *Journalism* 12 (1): 33–50. doi:10.1177/1464884910385188.

Russial, John, and Wayne Wanta. 1998. "Digital Imaging Skills and the Hiring and Training of Photojournalists." *Journalism and Mass Communication Quarterly* 75 (3): 593–605.

Sutton, Benjamin. 2015. "New French Report Zooms in on Field of Photography." http://hyperallergic.com/209257/new-french-report-zooms-in-on-field-of-photography/

Taylor, John. 2000. "Problems in Photojournalism: Realism, the Nature of News and the Humanitarian Narrative." *Journalism Studies* 1 (1): 129–143. doi:10.1080/146167000361212.

Vauclare, Claude, and Rémi Debeauvais. 2015. *Le Metier de Photographe* [Working as a Photographer]. http://culturecommunication.gouv.fr/Politiques-ministerielles/Etudes-et-statistiques/Publications/Collections-de-synthese/Culture-etudes-2007-2015/Le-metier-de-photographe-CE-2015-3

Yaschur, Carolyn. 2011. "Visualising the Future of Visual Journalism". In *The Future of News: An Agenda of Perspectives*, edited by Kelly Kaufhold, Amber Willard Hinsley, and Seth Lewis. 2nd ed. 127–138. San Diego, CA: Cognella Academic Publishing.

Zavoina, Susan, and Tom Reichert. 2000. "Media Convergence/Management Change: The Evolving Work Flow for Visual Journalists." *The Journal of Media Economics* 13 (2): 143–151.

TAKE FIVE

How *Sports Illustrated* and *L'Équipe* redefine the long-form sports journalism genre

Christopher Tulloch and **Xavier Ramon**

The consolidation of the counter genre that is long-form sports journalism (LFSJ) is of growing interest to the sports media researcher. In order to trace its expansion across the sports journalism landscape, this article offers a comparative transatlantic case study featuring the entire collection of long-form stories developed by two prestigious publications: the American magazine Sports Illustrated (SI Longform) and the French sports daily L'Équipe (L'Équipe Explore). The study considers the slow journalism heritage of LFSJ and its challenge to established Web interface theology while exploring key issues such as the sports agenda, sourcing and the use of immersive multimedia formats, aimed at improving the sporting culture of its users. The article concludes by considering the pivotal role of LFSJ in the brand-building strategies of the media outlets themselves.

Introduction

While it is true that lengthy sports feature articles have been a regular component in mainstream press outlets for decades, the vigorous expansion across the journalism landscape of long-form sports journalism (LFSJ) in its online multimedia capacity is a more recent phenomenon. In a media environment characterized by 24/7 production cycles, high-speed information flow and the impact of social media, the consolidation of this counter genre is of growing interest to the sports communication researcher. Legacy outlets such as *The New York Times* or *The Guardian*, along with prominent specialized platforms such as *Sports Illustrated Longform* (*SI Longform*), *L'Équipe Explore*, *SBNation*, *NBC SportsWorld*, *ESPN.com* or *Grantland*, have all invested human resources not only in multimedia formats which embrace innovation but also by lending priority to storytelling techniques which greater engage the reader thanks to the interface which LFSJ architecture offers.

The LFSJ Heritage: New-new Journalism, Slow Journalism

Long-form digital sports writing has paid its dues to recent wider dynamics in journalism praxis. A first nod can be made to the "new-new journalism" movement dating back a decade or so when a generation of disgruntled journalists took it on themselves to counter the anti-professional practices epitomized by the terms *binge journalism* or "churnalism" (Davies 2008) and imported, from the original "new journalism" of the 1960s, elements of narrative and ethical regeneration. These instruments include in-depth investigations for which the term "immersion journalism" is often coined together with a "greater attention to the subjective dimension of the experience and feelings of the actors of the events" (Neveu 2014) and an unapologetically literary reporting style which features the presence of the authors voice in the narrative (Sims 2007).

LFSJ is also compatible with one of the most fashionable under-swells in journalism production processes known as *slow journalism*. The slow journalism movement, which has been championed in recent years by publications such as *Delayed Gratification, Jot Down, Narratively, De Correspondent* or *The New York Times Magazine* (Dowling 2016; Harbers 2016), proposes a "new way of thinking about and producing journalism" (Le Masurier 2016, 405). Its identifying traits include:

- The possibility of a "proper time" (Ball 2016): the need to disassociate journalism from the current hyper-accelerated and algorithmic news rhythm (Ananny 2016; Le Masurier 2016), that is, the breaking news paradigm based on speed and instantaneity. According to Dowling and Vogan (2015, 218), "timeliness is moot. The digital long-form genre is untethered to the breaking news cycle".
- An interest in a high standard of writing and publication, accuracy, reflection, narrative, context, deep research, source checking and a rejection of interpretative clichés (Le Masurier 2015).
- A move away from pre-packaged public relations material and the overuse of wire services with the aim of amplifying "otherwise un-heard voices" (Belt and South 2016, 551).
- The preservation of prestige through an obsession with quality, the power of narrative and the setting of "the highest standards of storytelling craft" (Greenberg 2012, 382).
- The transparency and self-reflexivity of journalists. As Harbers (2016, 499) explains, "slow journalism is geared towards forms of reporting that do not conceal the underlying aspects of the reporting process". This "keeps the reader informed about the provenance of the information and how it was gathered" (Greenberg 2012, 381–382).
- The opportunity of engaging in acts of co-production between different journalists and news organizations (Boyles 2016).
- The aim of re-training "news audiences into investing in the benefits of patience and anticipation over instant gratification" (Dowling 2016, 535).
- The reader/user as participant-collaborator. While Vogan and Dowling (2016, 22) talk of how long-form journalism leads to the "empowerment of the fan", Nguyen (2012) considers it to have "broken the templates to build customized reading experiences". According to Meuret (2013), "it is no longer the journalists who find themselves embedded alone, but rather the readers, who, with a single click, can take over the controls of a story in which they assume the role of both observer and participant … Readers, thrown into the experience of others, seeing the world through the eyes of the journalist, find themselves taking part".

The combination of classic feature-reporting skills with digital interface possibilities has led many observers to consider long-form journalism as representing the interaction between "old" and "new" media typical of "convergent media culture", a phenomenon which "alters the relationships between existing technologies, industries, markets and genres" (Jenkins 2006, 15). In this sense, the blurring of technological distinctions that separate print and digital media has been referred to as "liquid journalism" (Deuze 2008). The hybrid character of the *Sports Illustrated* and *L'Équipe* long-form projects exemplifies this "bridging" role.

Challenging Web Theology

Interviewed in 2013 about the impact of long-form journalism, David Remnick, editor of *The New Yorker*, declared: "I think it's fantastic that the first law of evangelical Web theology, that no one would read anything long on the Web, has been overturned thoroughly" (Sharp 2013). One of the main reasons as to why this premise was overturned and which accounts for the positive reception of LFSJ has been the successful integration of multimedia applications into linear storytelling, a process which has led to an enhancement of the news consumption experience (Barnhurst 2010; Pauly 2014; Ramon and Tulloch 2016).

As Jacobson, Marino, and Gutsche (2016, 530) point out, "today's long-form journalism emerges at a dynamic time of technological advancement in the news industry, of conceptual understandings of visual studies and of journalism as a ritualized form of storytelling". Advances such as parallax scrolling, embedded video footage, high-resolution graphics work, audio documents and interactive photography embed the user into the warp and weft of the narrative, thus lending the Web greater potential for offering a seamless multi-sensorial experience. According to analysts, the key to the success of long form has been its capacity for "uniting print long-form narrative's novelistic technique with cinematic data visualization" and a move towards a "business model built on a carefully crafted multimedia product sensitive to users' appreciation of multimedia narrative aesthetics" (Dowling and Vogan 2015, 210, 220).

Some previous internet conventions are subverted along the way. For example, limits are placed on hyperlinks in order to reduce the risk of distraction. The driving idea here is that each feature long-form work should function as a "cognitive container" in which "media add-ons work to hold reader attention rather than scatter it to external Web sources", "digital long-form departs from online journalism's advertisement-littered and click-heavy customs ... and breaks from the distracting and superficial nature of online news" (Dowling and Vogan 2015, 211). According to Steve Duenes, Associate Managing Editor at *The New York Times*, it is essential that the interaction with the technology did not lead the user to "feel like you were taking a detour but [rather] that the multimedia was part of the one narrative flow" (Rue 2013). A key element here is that the capacity to engage the reader—what Rue refers to as the "triggering of an emotional response as you venture through the story"—is of greater importance than the spectacular nature of the design components themselves.

Methodology

The objective of the research is to consider to what extent *SI Longform* and *L'Équipe Explore* promote a wider agenda, an alternative narrative and a quality user experience through the multimedia resources available in digital LFSJ. To do so, content analysis has allowed researchers to read, interpret and make valid inferences in a systematic way of the manifest content of the messages included in the two websites, with the objective of contrasting the research questions with the empirical data obtained (Bryman 2012; Wimmer and Dominick 2011).

The sample was chosen in a non-probabilistic way by the researchers, who purposely selected two websites specifically devoted to LFSJ. *SI Longform* (United States) and *L'Équipe Explore* (France) were selected considering strategic criteria such as the relevance, tradition and respectability of their parent companies; the quality of their Web-based sports journalism; the volume of publication; and their innovation in terms of multimedia and interactive resources. In a high-speed media landscape these platforms represent an alternative space to articulate a different kind of journalism, based on in-depth research, long-form narratives and tailor-made consumption of content by the user.

The New York-based *Sports Illustrated*, property of Time Inc., was founded in 1954. Its high circulation figures can be traced to its in-depth sports reporting and richness in photography, aspects that still impregnate its journalistic approach. At the time of writing, it has a print circulation of 3,004,430 and an audience of 27 million unique users on its website. In October 2013, the magazine launched its long-form platform (http://www.si.com/longform/). This website is presented under the cachet "Longform since 1954", an expression that reinforces the brand identity of the company by suggesting that "the magazine had been producing such relatively complex works for decades" (Dowling and Vogan 2015, 217). Since its creation, *SI Longform* has published 58 articles, averaging 1.81 articles per month.

The French sports daily *L'Équipe* was created in 1947 as a successor to the newspaper *L'Auto*, initially founded in 1900 as *L'Auto-Vélo*. The outlet, owned by Éditions Philippe Amaury, "has acquired the reputation of being a quality newspaper providing an excellent coverage of sports news, with which no 'generalist' newspaper can compete" (Ranc 2012, 40). *L'Équipe* has a circulation rate of 217,456 copies at the time of writing and its website has an audience of 5.6 million unique users. *L'Équipe Explore* (http://www.lequipe.fr/explore/), the specific website devoted to long articles and interactivity, was launched in April 2013. Since then, 39 articles have been published, for an average periodicity of 1.03 pieces per month.

The object of study has been the entire collection of long-form stories published by *SI Longform* and *L'Équipe Explore* (N = 97) up until May 2016. In order to conduct the empirical analysis, two methodological tools were designed: a codebook and a coding form. The codebook specified with detail the instructions and criteria used to identify and evaluate each category, so that researchers could register the information following a uniform approach. This coding scheme enabled the further comparison between the data obtained in the two outlets. A coding sheet was created to allow the relevant aspects of each article to be registered. Additional observations about the production and the display of contents were also coded. Taking into account the requirement to test the form to assure the inter-coder reliability, 10 pieces (5 from *SI Longform* and 5 from *L'Équipe Explore*) were codified by the two researchers before starting the systematic analysis of the whole sample.

After coding the 97 articles that compose the sample, researchers exported the data to a common file from which they proceeded to extract the quantitative and qualitative data, generating the tables, examples and observations presented here. Finally, following Brennen's (2013, 24) indications, the researchers proceeded to analyse the information and interpret the results, extracting the relevant conclusions drawn from the empirical study.

Results

Agenda and Sourcing

A comparative glance at Table 1 shows that the French website promotes a more diverse sporting agenda given that *SI Longform* has given space over to 14 different sports in the 58 feature articles that it has published so far while *L'Équipe Explore* has

TABLE 1
Sports agenda

	SI Longform		***L'Équipe Explore***	
Sport	*N*	%	*N*	%
Athletics	2.25	3.88	2	5.13
Base jumping	0	0.00	1	2.56
Baseball	7.25	12.50	0	0.00
Basketball	14.25	24.57	2	5.13
Bass fishing	1	1.72	0	0.00
Boxing	3	5.17	1	2.56
Chess	0	0.00	1	2.56
Dancing	0	0.00	1	2.56
E-sports	0	0.00	1	2.56
Cycling	0	0.00	5	12.82
Fighting	0	0.00	1	2.56
Football (US)	13.25	22.84	0	0.00
Golf	0	0.00	1	2.56
Hockey	3	5.17	0	0.00
Horse riding	2	3.45	1	2.56
Mountaineering	0	0.00	1	2.56
Racing	1	1.72	1	2.56
Rodeo	1	1.72	0	0.00
Rugby	0	0.00	4	10.26
Sailing	0	0.00	1	2.56
Scuba diving	0	0.00	1	2.56
Soccer	4	6.90	7	17.95
Surfing	0	0.00	1	2.56
Swimming	0	0.00	1	2.56
Tennis	1	1.72	1	2.56
Trailing	0	0.00	1	2.56
Winter sports	4	6.90	2	5.13
Wrestling	1	1.72	0	0.00
Multisport	0	0.00	1	2.56
Total	58	100.00	39	100.00

published 39 articles devoted to 23 disciplines. The statistics also reveal a broad definition of "sports" as both media outlets feature articles on traditionally lesser-covered disciplines such as base jumping, bass fishing, dancing, e-sports, rodeo or trailing. However, when it comes to priority sport selection, each of the outlets has focused prominently on three sports to build their agendas. In the case of *SI Longform*, 59.91 per cent of the pieces concern basketball (24.57 per cent), football (22.84 per cent) and baseball (12.50 per cent), while at *L'Équipe Explore*, 41.03 per cent of the sample has been devoted to soccer (17.95 per cent), cycling (12.82 per cent) and rugby (10.26 per cent).

While a surface observation shows that by focusing on a "big three" format, the two outlets seem to reproduce and reinforce the preponderance of revenue sports, a deeper look at the sample reveals that the two websites have provided original angles and unique perspectives on well-known sports figures alongside the profiles of unfamiliar or even forgotten protagonists.

Promoting Original Angles and Unique Perspectives on Dominant Sports

In the case of basketball, we can see how these two outlets revisit history and use the human-interest angles to focus not only on the life of Kobe Bryant or Lebron James' return to Cleveland but also on alternative stories such as the Patrick Ewing conspiracy in the 1985 National Basketball Association (NBA) draft or the unsolved mystery of the death of Bison Dele. College basketball receives similar treatment from *SI Longform* as seen by its reporting on Princeton's near upset of Georgetown in the first round of the 1989 NCAA Basketball or coach Bob Knight's chair-throwing incident. In addition, *Sports Illustrated* has even converted its reporters into protagonists of basketball stories, as happened with Michael McKnight's 363-day quest to learning how to dunk or Alexander Wolff's adventure of owning an American Basketball Association team, the Vermont Frost Heaves.

As for its angle on American football, *SI Longform* exploits its archives when recounting the stories of quarterback Dan Marino, who only made one Super Bowl career appearance, the key value of the halftime segment of the Super Bowl or the Bears' memorable Super Bowl shuffle, which became a cultural landmark in 1985. College football is also seen through a historical frame. A salient example here is the then-versus-now historical photograph sequence taken at the 1957 Cotton Bowl between TCU and Syracuse. A relevant human-interest collegiate story is the "Ghost of Speedy Cannon" about an African-American football player at Jacksonville High School (Alabama), who died in a football match in 1972 but whose death can be connected to racism, as journalist Thomas Lake argues after a 12-month investigative task to shed new light on the case.

Human-driven stories and historical elements are also translated into baseball, as evidenced by long articles on the rebuilding of the Houston Astros, the retirement of Derek Jeter as an opportunity to reflect on the changes in the Major League Baseball or the suicide of pitcher Donnie Moore in 1989.

As for its "Big Three", *L'Équipe Explore* delves into the archives to reveal unknown aspects of the 1970 Brazilian World Cup soccer team or the state of football in the former Yugoslavia, assessing how the transformation of the country into six republics impacted sport in general. *L'Équipe Explore*'s coverage of cycling is also impregnated with a historical spirit as shown by articles on the most remarkable climbers in the Tour de France's history or the tragic death of Tom Simpson on Mont Ventoux. As for more intimate human-interest stories, the French platform reveals the psychology of cycling's final sprint or the African origins of Chris Froome. As regards rugby, the outlet recalled the 1999 Rugby World Cup and the victory of France over New Zealand, and discovered for its readers the day-to-day life of the amateur club US Finhan.

Gender and Nationality Issues

Mediasport has traditionally been constructed as a predominantly masculine territory, where gender inequalities have not only been legitimized but also accentuated (Bruce 2013). Quantitatively, the space devoted to male sporting achievements has been a lot more extensive than that of women (Messner and Cooky 2010; O'Neill and Mulready 2015). Although the figures vary depending on the social, historical and sporting contexts of each country, women still receive less than 10 per cent of the sporting coverage both in newspapers and television (Markula 2009).

Unfortunately, *SI Longform* and *L'Équipe Explore* have not provided more opportunities for sportswomen to be showcased (see Table 2). At *SI Longform*, 77.59 per cent (*N* = 45) of the pieces have been devoted to men. Only two stories (3.45 per cent) have sportswomen as protagonists and nine stories (15.52 per cent) have both genders as protagonists. The gender gap is even wider at *L'Équipe Explore*, where men have accounted for 87.18 per cent (*N* = 34) of the stories and only one piece has been exclusively devoted to women. Therefore, it can observed that from the 97 pieces that integrate the sample, only three articles, starring the US skier Mikaela Shiffrin, the US tennis player Serena Williams and the ballet dancer Mathilde Froustey have been devoted to sportswomen.

It should be noted that *SI Longform* and *L'Équipe Explore* are not an exception when it comes to the structural underrepresentation of women in media organizations (Whiteside and Hardin 2013). There are no female reporters among the authors of *SI Longform*'s articles. Among the authors at *L'Équipe Explore*, only two female journalists authored a piece.

In terms of nationality, media have commonly been prone to maximize their countries' stories over the rest. Due to the financial logic of media and the news criteria of cultural proximity (Angelini, Billings, and MacArthur 2012), media organizations have

TABLE 2
Gender of protagonists

	SI Longform		*L'Équipe Explore*	
Gender	*N*	%	*N*	%
Men	45	77.59	34	87.18
Women	2	3.45	1	2.56
Mixed	9	15.52	4	10.26
Neutral	2	3.45	0	0.00
Total	58	100.00	39	100.00

TABLE 3
Nationality of protagonists

	SI Longform		***L'Équipe Explore***	
Nationality	***N***	**%**	***N***	**%**
Home athletes	49	84.48	13	33.33
International	9	15.52	26	66.67
Total	58	100.00	39	100.00

primarily tailored their agenda "towards nationally constituted and regional/local readerships" (Rowe 2013, 166). Within this trend, the investigation reveals the high level of ethnocentrism displayed by *SI Longform*. As can be seen in Table 3, American athletes have been protagonists in 84.48 per cent of the articles (N = 49) while international athletes have only accounted for the remaining 15.52 per cent of the pieces (N = 9). In stark contrast, *L'Équipe Explore* showed a greater international approach in its agenda. From the 39 articles published, 13 have been devoted to French athletes (33.33 per cent) while 26 pieces (66.67 per cent) have had international athletes as protagonists.

Contextual Issues

According to Boyle (2006, 143), "at its best, sports journalism is about making sense of the wider context within which events have occurred". That is, the role of the journalist should be "to place athletic performances within broader contexts in order to enhance the overall understanding of sport" (Billings 2008, 56). Our research shows that *SI Longform* and *L'Équipe Explore* have made sense of the larger framework of sport, expanding their coverage to embrace the complexity and salient issues of a social, historical, geopolitical and cultural nature.

First and foremost, race issues have been rendered as one of the prominent contextual areas in the coverage, especially at *SI Longform*. In "Ghost of Speedy Cannon", Thomas Lake delved into the climate of racism and hatred against African-Americans in Alabama in the early 1970s. In "Faster Than the Fastest", McKnight recalls the types of expressions that journalists employed in the 1930s to refer to African-American athletes, while Gregory and Wolff's "The Game That Saved March Madness" shed light on the connection between the Georgetown Hoyas black players and the rise of the "gangsta rap" culture, which made many people associate basketball players with "thugs".

Health issues also receive major attention. "Shane Comes to the Metrodome" covers the negative long-term effects of American football on health and, in particular, how chronic traumatic encephalopathy destroys parts of the brain and generates memory loss, depression and even dementia. Through the article "Jeu de Massacre?", *L'Équipe Explore* raises the public awareness of the effects of rugby on health. Other health issues explored involve the role of psychology in football and golf; the risks of apnea on health; doping in cycling, baseball and basketball; the safety measures in dirt-track racing; the mental illness of the baseball player Donnie Moore and the brain injury suffered by the horse breeder Jeff Lucas.

Thirdly, geopolitical and historical issues are major components of the contextual approach displayed by the two websites. In "Yougo Football", *L'Équipe Explore* provided contextual information about the Balkan war and its effects on sports. "On the Edge" focuses on the tensions and deteriorating relations between Georgia and Russia and the instability caused by the conflicts over the disputed regions of Abkhazia and South Ossetia. The context of the Cold War and how it made it impossible for Arvydas Sabonis to play college basketball in the United States is also featured, along with "L'Appel de l'Irlande", which explains the division of Ireland and how the Irish rugby team and the common anthem play a key role in building bridges of respect and tolerance between the two countries. "Kasparov contre le reste du monde" explains how the chess master took advantage of the historical and geopolitical circumstances of the time, becoming a symbol of the change accompanying the upheavals that led to the collapse of the Soviet Union.

The economic impact of sport is also brought to the fore. In "Masters of Bass", Steve Rushin explains the industry of bass fishing, which now includes 250,000-square-foot Bass Pro Shops and multimillionaire professional bass anglers. *L'Équipe Explore*'s Xavier Colombani contextualized his piece on Lebron James with the economic effect of his comeback to Cleveland on local business while the economics of horse riding, the Super Bowl halftime show and the emerging market of soccer statistics are also examined by *SI Longform*.

Sources

This study reveals that both sites use a wide range of relevant sources to build well-documented coverage and provide the most complete picture possible. In contrast to previous studies, which pointed out the scarce number of different sources employed in sports journalism (Rowe 2007), the media studied here use an average of 5.03 and 5.85 sources in each article.

As shown in Table 4, the most widely used sources have been sporting figures (former athletes, athletes, coaches, performance directors, and so on). At *SI Longform*,

TABLE 4
Types of sources quoted

	SI Longform		***L'Équipe Explore***	
Sources	***N* pieces**	**%**	***N* pieces**	**%**
Sports reporters (past and present)	30	51.72	13	33.33
Journalists/editors from other news desks	6	10.34	4	10.26
Athletes	26	44.83	29	74.36
Former athletes	37	63.79	31	79.49
Coaches and performance directors	34	58.62	28	71.79
Institutions/organizations	24	41.38	24	61.54
Private companies	8	13.79	7	17.95
News agencies	31	53.45	11	28.21
National and international media	35	60.34	25	64.10
Websites	6	10.34	1	2.56
Social networking sites and blogs	3	5.17	3	7.69
Scholars, experts and analysts	8	13.79	13	33.33
Books and specialized publications	16	27.59	18	46.15
Other sources	28	48.28	23	58.97

former athletes are included in 63.79 per cent (N = 37) of the sample, coaches and performance directors are featured in 58.62 per cent (N = 34) of the articles and current athletes appear in 44.83 per cent (N = 26) of the pieces. Likewise, *L'Équipe Explore* has counted on past and present athletes (used as sources in 31 and 29 out of 39 pieces, respectively) as well as coaches and performance directors (N = 28) to provide the needed background and analysis in their stories.

Sporting actors aside, national and international media are frequently quoted by the two outlets. At *SI Longform*, these sources were included in 60.34 per cent (N = 35) of the pieces, while at *L'Équipe Explore*, national and international media organizations were reflected in 64.10 per cent (N = 25) of the articles. The insights provided by veteran journalists and the extensive photographical material provided by major news agencies and other newswire services also allows *SI Longform* and *L'Équipe Explore* to round out their coverage. Sports institutions and organizations are also frequently cited by both websites alike (N = 24). Executives, representatives and former representatives from clubs and franchises, national teams, governmental institutions, universities and collegiate institutions, Olympic and Paralympic Committees, national and international federations of different sports, professional leagues and competitions, and foundations are all present in LFSJ sourcing routines.

Scholars, experts and analysts are also relevant especially at *L'Équipe Explore*, where they have been consulted in 33.33 per cent (N = 13) of all cases. Outside academia, prominent experts from different fields (law, neurosurgery, psychology or data analysts) have also been consulted. The sources with the least impact are journalists and editors from other news desks, private companies, websites and social networking sites and blogs. Given that human interest is a cornerstone promoted by *SI Longform* and *L'Équipe Explore*, family members and friends have often been quoted during the timeframe of the observation in their crucial story-building role along with fans, spectators, referees, scouts and practitioners from different professional sectors (teachers, engineers, businessmen, illustrators, attorneys, film-makers, and so on).

Digital Convergence

A detailed examination of both platforms shows that both outlets are geared towards blending text with images, videos and sophisticated multimedia/interactive elements to deliver their products. The formats employed and the digital tools provided allow for a creative licence which enhances the quality and appeal of information, as well as enriching the users' reading experience.

Formats. Each one of the stories published presents a unique look, a distinctive template and a specific content organization. To display the information, *SI Longform* has prioritized the vertical scrolling model, including parallax, an attractive type of curtain effect in which the background moves more slowly than the foreground. *L'Équipe Explore* has mostly employed a hybrid approach, which allows readers to scroll down using parallax transitions or have direct access to the different chapters of the stories. Stories are structured in five sections and the reader can jump between them, thus creating his or her own reading chronology.

Texts. While length does not necessarily imply quality, literary sports writing does require a certain breathing space in order to provide comprehensive analysis and interpretation of all the significant issues of both a sporting and contextual nature (Le Masurier 2015). As can be perceived from Table 5, in broad terms *L'Équipe Explore* has provided longer pieces than *SI Longform*. The articles with an extension inferior to 45,000 characters (*N* = 44) represent 75.86 per cent of *SI Longform*'s sample, whereas the articles of the same length only account for 46.15 per cent of content published at *L'Équipe Explore*. The French site's articles ranged from 45,000 to 65,000 characters (*N* = 24) and represented 61.54 per cent of total production.

Use of Images. As for extra-textual features, both sites used more than 31 photos on average in each article. The types of images published, which were coherently integrated in the narrative flow of the stories, include large-format photographs (combination of action shots and portrait shots, both contemporary and archival), screen capture shots of video footage, symbols and icons, diagrams, collages, images of tickets and clips from old newspapers, among others. Poignant examples include the 25 front-page covers employed by Neil Leifer in his panoramic over the history of boxing photography or those that allow readers' to focus on one protagonist of the picture, as happened with the case of Bison Dele. While many of the photographs have been provided by major news agencies, others have been taken specifically for the articles, such as "Astro-Matic Baseball" or "A Place in the Game".

Use of Videos. While video is an integral component of the long-form storytelling provided by *SI Longform* and *L'Équipe Explore*, research reveals significant differences between the two media platforms (see Table 6). At *SI Longform*, two of every three pieces include video (65.52 per cent) whereas the French site uses video in all 39 of its articles.

The amount of video material in the articles shows how LFSJ considers this to be a useful resource. Of its 38 feature articles, *SI Longform* has published 224 videos for an average of 5.89 per article. By contrast, *L'Équipe Explore* has included 278 videos in 23

TABLE 5
Extension of the texts

	SI Longform		*L'Équipe Explore*	
Length of the articles (characters)	*N*	%	*N*	%
≤20,000	9	15.52	12	30.77
20,001–25,000	7	12.07	0	0.00
25,001–30,000	6	10.34	0	0.00
30,001–35,000	10	17.24	1	2.56
35,001–40,000	8	13.79	2	5.13
40,001–45,000	4	6.90	3	7.69
45,001–50,000	7	12.07	7	17.95
50,001–55,000	0	0.00	7	17.95
55,001–60,000	2	3.45	3	7.69
60,001–65,000	1	1.72	4	10.26
65,001–70,000	1	1.72	0	0.00
70,001–75,000	0	0.00	0	0.00
>75,000	3	5.17	0	0.00
Total	58	100.00	39	100.00

TABLE 6
Number and percentage of pieces where videos were included

	SI Longform		*L'Équipe Explore*	
Videos	***N* pieces**	**%**	***N* pieces**	**%**
Yes	38	65.52	39	100.00
No	20	34.48	0	0.00
Total	58	100.00	39	100.00

TABLE 7
Length of the videos

	SI Longform		*L'Équipe Explore*	
Length of the video footage (seconds)	***N* pieces**	**%**	***N* pieces**	**%**
1–60 (1 minute or less)	4	10.53	1	2.56
61–300 (1–5 minutes)	9	23.68	1	2.56
301–600 (5–10 minutes)	10	26.32	2	5.13
>600 (>10 minutes)	15	39.47	35	89.74
Total	38	100.00	39	100.00

pieces, for an average of no less than 12 pieces of video footage per article. *L'Équipe Explore* also posted lengthier clips, mostly beyond 10 minutes of length in almost 90 per cent of all articles and published three pieces where video is the primary tool. In those pieces, focused on ultra-trailing, track cycling and pole vaulting, videos of over 20 minutes duration are the main resources of the articles (see Table 7).

So what is video footage deployed for? Historical footage of sporting action is one of its main uses. An example of the latter is "Ghost of Speedy Cannon", which employed footage recorded on 16-mm that was kept for decades before being digitized by *Sports Illustrated*. Interviews with past and present protagonists are also frequently used. Contemporary television clips also enrich articles while some even include embedded videos of entire matches, such as the 1986 United States Football League Championship game between Baltimore and Oakland. Video is also used to showcase the profiles of lesser-known athletes as in "The Very Best", which includes 40 minutes of video footage on the Sochi 2014 Winter Olympics.

Video also offers a space for innovation. Some pieces incorporate audiovisual footage made with Instagram while others, particularly at *L'Équipe Explore*, include animations and infographics. To illustrate, "À Bout de Souffle" includes a video with an animation that explains the details of how diver Herbert Nitsch descended to 253 metres, while in "Clock Hunters", video animation presents the evolution from Eddy Merckx's time trial bike (1974) to Bradley Wiggins' bike (2012), showing the dramatic changes in aerodynamics.

Multimedia and Interactive Elements

Along with images and video, *L'Équipe Explore* and *SI Longform* use a wide range of other multimedia elements that enhance the aesthetic attractiveness of stories and reveal the high level of creativity and technical evolution that the two organizations have undergone in the recent years. As is evident in Table 8, *SI Longform* has embedded photo-galleries in 41.38 per cent of its pieces (*N* = 24), followed by audios (*N* = 9), timelines/chronologies (*N* = 7), and graphics and infographics (*N* = 4). *L'Équipe Explore* creates graphics and infographics for 79.49 per cent of its pieces (*N* = 31) and makes extensive use of photo-galleries and maps followed by timelines/chronologies (*N* = 8), other interactive applications (*N* = 7) and audios (*N* = 2).

These applications enhance the quality of information in various ways. Photo-galleries allow readers to visually revisit key moments and protagonists in the history of sport. Timelines permit users to easily navigate through the careers of athletes and the history of competitions. Maps provide valuable contextual information about the location of sporting events. A pertinent example is the article "3-on-3", focused on FIBA's half court basketball World Tour where seven Google interactive maps enable users to explore each of the venues.

Graphics, especially at *L'Équipe Explore*, have been crucial in the strategy of enhancing the richness of content. Visually attractive infographics prove very useful to explain specific data such as the Freeride World Tour article "Freeride. Oserez vous les suivre?" Other significant examples of data visualization can be found at "Nous Étions si haut, perches", where an infographic shows the records obtained in the pole vault from 1898 to 2014, or at "Tahiti Surf Club", where a two-image graphic explains the formation of the Teahupoo wave. The implementation of interactive infographics has enhanced the possibility of transmitting additional data. To illustrate, at "Chasseurs de Temps", dynamic infographics allow readers to see Lapierre's aerodynamic innovations where users can click on seven different parts of the bike.

As part of its interactive package, *SI Longform* includes articles such as "Sending Our Very Best" where, in order to learn more about the profiles of 26 Winter Olympians and Paralympians who took part in the Sochi 2014 Olympics, readers can navigate scrolling horizontally, discovering the profiles of the athletes, which include videos and hyperlinks to their social media accounts. A second interactive feature, "Boston: One Year Later", enables readers to choose between using a more linear pattern or navigating through the course map of the Boston Marathon, which includes different textual and visual materials of the stories of the people involved in the race. Other tools worth highlighting include embedded audios (when no video footage is available), glossaries

TABLE 8
Deployment of multimedia elements

	SI Longform		***L'Équipe Explore***	
Multimedia elements	***N* pieces**	**%**	***N* pieces**	**%**
Photo-galleries	24	41.38	15	38.46
Timelines/chronologies	7	12.07	8	20.51
Maps	2	3.45	12	30.77
Graphics and infographics	4	6.90	31	79.49
Interactive videos	0	0.00	2	5.13
Interactive collages	2	3.45	2	5.13
Audio	9	15.52	4	10.26
Other interactive applications	6	10.34	7	17.95

TABLE 9
Number of LFSJ articles that include hyperlinks

	SI Longform		***L'Équipe Explore***	
Hyperlinks	***N* pieces**	**%**	***N* pieces**	**%**
Yes	4	6.90	8	20.51
No	54	93.10	31	79.49
Total	58	100.00	39	100.00

for explaining jargon or interactive images enhanced with richer content. An ingenious example of interactive image use can be found at "Mortelle Sant Valentin", which motivates readers to discover clues on Oscar Pistorius' case as if they were detectives.

Use of Hyperlinks. In contrast to this display of multimedia applications, hyperlinks have been scarcely used, despite being generally regarded as core elements in Web journalism (see Table 9). At *SI Longform*, 93.1 per cent of the pieces ($N = 54$) do not provide any hyperlinks. Following a similar pattern, at *L'Équipe Explore*, 79.49 per cent of the pieces ($N = 31$) do not include any links.

The French outlet has only employed 13 hyperlinks throughout the sample and most of them give access to PDF articles that were originally published at either *L'Équipe* or *L'Équipe Magazine*. In the case of *SI Longform*, 98 hyperlinks were codified. However, it should be noted that one piece alone (on the Sochi 2014 Olympians) includes 52 links to their social media profiles on Twitter and Instagram. The major absence of hyperlinks at both sites indicates that both media pursue self-contained products, capable of retaining readers' attention through their convergent narratives. By doing so, they also constrain the users' opportunities to obtain further information from other relevant online platforms.

Discussion

Both the qualitative and quantitative content analyses presented in this study allow us to highlight some of the most salient issues in current online LFSJ. In order to structure the discussion of the findings, we have divided our analysis into four blocks: story content itself, the LFSJ agenda, the digital convergence issue and the role long-form plays in the commercial strategy of media companies.

Content

As for content, the (re)creation of sporting history, the construction of legend and a certain nostalgia are constant features of the works present in the sample. There is a proliferation of cross-generational stories, particularly in the case of *SI Longform*, such as the 1957 Cotton Bowl story which features the same photo in the same locker room taken five decades later or the "time capsule" used to transport the reader back to 1985 considered as a "Great Year in Sports". Cross-generational pieces include the father and son story of Lithuanian basketball star Sabonis or the Derek Jeter feature on how the game of baseball has changed. This emphasis reinforces the idea that "slow journalism" is as interested in "the old" as it is in "the new" (Le Masurier 2015, 138).

Many stories carry a "journey" *leitmotif* such as McKnight's slam dunk torture, Kobe Bryant's journey into "twilight", the recovery made by Boston Marathon runners or the evolution of US soccer fans. This allows users to gain perspective on sporting events and delves into personal memory association with a shared sports culture. While it is true that positive stories regarding personal endeavour and the strength of the human spirit do prevail, sporting tragedy is also present in the long-form sample, such as the stories surrounding the deaths of pitcher Donnie Moore, the NBA's Bison Dele, Alabama football star Speedy Cannon or the Memorial day weekend deaths at the dirt-track circuit.

Examples of sporting failure are also present in the sample, as can be seen in the features dedicated to one-off quarterback wonders Tim Tebow or Dan Marino or the decline of Russian ice hockey. What unites these evocative stories is the focus on the human dimension, the zoom-in on the motivations for personal actions that may lead equally to sporting glory or unexpected failure. In the words of Meuret (2013), "the existential questions they are faced with apply to everybody. The deep humanity and the long narrative development of these stories touch us. They reveal the world to us and give meaning to its joys and tragedies."

Agenda

Regarding the LFSJ agenda on show in this 97-article sample, we would like to make three divergent observations. The first is that while the initial hypothesis that LFSJ could be used as a platform for a wider sporting menu held true in the case of *L'Équipe Explore*—with 23 sports covered in just 39 articles—this is not necessarily the case for *SI Longform* where the stats show that not only are fewer sports covered (14 out of 58 articles) but that nearly 60 per cent of them are exclusively dedicated to basketball, football and baseball. The *SI Longform* project is therefore more conservative in its editorial choices than its French counterpart, in part down to the overwhelming nature of the coverage dedicated to the Big Three by its parent company publication and its demographic—moneyed, professional, white male—profile. That said, minority sports do get a fair look in: bass fishing, rodeo and wrestling in the US case and mountaineering, sailing, surfing, trailing, base jumping, chess, dancing, free diving and e-sports in *L'Équipe*. The intelligent use of multimedia applications and the deployment of engaging storytelling techniques is of heightened importance here as the writer must convince an initially more sceptical reader that their subject matter is worth reading to the end.

Secondly, while the sample does offer a variety of sports, we can observe the concessions made to the respective local audiences. *L'Équipe Explore* elevates soccer and cycling to the top of the list while in the case of *SI Longform* this can be seen in the number of stories dedicated to US sports industries such as the NBA or National Football League (NFL) but also in its dedication to US-only stories such as rodeo riders, college basketball or American horse races, editorial decisions which, while well narrated, still limit the possibilities of transcending the national sports fan market.

Thirdly, the inclusion of wider contextual issues on the LFSJ agenda also offers material for discussion. For example, the dramatic results regarding gender on the agenda offers a clear indication of one field where LFSJ has a large margin for improvement. Not only are female athletes absent—3 out of 97 stories—but so too are female sports writers. When women do appear it is often in secondary roles as fans or halftime entertainers. However, race issues are prominent (particularly in *SI Longform*), health stories abound (quarterback concussions, rugby tackles, doping in cycling) as do geopolitical themes (Sochi Olympics, the Cold War background to the Sabonis story) which are constantly present. Pop culture issues appear in *SI Longform*'s street basketball feature along with the YouTube-fest dedicated to the NFL halftime show. In this sense, the common denominator of both LFSJ platforms is their parallel telling of a specific sports story in a wider social context, a technique necessary to fully understand the impact and relevance of the story in hand.

Multimedia Applications

Results show that multimedia convergence is a clear feature of the long-form digital sports story. As Chris Stone, editorial director at *Sports Illustrated* put it, "How can we begin to cover sports without understanding, appreciating and explaining the role of the nexus of tech and sports"? (Baysinger 2016). The list of techniques employed from formats to templates, extra-textual features such as large-format photography, diagrams, interactive collages, YouTube footage and the whole range of interactive elements from parallax scrolling to infographics lead the reader-user on an immersive multi-sensory experience. However, beyond the aesthetic pleasure of navigating through such design embellishments, many of the LFSJ stories in the sample benefit directly from such applications thanks to their capacity for helping the reader visualize the dimensions of an avalanche or a tidal wave. The multimedia applications allow the user to return to the stories or skip elements in which they have lesser interest. A click on visual media or photo galleries allows the reader to dictate how far he or she wishes to delve into a story, taking them to a different temporal interface with the text. The sense of control and the ability to explore the story in a customized fashion is of undoubted appeal to the tablet-bearing public to which it addresses itself. The results are uneven when it comes to multimedia use. There is no "standard template". *L'Équipe Explore* uses more—and much longer—videos and more photos. A third of all *SI Longform* stories have no video links at all. Hyperlinks are limited to maintain reader loyalty. As regards the use of multimedia convergent technology, both *SI Longform* and *L'Équipe Explore* have found a comfortable midway point between the excesses of John Branch's 2012 ground-breaking but logistically unrepeatable "Snowfall" piece in *The New York Times* and the random incorporation of YouTube and photo archive material. In almost all the sample stories, multimedia use is controlled, relevant and journalistically justifiable.

The Role of Long-form in the Commercial Strategy of Media Companies

The self-referencing nature of many of the stories—particularly in the case of *SI Longform*—is also a standout feature of their long-form projects. According to Bourdieu, "an art which ever increasingly contains reference to its own history demands to be perceived historically; it asks not to be an external reference ... but to the universe of past and present works of art" (Bourdieu 2013, 27). This phenomenon manifests itself in many different ways, particularly in the case of *SI Longform*. Firstly, the site constantly pushes its "From the Vault" section featuring its self-proclaimed "classic articles" in a strategic attempt to link history, tradition, authority and prestige as part of what Chris Stone, the editorial director of *Sports Illustrated*, refers to as a "premium content experience" (Lichterman 2016).

Secondly, some articles contain video links to Sports Illustrated TV where *SI Longform* writers discuss aspects of the story under consideration from a small television set. Thirdly, some of the *SI Longform* writers convert themselves into the main protagonists of the story. Three striking examples come to mind here: reporter Michael McKnight's 363-day journey to learn how to slam dunk, a feature article on *Sports Illustrated* photographer Neil Leifer and *Sports Illustrated* writer Alexander Wolff's purchase of an American Basketball Association team.

L'Équipe Explore also displays a wide range of self-referencing techniques. In this sense no less than 15 members of staff are dedicated to the marketing side of the Web (Alyce 2014). Staff journalists are fully versed in search engine optimization (SEO) techniques when writing their articles and, as Frederic Waringuez, assistant editor at the French sports daily recognizes, "we use all possible forms of leverage to optimize our traffic. The notoriety of a brand such as *L'Équipe* allows us to generate a high number of direct visits and SEO strategies are one of our main priorities." In an attempt to make this project profitable, production costs are reduced by pooling human resources, by extending coverage on articles previously covered in shorter form for the print version of the brand and by delving further into the archives. Every edition of *L'Équipe Explore* receives a full-page article in the print version and in the case of the major webdocs, a 52-minute televised version is edited for the brand's own channel—*L'Équipe 21*—as part of a multimedia synergy package (Hacquin 2013). External sponsors are also now a feature as *L'Équipe Explore* is averaging close to 500,000 unique visits per article (Poiroux 2014) alongside the gradual expansion of the MyLEquipe app available on IOS and Android. Access is offered to PDF articles originally published at either *L'Équipe* or *L'Équipe Magazine* or by paying homage to *L'Équipe* newspaper in "Joyeux anniversaire. 70 ans d'histoire(s)" which offers a detailed history of the publication from 1946 to 2016 and its milestones throughout the years. The article presents several historical materials from *L'Équipe* newspaper, including front pages (which readers can download in high resolution), articles, images and video archives. As a further element of brand reinforcing, one of the videos also features images of high-profile athletes and coaches reading *L'Équipe*. All these self-referencing strategies form part of a concerted effort to further widen the *L'Équipe* brand through the internet. In this sense, the publication also offers subsidiary products such as the Ebillet ticketing service, EVoyages for sports-related trips or the sale of sports shirts all through the online brand called the EStore which, in the words of Emmanuel Alix, Director of the group's Digital Hub, all respond to the "qualified and influential nature of the audience of L'Équipe's website" (*Internet Retailer* 2016).

This constant self-citation forms part of the deployment of the long-form option as a commercial brand-building tool and is further evidence as Stone at *Sports Illustrated* recognizes that the core print product is no longer a "sustainable business model" (Lichterman 2016). As Dowling and Vogan point out, the very use of the subtitle "Longform since 1954" by *Sports Illustrated* is a way of cultivating prestige, reaffirming its position as the dean of long-form journalism and is

> an initiative that exploits long form's meaning to suggest the magazine had been producing such complex works for decades using long form's cachet to expand on its traditional reputation as a relatively highbrow sports publication ... [it] functions as an opportunity for these prominent media organizations to build a branded sense of renown in an increasingly competitive market. (Dowling and Vogan 2015, 217)

Academics aside, specialists in the commercial field also recognize the leveraging power that long-form journalism provides when communicating an organization's brand. In this sense, Barb Palser, vice president of Internet Broadcasting, which provides digital publishing, content and advertising operations services to local media companies told *USA Today* that "investing in quality talent and producing great examples of reporting and interactive storytelling can have an important brand-building effect" (Rieder 2013). The strategic option for LFSJ goes beyond profit concerns as it constitutes a useful weapon in the race for the growing demographic of (largely male) tablet users and the sustenance of a carefully constructed institutional identity that operates across all platforms. As Dowling and Vogan (2015, 211) point out, "digital longform features often operate as loss leaders for their parent companies ... they do not directly generate profits but build a branded sense of symbolic capital that leads to economic profits in less direct ways". Sport itself is particularly useful as it has "historically delivered moneyed adult male consumers to advertisers more effectively than other mainstream media genres" (Dowling and Vogan 2015, 212). From a brand positioning angle, long form is a win–win option in that it brings prestige to the stereotyped low-brow reputation of sports journalism and serves to expand the demographic reach and market share of the parent company under which it operates.

Conclusion

This article has attempted to trace the emergence of online LFSJ as an exponent of slow journalism and other contemporary dynamics in the profession. A thorough examination of the stories published by two prestigious media outlets has been provided, allowing the researchers to present a comprehensive radiography of both publications. The research has revealed the similarities and differences used by the two online platforms in terms of agenda and convergence. Fundamental cornerstones, such as the range of disciplines and relevant contextual issues covered, the salient angles and approaches chosen, the sources employed, the alternative narratives and multimedia applications displayed or the brand-building strategies underlying the contents have been identified. While the study presents a largely positive vision of the LFSJ projects under consideration here, it does not shy away from highlighting areas where the authors feel changes could be made, particularly in the fields of gender representation and an excessive ethnocentrism in the choice of sports to be showcased.

To widen the scope of the comparative analysis presented here and to capture an even greater idea of the LFSJ community, further work could be carried out to include the contents published by other specialized outlets such as *ESPN.com*, *SBNation* or *NBC SportsWorld*. Content analysis could be supplemented by in-depth interviews with editors and journalists to allow for an in-depth examination of their values, the newsrooms' cultures in which they operate, their creation processes, professional routines and their attitudes towards LFSJ. Ethnographic data regarding reader reception would also help to discern their expectations about and interface with long-form products. It will also enable researchers to know more about the users' experience as consumers and the ways in which they engage with the digital long-form narratives, and will allow us to make solid projections regarding the future consolidation of this genre.

DISCLOSURE STATEMENT

The authors report no financial interest or potential conflicts of interest.

REFERENCES

Alyce, Anthony. 2014. "Le modèle économique de lequipe.fr" [The economic model of l'equipe.fr]. *Ecofoot.fr*, March 31. https://www.ecofoot.fr/modele-economique-lequipefr/

Ananny, Mike. 2016. "Networked News Time." *Digital Journalism* 4 (4): 414–431.

Angelini, James R., Andrew C. Billings, and Paul J. MacArthur. 2012. "The Nationalistic Revolution Will Be Televised: The 2010 Vancouver Olympic Games on NBC." *International Journal of Sport Communication* 5 (2): 193–209.

Ball, Benjamin. 2016. "Multimedia, Slow Journalism as Process, and the Possibility of Proper Time." *Digital Journalism* 4 (4): 432–444.

Barnhurst, Kevin. 2010. "The Form of Reports on US Newspaper Internet Sites, an Update." *Journalism Studies* 11 (4): 555–566.

Baysinger, Tim. 2016. "Q&A: How the New Chief Editor of *Sports Illustrated* Plans to Keep It at the Forefront." *Adweek*, June 15. http://www.adweek.com/news/press/qa-how-new-chief-editor-sports-illustrated-plans-keep-it-forefront-171992

Belt, Don, and Jeff South. 2016. "Slow Journalism and the Out of Eden Walk." *Digital Journalism* 4 (4): 547–562.

Billings, Andrew C. 2008. *Olympic Media: Inside the Biggest Show on Television*. Abingdon: Routledge.

Bourdieu, Pierre. 2013. *Distinction. a Social Critique of the Judgment of Taste*. Abingdon: Routledge.

Boyle, Raymond. 2006. *Sports Journalism: Context and Issues*. London: Sage.

Boyles, Jan Lauren. 2016. "Resiliency in Recovery." *Digital Journalism* 4 (4): 478–493.

Brennen, Bonnie S. 2013. *Qualitative Research Methods for Media Studies*. New York: Routledge.

Bruce, Toni. 2013. "Reflections on Communication and Sport: On Women and Femininities." *Communication & Sport* 1 (1-2): 125–137.

Bryman, Alan. 2012. *Social Research Methods*. 4th ed. Oxford: Oxford University Press.

Davies, Nick. 2008. *Flat Earth News*. London: Vintage.

Deuze, Mark. 2008. "The Changing Context of News Work: Liquid Journalism and Monitorial Citizenship." *International Journal of Communication* 2: 848–865.

Dowling, David. 2016. "The Business of Slow Journalism." *Digital Journalism* 4 (4): 530–546.

Dowling, David, and Travis Vogan. 2015. "Can We 'Snowfall' This? Digital Longform and the Race for the Tablet Market." *Digital Journalism* 3 (2): 209–224.

Greenberg, Susan. 2012. "Slow Journalism in the Fast Lane." In *Global Literary Journalism*, edited by Richard L. Keeble and John Tulloch, 381–393. New York: Peter Lang.

Hacquin, Arnaud. 2013. "L'Équipe inaugure un service consacré aux nouvelles écritures" [L'Équipe inaugurates A Service Devoted to New Writing]. The Rabbit Hole. L'actualité du transmédia, October 21. http://www.therabbithole.fr/webdocs/lequipe-inaugure-un-service-consacre-aux-nouvelles-ecritures/

Harbers, Frank. 2016. "Time to Engage." *Digital Journalism* 4 (4): 494–511.

Internet Retailer. 2016. "L'Équipe launches L'Équipe Store, the Benchmark Marketplace for Sports Products". *Internet Retailer*, March 22. https://www.internetretailer.com/2016/03/22/lequipe-launches-lequipe-store-benchmark-marketplace

Jacobson, Susan, Jacqueline Marino, and Robert E. Gutsche. 2016. "The Digital Animation of Literary Journalism." *Journalism* 17 (4): 527–546.

Jenkins, Henry. 2006. *Convergence Culture: Where Old and New Media Collide*. New York: New York University Press.

Le Masurier, Megan. 2015. "What is Slow Journalism?" *Journalism Practice* 9 (2): 138–152.

Le Masurier, Megan. 2016. "Slow Journalism." *Digital Journalism* 4 (4): 405–413.

Lichterman, Joseph. 2016. "'We're Not the Monolith That We Once Were': *Sports Illustrated*'s New Boss on Plans for Digital Growth". *NiemanLab*, June 16. http://www.niemanlab.org/2016/06/were-not-the-monolith-that-we-once-were-sports-illustrateds-new-boss-on-plans-for-digital-growth/

Markula, Pirkko, ed. 2009. *Olympic Women and the Media: International Perspectives*. London: Palgrave Macmillan.

Messner, Michael A., and Cheryl Cooky. 2010. *Gender in Televised Sports: News and Highlight Shows, 1989–2009*. Los Angeles, CA: USC Center for Feminist Research.

Meuret, Isabelle. 2013. "A Short History of Long-Form Journalism." *INA Global*, December 17. http://www.inaglobal.fr/en/press/article/short-history-long-form-journalism

Neveu, Erik. 2014. "Revisiting Narrative Journalism as One of the Futures of Journalism." *Journalism Studies* 15 (5): 533–542.

Nguyen, Kevin. 2012. "The Future of the Feature: Breaking out of Templates to Build Customized Reading Experiences." *Nieman Lab*, November 16. http://www.niemanlab.org/2012/11/the-future-of-the-feature-breaking-out-of-templates-to-build-customized-read ing-experiences

O'Neill, Deirdre, and Matt Mulready. 2015. "The Invisible Woman? A Comparative Study of Women's Sports Coverage in the UK National Press Befnore Ad after the 2012 Olympic Games." *Journalism Practice* 9 (5): 651–668.

Pauly, John J. 2014. "The New Journalism and the Struggle for Interpretation." *Journalism* 15 (5): 589–604.

Poiroux, Jérémie. 2014. "L'Équipe peut-il encore innover dans l'information sportive [Can L'Equipe still innovate in the field of sports reporting]?" *INA Global*, July 4. http://www.inaglobal.fr/presse/article/l-equipe-peut-il-encore-innover-dans-l-information-sportive-7685

Ramon, Xavier, and Christopher Tulloch. 2016. "Periodismo de largo formato en la era Digital" [Long-form sports journalism in the digital era]. *El Profesional de la información* 25 (3): 404–412.

Ranc, David. 2012. *Foreign Players and Football Supporters: The Old Firm, Arsenal, Paris Saint-Germain*. Oxford: Oxford University Press.

Rieder, Rem. 2013. "Long-Form Journalism Makes Comeback." *USA Today*, June 5. http://www.usatoday.com/story/money/columnist/2013/06/05/rem-rieder-longform/2389995/

Rowe, David. 2007. "Sports Journalism: Still the 'Toy Department' of the News Media?" *Journalism* 8 (4): 385–405.

Rowe, David. 2013. "The State of the Sports Press. Reflections on an International Study". In *Routledge Handbook of Sport Communication*, edited by Paul M. Pedersen, 165–177. Abingdon: Routledge.

Rue, Jeremy. 2013. "The 'Snow Fall' Effect and Dissecting the Multimedia Longform Narrative." *Multimedia Shooter*, April 21. http://multimediashooter.com/wp/2013/04/21/the-snow-fall-effect-and-dissecting-the-multimedia-longform-narrative/

Sharp, Naomi. 2013. "The Future of Longform." *Columbia Journalism Review*, December 9. http://www.cjr.org/behind_the_news/longform_conference.php

Sims, Norman. 2007. *True Stories: A Century of Literary Journalism*. Evanston, IL: Northwestern University Press.

Vogan, Travis, and David Dowling. 2016. "Bill Simmons, Grantland.Com, and ESPN's Corporate Reinvention of Literary Sports Writing Online." *Convergence* 22 (1): 18–34.

Whiteside, Erin, and Marie Hardin. 2013. "The Glass Ceiling and beyond. Tracing the Explanations for Women's Lack of Power in Sports Journalism". In *Routledge Handbook of Sport Communication*, edited by Paul M. Pedersen, 146–154. Abingdon: Routledge.

Wimmer, Roger D., and Joseph R. Dominick. 2011. *Mass Media Research: An Introduction*. 9th ed. Boston, MA: Wadsworth, Cengage Learning.

Index

Note: **Bold** page numbers refer to tables; *italic* page numbers refer to figures and page numbers followed by "n" denote endnotes.